D1457313

PRAISE FOR

HERE'S TO MY SWEET SATAN

"If you think belief in the occult and supernatural faded in the late seventeenth century after the murderous Salem Witch Trials, think again. America went through a second wave of paranormal beliefs in the late twentieth century, resulting in disastrous moral panics over satanic cults and recovered memories of sexual abuse. Beliefs have consequences and George Case has documented this period in exquisite detail and compelling prose. The best book I've read all year."

—**Michael Shermer**, publisher of *Skeptic* magazine, monthly columnist for *Scientific American*, and author of *Why People Believe Weird Things* and *The Moral Arc*

"George Case has assembled, contextualized and made clear more disparate occult references and examples across multiple disciplines than has been proposed in any other book on the subject thus far. What's more, he brings back to the modern world the press reactions of the day, making for a lively read that takes us right back to the sixties and seventies. *Here's to My Sweet Satan* is a swift-moving read that re-conjures dozens of key story lines linking pop culture to the Satanic, that you thought you knew, but now realize you never knew this richly."

—**Martin Popoff**, author of *Who Invented Heavy Metal?* and *The Big Book of Hair Metal*

"Horns in the air! Case takes us to a veritable witches' sabbat of obsession with satanic themes in late twentieth century culture. His well researched work encompasses everything from the growth of modern nihilistic philosophy to the 'horror gimmicks' of 1970s toys. Get ready to break out your Black Sabbath albums, rewatch *Rosemary's Baby* and see contemporary culture in its darkest hues. You're in for a hell of a ride."

—**W. Scott Poole**, historian and author of *Satan in America* and *Vampira: Dark Goddess of Horror*

HERE'S TO MY SWEET SATAN

How the Occult Haunted Music, Movies and Pop Culture, 1966–1980

George Case

Fresno, California

Here's to My Sweet Satan
Copyright © 2016 by George Case. All rights reserved.

Published by Quill Driver Books
An imprint of Linden Publishing
2006 South Mary Street, Fresno, California 93721
(559) 233-6633 / (800) 345-4447
QuillDriverBooks.com

Quill Driver Books and Colophon are trademarks of
Linden Publishing, Inc.

ISBN 978-1-61035-265-9

135798642

Printed in the United States of America
on acid-free paper.

Library of Congress Cataloging-in-Publication Data

Names: Case, George, 1967- author.
Title: Here's to my sweet Satan : how the occult haunted music, movies, and
    pop culture 1966-1980 / George Case.
Description: Fresno : Quill Driver Books, 2016. | Includes bibliographical
    references and index.
Identifiers: LCCN 2015042350 | ISBN 9781610352659 (hard cover : alk. paper)
Subjects: LCSH: Occultism. | Arts. | Popular culture.
Classification: LCC BF1429 .C36 2016 | DDC 130.973--dc23
LC record available at http://lccn.loc.gov/2015042350

MIX
Paper from
responsible sources
FSC
www.fsc.org   FSC® C011935

Forthwith from every squadron and each band
The heads and leaders thither haste where stood
Their great commander; godlike shapes and forms
Excelling human, princely dignities,
And powers that erst in Heaven sat on thrones;
Though of their names in heav'nly records now
Be no memorial, blotted out and razed
By their rebellion, from the Books of Life.
Nor had they yet among the sons of Eve
Got them new names, till wand'ring o'er the earth
Through God's high sufferance for the trial of man,
By falsities and lies the greatest part
Of mankind they attempted to forsake
God their Creator, and th' invisible
Glory of him that made them, to transform
Oft to the image of a brute, adorned
With gay religions full of pomp and gold,
And devils to adore for deities:
Then were they known to men by various names
And various idols through the heathen world.

John Milton,
Paradise Lost

Contents

Foreword

When I was in high school in the late 1960s and early 1970s ,a craze swept the nation for playing vinyl records backwards in search of hidden messages allegedly buried within by rockers under the influence of more than just mind-altering substances. On a cheap turntable one could shift the speed switch midway between $33^{1/3}$ and 45 to disengage the motor drive (while the amplifier remained active), then manually turn the record backward in hopes of plucking out of the noise something meaningful.

One of the eeriest comes from the Fab Four's *White Album*, by which time the lovable mop tops from Liverpool had morphed into darker incarnations of the Beatles, most notably in the nearly nonsensical "Revolution No. 9." Forward, an ominously deep voice endlessly repeats *number nine... number nine...number nine....* But spin the platter counterclockwise and you get *turn me on, dead man...turn me on, dead man...turn me on, dead man....*

To a wide-eyed school kid without an ounce of skepticism, this fueled the rumor then circulating that Paul McCartney was dead. You see, the future Sir Paul was actually killed in an automobile accident in 1966 and subsequently replaced by a look-alike. The clues were there in the albums, if you knew where to look. It didn't take us long. *Sgt. Pepper's* "A Day in the Life," for example, recounts the accident:

He blew his mind out in a car
He didn't notice that the lights had changed
A crowd of people stood and stared
They'd seen his face before
Nobody was really sure if he was from the House of Lords.

The cover of the *Abbey Road* album, released late September 1969, shows the one-time Quarry Men walking across a street in what looks like a funeral procession. According to legend, John was dressed in white as the preacher, Ringo in black as the pallbearer, a barefoot and out-of-step Paul as the corpse (appropriately holding a cigarette), and George in work clothes as the gravedigger. In the background one sees a Volkswagen Beetle whose license plate reads 28IF—the age Paul would have been "if" he had not been killed in the 1966 accident. (Type into a search engine the word string "Paul is dead" for countless more examples.) As these things go, when legends become fact, it is the legend that gets printed, despite John Lennon's disclaimer to *Rolling Stone* magazine in 1970: "That was all bullshit, the whole thing was made up." But made up by whom?

Darker still were satanic messages purportedly buried in rock songs, most improbably (or was it?) in Led Zeppelin's "Stairway to Heaven." The stanza in question, when played forward, reads:

> *If there's a bustle in your hedgerow*
> *Don't be alarmed now*
> *It's just a spring clean for the May queen*
> *Yes, there are two paths you can go by*
> *But in the long run*
> *There's still time to change the road you're on.*

Frankly, I'm not sure what the lyrics mean forward, but when I was in high school this and many other now-classic rock tunes were deeply meaningful. ("What did John mean when he said 'the walrus was Paul'?") Play this portion of Jimmy Page and Robert Plant's masterpiece in reverse and you get this:

> *Oh...here's to my sweet Satan*
> *The one whose little path will make me sad*
> *whose power is Satan*
> *He'll give you...give you 666*
> *There was a little tool shed where he made us suffer*
> *sad Satan.*

Interestingly, if you listen to this section backwards without the words on the screen, your brain will only pluck out a few words or fragments, such as "Satan" and "666" (or "sex, sex, sex" in some hearings). But bring up the reverse words on the screen and the lyrics are nearly as clear as when played forward (although, tellingly, different "interpretations" of the words yield equally clear lyrics). It's a striking example of what cognitive psychologists call "priming": prime the brain to see or hear something by providing guiding cues (such as lyrics to accompanying vocals) and it will obey. I have long used this particular example in my public talks (see my first TED talk, for example), and there are entire web pages dedicated to finding reverse lyrics and words in songs and speeches, for example, reversespeech.com. (Most amusing is one of President Clinton's speeches that when played in reverse supposedly reveals his peccadillo with a certain White House intern, as if that was the smoking gun needed to convict.)

I hadn't given much thought to the origin of my youthful enthusiasm for such turntable tinkering until I read George Case's marvelous history of the period, *Here's to My Sweet Satan*. Not only an entertaining return to the most culturally turbulent decades of the century, the book reinforces the necessity of finding purchase on an Archimedean lever to move the world far enough away to see the larger historical forces at work. Case does this with artful brilliance. The resurgence of belief in the occult and supernatural not only led us to search rock records for secreted evidences of the Prince of Darkness, it drove countless films, TV shows, novels, magazine articles, and other products of pop (and even high) culture. Mephistopheles was everywhere, and today's *Harry Potter*, *Twilight*, and *Walking Dead* vogues have their origin in the epoch so elegantly recalled by the author.

Case begins—appropriately enough for those of us who lived through the rise and fall of the evangelical Christian movement (I was once a born-again myself)—with *Time* magazine's infamous "God is Dead" cover. From there he tracks pop culture's proxies for these deeper historical trends that will trigger vivid memories for baby boomer readers: *The Exorcist, Rosemary's Baby, The Other, The Omen, Carrie, Salem's Lot, The Shining, The Stand, The Dead Zone, Firestarter, The Chosen, The Devil's Rain, The Devil in Miss Jones, The Reincarnation of Peter Proud, The Late Great Planet Earth, Interview With the Vampire, The Amityville Horror*, Ouija boards, Black Sabbath, Aleister Crowley, Alice Cooper, the Rolling Stones' "Sympathy for the Devil" and, of course, Led Zeppelin's "Stairway to Heaven." (And Case notes that Jimmy Page's insistence to *Rolling Stone* magazine that "I do not worship the Devil" had as much effect on the public's paranoia as Lennon's earlier denial that Paul was dead.)

In short, if you think belief in the occult and supernatural faded in the late seventeenth century after the murderous Salem Witch trials, think again. America went through a second wave of paranormal beliefs in the late twentieth century, and George Case has document this period in exquisite detail and compelling prose. The best book I've read all year.

—Michael Shermer, Altadena, December 2015

Author's Note

At some unconscious level I probably began writing this book in 1976, at the age of nine, when I read and was profoundly affected—or damaged—by William Peter Blatty's *The Exorcist*. Combine that with a preceding childhood of viewing *Scooby-Doo, Where Are You!* every Saturday, flipping through the pulpy pages of *Creepy* and *Eerie*, and faithfully attending to documentaries about the Sasquatch, then follow with an adolescence of arranging Tarot cards, listening obsessively to Led Zeppelin and Black Sabbath, and investigating the works of Aleister Crowley, and the basic research for *Here's to My Sweet Satan* was completed twenty-five years before I composed a single sentence of it.

As an adult it eventually occurred to me that my youthful fascination with the occult might have been a way of channeling an inherent anxiety or shyness through supernatural terrors rather than confronting the genuine phobias of my everyday life. If so, I'd been born at the right moment: the occult was a big business when I was a kid, and it turned up across the media landscape (though few called it that then) of the era. To me and millions of others, this was a unique period of magic, monsters, and mystery, when the forces of the unknown were as real as the local movie theater, the bedroom bookshelf, the daily horoscope, and the nightly news. It was a great and terrible time to be alive.

But *Here's to My Sweet Satan* is only partly about my nostalgia for a lost world. In documenting the multifaceted expressions of the occult that coincided with my growth—and, it could be argued, with the inexorable decay of the larger culture around me—I bid an autumnal farewell to both my earliest self and to a fading ideal of ourselves in the universe. In tracing the back stories and objective evidence behind the occult boom, as I have attempted here, I also discovered different, more complicated dimensions to the phenomenon that went unrecognized in its day, or dimensions that would become apparent only after its initial popularity waned. In evolving away from my boyish nightmares and toward what I hope is a more mature understanding of the occult, I have recalled its attractions from a fresh perspective, yet I am still glad to have had those first, fearful encounters that so moved me then and so shaped me ever afterward.

In forgetting, I have tried to remember.

Introduction:
The Return of the Repressed

And I saw an angel come down from heaven, having the key of the bottomless pit and a great chain in his hand.

And he laid hold on the dragon, that old serpent, which is the Devil, and Satan, and bound him a thousand years.

And cast him into the bottomless pit and shut him up, and set a seal upon him, that he should deceive the nations no more, till the thousand years be fulfilled, and after that he must be loosed a little season.

Revelation 20:1–3

On April 8, 1966, during the year's Easter and Passover season, the cover of that week's *Time* magazine was different. For the first time in its long run, no one person was depicted on the front of America's leading news periodical. Instead of featuring the usual portrait of some powerful or newsworthy figure, like a president, a civil rights leader, an astronaut, or an athlete, the issue displayed only text, in the form of a single unanswerable question, printed in evocative red letters across a black background:

Is God Dead?

The bold graphics of the cover and the bolder implications of its words made the issue *Time*'s biggest seller for the year and drew nearly 3,500 mailed responses from readers, both positive and negative. "Toward a Hidden God," the cover story of a journal that then had a worldwide circulation of four million copies, reported on a new trend of "Christian atheists" who were beginning to reject the age-old conception of an omniscient, omnipotent deity that underpinned most of the world's religious traditions. The nameless author of the article (in fact, it was the magazine's theology editor, John T. Elson) observed that "If nothing else, the

Christian atheists are waking the churches to the brutal reality that the basic premise of faith—the existence of a personal God, who created the world and sustains it with his love—is now subject to profound attack . . . . From the scrofulous hobos of Samuel Beckett to Antonioni's tired-blooded aristocrats, the anti-heroes of modern art endlessly suggest that waiting for God is futile, since life is without meaning."[1]

The "Is God Dead?" controversy inflamed an already heated discourse on belief and ethics through the rest of the 1960s and throughout the following decade. But the *Time* cover story also prefigured the rise—or revival—of another kind of belief in the same period. While secular thought seemed to be displacing the Judeo-Christian monotheism that had held sway for millennia, it also left a vacuum that made room for a range of other values. God, perhaps, had died, but His old rivals were being resurrected. During this era, a variety of suppressed, discredited, or half-forgotten spiritualities came to the forefront of popular imagination in an unprecedented wave of media. For some twenty years after 1966, the Western world was captivated and distracted by ideas and expressions that had not held widespread credence for centuries, if ever: arcane rites of magic and sorcery, unexplained natural phenomena, esoteric practices of healing or divination, secretive religions, medieval witchcraft, and ancient demonology. The general term that encompassed all of these was the occult.

From the Latin for "covered" or "hidden," the occult was largely defined by the established creeds it stood apart from. Christianity, after all, invoked spirits, miracles, and the devil, and the Old Testament told of giant beings, human sacrifices, divine interventions, and a mysterious and wrathful deity. Anthropology and archaeology had uncovered primitive methods of imposing human will on the outside world—rain dances, shamanic cures, and fertility ceremonies—and paleontologists had confirmed the long-gone existence of monstrous reptilian creatures and semi-human ancestors. Historians researched shameful episodes of official witch persecution in Europe alongside a few verifiable cases of Satanism. Intrepid travelers documented exotic forms of knowing that were common in Japan, China, or the subcontinent. None of these had been fabricated in the twentieth century. They were long-standing facts of human culture and knowledge.

But the occult did not relegate them to myth, or to the Bible or the Middle Ages or the Orient. The occult posited that such things belonged not safely in the unreachable past or sanctioned doctrine or the inscrutable East, but in the modern West's present and outside its familiar scriptures.

The occult was the wayward, the abandoned, and the alternative versions of reason and revelation that most people had dismissed as obsolete but that nevertheless insisted on their right to be revered. The occult was the terminus of skepticism's full-circle journey back into faith. The occult was disbelief suspended. The occult was all that was unholy.

Between 1966 and 1980, the occult was manifested in blockbuster movies, hit records, and bestselling books. But it was also present in neighborhood hobby shops, small-town department stores, and children's breakfast cereals. The occult made headlines, but it also pervaded a covert underground. The occult attracted eccentrics and reckless youth, but it also gave pause to the middle class and the middle-aged. The occult was condemned from pulpits, but it thrived in suburban basements. The occult was front and center in horrific murder trials, but it preoccupied, and divided, ordinary families. The occult boom may have been largely driven by Hollywood and Madison Avenue, but it took root in Peoria and Main Street. Some, perhaps most, of the occult infatuation in these years was no more than an ephemeral commercial gimmick, which in some ways makes it more interesting and certainly more entertaining. But some of it was born of real moral and intellectual developments that had swept across everyday society and whose lingering effects still resonate today.

Now, wait a second. It can be very easy, and very wrong, to scan the theater marquees and Top 40 charts of a given epoch and extract a single defining theme. A scattering of vaguely related famous names and titles does not a groundswell make. Weren't the sixties and seventies better known as the time of an ascendant black consciousness? What about the impact of feminism? The sexual revolution? The me generation? Weren't blaxploitation movies, women's liberation, singles bars, and selfishness the true markers of the period? What about the new visibility of "ethnic" actors and films, for example, Woody Allen, Al Pacino, Dustin Hoffman, *The Godfather*, and *Mean Streets*? Or the expanding pornography industry, with the taboo-busting *Penthouse* magazine and hit skin flicks like *Deep Throat*? What about singer-songwriters, the ecology, inflation, jogging, disaster movies, and disco? Indeed. Yet the occult was pervasive enough to be regarded very seriously by contemporary observers; its impact wasn't just perceived in hindsight. And if the occult was only one of numerous social and artistic movements during its day—part cultural phenomenon, part exploitative fad—it may have been the one with the most consequential implications. It was certainly the one that provoked the strongest backlash.

Likewise, much of what emerged from the occult mania was pretty silly: rejuvenated superstitions, rediscovered pulp fiction, simplistic or opportunistic interpretations of far deeper doctrines, and old stories retold with more graphic literal and visual language for a more "uninhibited" age. Some of what passed for the occult during the sixties and seventies was just deliberately fraudulent. But some of it raised serious questions about good and evil, about man's place in the cosmos, and about the very nature of reality itself. The point here is less that there really were demonic possessions, witch covens, or a Loch Ness monster, but that hundreds of thousands of people believed there to be, and millions more at least had to consider such things as part of their ordinary understanding of the world. For some the occult was a hysteria, for others it was a sideshow, but it could seldom be ignored.

Of course, public interest in the occult did not suddenly begin in 1966 and just as suddenly die out fourteen years later. There had long been ghost stories, horror movies, and weird or macabre legends derived or exaggerated from supposedly authenticated facts. In America in the 1950s alone, news sensations included a veritable flying saucer craze, a major subgenre of low-budget monster films, and the alleged "menace" posed by the market for gory and titillating comic books. Over the next couple of decades, however, the occult moved from juvenile fantasy into adult obsession. It remained in lurid magazines and B-grade motion pictures, but it also entered the fields of theology and politics; the occult became the stuff of respectable literature, prestige cinema, and scholarly inquiry. This had never happened before.

And many would argue that the occult has never gone away as a social current. Post-*Celestine Prophecy*, post-*Blair Witch Project*, post-*X-Files*, post-*Da Vinci Code*, and post-*Harry Potter*, its various offshoots and subcategories appear to be more popular than ever today. But this is because the barriers to belief have already been broken down. During the late sixties and throughout the seventies, the provocations of writers, musicians, filmmakers, philosophers, and (it must be considered) serial murderers were up against a culture far less prepared for them. The reason we are so entranced by *Twilight* or *The Walking Dead* now, the reason schoolchildren wear skull logos on their clothing, and the reason police look for bizarre motives in otherwise inexplicable crimes is that Stephen King, Alice Cooper, and Charles Manson set the standards and pointed the way. Our present mainstream readily accepts the occult because of a past when it had to creep in from the fringe.

What precipitated it? What happened in the real world to make the next world or the alternative worlds so attractive? Even "Is God Dead?" on the newsstands of 1966 had a distant precedent in the philosopher Friedrich Nietzsche's 1882 pronouncement in *The Gay Science,* "God is dead." The essence of modernity was its drift away from revealed wisdom toward science and empiricism, evidenced in the biology of Darwin, the political theory of Marx, and the psychology of Freud. Those rationalist advances of the nineteenth century, though, had spurred their own irrational occult revival, as personalities such as Eliphas Lévi, Edward Bulwer-Lytton, Helena Blavatsky, and J. K. Huysmans explored realms of forbidden or foreign knowledge, and authors Mary Shelley (*Frankenstein*, 1818), Robert Louis Stevenson (*The Strange Case of Dr. Jekyll and Mr. Hyde*, 1886), and Bram Stoker (*Dracula*, 1897) created a trio of enduring occult archetypes. And that revival would be echoed by the latter half of the twentieth century, when a new and even more dislocating set of factors was in play.

After World Wars I and II, fascism and the Final Solution, and the atomic bomb, the presence of a benign God watching over humanity became less plausible to the average mind than ever. In the face of a science that threatened all life on the planet and a social order that reduced men to machines, the illogical and the disorderly once again looked appealing. The ongoing threat of nuclear annihilation; the assassinations of John F. Kennedy, Martin Luther King Jr., and Robert F. Kennedy; and the revelations of the Pentagon Papers and the Watergate scandal—each undermined citizens' faith in the purposefulness of life, the stability of government, and the integrity of authority. Meanwhile, the automotive and aeronautical mobility of the postwar era brought many Westerners into contact with the insoluble mysticism of Asian religions, notably Zen Buddhism and Hinduism, while Beat writers Jack Kerouac, Allen Ginsberg, and their peers wrote and spoke of a sort of sense to be found in senselessness. Later in the sixties came the increased use among the young of the psychotropic drugs marijuana, LSD, psilocybin, and mescaline, which left already impressionable people yet more open to distorted or hallucinatory perceptions of experience. Technocrats and military men had devised elaborate space programs that seemed to have cruelly quantified the infinite wonders of the universe. The time was right for a reintroduction of the fantastic into public discourse. The structure of the state and the precepts of the church could no longer be trusted. If there was no longer anything or anyone to believe in, the unbelievable was a viable option. If God was dead, Death and its attendants were viable Gods.

Strange, then, that the key point in the modern origins of something as dark and disturbing as the occult lies—like so much else that arose in the sixties—with none other than the bright and beatific Beatles.

1

Diabolus in Musica

Look into my eyes
You'll see who I am
My name is Lucifer
Please take my hand
—Black Sabbath, "N.I.B."

Before 1967, the occult usually turned up in popular music as a romantic metaphor or as a joke. There was Frank Sinatra's "Witchcraft," Elvis Presley's "(You're the) Devil in Disguise," Screamin' Jay Hawkins's "I Put a Spell on You," and Bobby Pickett's comic Halloween hit, "Monster Mash." There was Bobby Vinton's "Devil or Angel" and Neil Sedaka's "Little Devil," and there were chestnuts like "That Old Devil Moon," "That Old Black Magic," "Bewitched, Bothered, and Bewildered," and "Ghost Riders in the Sky." The African-American blues tradition took the subject rather more seriously, imparting a biblical resonance to material that included Robert Johnson's "Hellhound on My Trail" and "If I Had Possession Over Judgment Day," as well as Albert King's "I Ain't Superstitious," Howlin' Wolf's "Evil (Is Goin' On)," and the spirituals "Satan, Your Kingdom Must Come Down" and "John the Revelator." For a majority of listeners, however, there was little in their favorite songs and artists truly espousing a non- or anti-Christian outlook. The lyrics and titles sometimes suggested devils or ghosts or the supernatural, and many of the musicians' personal lives were far from upright, but nothing in the medium seriously addressed unconventional religion or illicit observance.

But on June 1, 1967, the most famous musicians in the world released a new long-playing record whose jacket depicted a gallery of unconventional personalities and one individual whose unconventionality was infamous. The Beatles' *Sgt. Pepper's Lonely Hearts Club Band* was a widely anticipated album that confirmed the band's status as the defining taste-makers of their time. It was the soundtrack to the blissful "Summer of Love," it firmly established the primacy of psychedelic rock music, and it was hailed as a musical breakthrough that offered a mass audience a representation of the marijuana and LSD sensation in sound. Today *Sgt. Pepper* is remembered as *the* classic album of the classic rock era, notable for its pioneering recording techniques and enduring Beatle songs ("With a Little Help from My Friends," "Lucy in the Sky with Diamonds," "A Day in the Life"), although the group's earlier and later music has aged more successfully. Even the album's cover is considered a landmark in the field of record packaging—from the years when music was actually presented on physical discs in physical sleeves—and millions of fans studied the jacket photo and the puzzling assembly of figures it depicted.

Photographed by Michael Cooper, the *Sgt. Pepper* cover shot had taken place on March 30, 1967. The Beatles, innovating with every step, decided on a layout that broke with their habit of simply posing the quartet alone in a single portrait. Designer Peter Blake, a rising star in London's Pop Art world, later recalled conferring with the Beatles and art gallery owner Robert Fraser on a different approach to the design: "I think that that was the thing I would claim actually changed the direction of it: making a life-sized collage incorporating real people, photographs, and artwork. I kind of directed it and asked the Beatles and Robert (and maybe other people, but I think it was mainly the six of us) to make a list of characters they would like to see in a kind of magical ideal film, and what came out of this exercise was six different sets of people."[1] The result was a group shot of almost seventy people, with the four costumed Beatles as the only live bodies in the picture. Among the selections picked by the Beatles, Blake, and Fraser were admired contemporaries Bob Dylan and writer Terry Southern; movie stars Fred Astaire, Laurel and Hardy, Tony Curtis, Marlon Brando, and Marilyn Monroe; and a number of artistic and literary outlaws—Edgar Allan Poe, William S. Burroughs, Aubrey Beardsley, Dylan Thomas, and Oscar Wilde. And in the top left corner of the collection, between the Indian yogi Sri Yukteswar Giri and the thirties sex symbol Mae West, glared the shaven-headed visage of a man once known as "the Wickedest Man in the World." His name was Aleister Crowley.

Most accounts name Paul McCartney as the Beatle who picked Crowley, although the foursome's more controversial choices of Adolf Hitler, the

Marquis de Sade, and Mahatma Gandhi were dropped from the collage. What McCartney knew of Crowley was probably superficial—his subsequent life and work make no reference to Crowley whatsoever—but in 1967 the Beatle was highly attuned to the prevailing vogues of young Britain and America and the burgeoning counterculture. At the same time, Peter Blake's specialty was in "found" pictures from decades past: the Pop sensibility of exhibiting rediscovered advertising and newspaper illustrations with a distancing layer of irony. Together the musician and the designer were sensitive to the revival of Victoriana that characterized British graphics and style in the later sixties (seen, for example, in the uniforms of the *Sgt. Pepper* bandsmen and the circus poster that inspired the lyrics to the album's "Being for the Benefit of Mr. Kite!"), and Aleister Crowley, born in 1875, was part of that revival. The Crowley photo used by Blake had been photographed by Hector Murchison in 1913 and, thanks to its promotion by the Beatles, became the most recognizable image of him. Like the reputations of three of the other cover subjects, the "decadent" artist Aubrey Beardsley, the proto-surrealist author Lewis Carroll, and the scandalous writer Oscar Wilde, Crowley's was gradually being rehabilitated for a more tolerant time. He was no longer an affront to Britannic majesty but a martyr to moral hypocrisy.

Born into a brewing fortune and raised in a fanatically religious household, Edward Alexander Crowley was, in some ways at least, a typical product of his class. He was wealthy enough to avoid regular employment from youth onward; studied at Cambridge and traveled broadly (sometimes on perilous climbing expeditions in Britain, Europe, and Asia); wrote and self-published prose and poetry; adventured sexually with women and men; and freely partook of alcohol, stimulants, and opiates. Had this been all there was he might have been remembered as just another fin de siècle libertine, but Crowley had another pursuit that was not merely the vice of a privileged dandy but an all-consuming passion. Such was his irreverence and appetite for transgression, obvious even as a child, that his mother labeled him as "the Great Beast," taken from the apocalyptic Book of Revelation. For the remainder of his life Crowley adopted and sought to live up to the designation, preaching and practicing his abiding tenet: "Do what thou wilt shall be the whole of law."

Aleister Crowley's earthly exploits were a story of substantial literary gifts and metaphysical scholarship in service to an arrogant and abrasive personality. He could both impress with his brilliant mind and intimidate with his vicious head games. "I took an immediate dislike to him," recounted the novelist Somerset Maugham of his meeting Crowley in Paris in the early 1900s, "but he interested and amused me. He was a great talker and he talked uncommonly well. . . . He was a liar and unbecomingly boastful, but the odd thing was that he had actually done some of the things he boasted of. . . . Crowley told fantastic stories of his experiences, but it was hard to say whether he was telling the truth or merely pulling your leg."[2] Maugham would go on to base the villainous title character of Oliver Haddo in his *The Magician* on Crowley.

Intelligent and cultured yet selfish and domineering, Crowley had joined the Order of the Golden Dawn mystical sect but fell afoul of its leadership and formed his own circle, the Order of the Silver Star; his "Great Operation" was the transcription of *The Book of the Law*, as dictated by the spirit Aiwass through his wife, Rose, in Cairo in 1904. A succession of spouses, lovers, disciples, and intimates passed through his life. He exiled himself to America during World War I, formed a ragtag cult of believers at a Sicilian abbey in the early 1920s, and lost a much-publicized libel suit in 1933. At his height he was a figure of international notoriety for the diabolic excesses of his lifestyle and his gleefully blasphemous writings and art (he even signed his name with an unmistakably phallic A), but his money and press appeal gradually ran out. Crowley's voluminous treatises on yoga, chess, poetry, Tantric sex, mountaineering, and the lost arts of what he always called "magick" drew a steady audience of devotees, yet by the end of his life only a few remained committed. He died in a boarding house near Hastings, England, in 1947, addicted to heroin and largely forgotten by the countrymen he had once so shocked. To one witness, his last words were "Sometimes I hate myself."[3]

But it was Crowley's "Do what thou wilt" that the youth of 1967—both the members of the Beatles and the group's countless listeners across the globe—most appreciated. To them, Crowley was not a wicked man but one well ahead of his time, who anticipated the later generation's rejection of outmoded pieties of duty and restraint. What Crowley stood for, ultimately, was self-gratification: no mere aimless indulgences but the healthy and liberating pursuit of one's deepest will and desires against the soulless and shallow expectations of authority. Crowley's elaborate credo of Thelema (Greek for "will") gave young people's enjoyment of sex, drugs, and rock 'n' roll a dimension beyond their immediate pleasures—from a Crowleyan perspective, such joys could be considered sacred. "We suppress the individual in more and more ways," ran Crowley's 1938 introduction to *The Book of the Law.* "We think in terms of the herd. War no longer kills soldiers, it kills all indiscriminately. Every new measure of the most democratic and autocratic governments is Communistic in essence. It is always restriction. We are all treated as imbecile children."[4] These sentiments underlay the complaints voiced by the marchers and demonstrators of the sixties. Though Crowley is but a footnote in the Beatles' legacy, it was inevitable that many of the buyers who scooped up *Sgt. Pepper's Lonely Hearts Club Band* and gazed through expanded minds at its cover would investigate his biography and apply his teachings to their own circumstances. If Aleister Crowley had incidentally also conducted animal sacrifice, vociferously denounced Christianity, and claimed to have called up demons out of the nether worlds, well, those too became part of his legend. That baleful face on the jacket of a milestone collection of popular music was to be the one that launched a million trips.

The Beatles' nearest rivals in rock 'n' roll were the Rolling Stones. It was the Stones who really seemed to symbolize the dangerous glamour of the genre and the time. They had no need to put Aleister Crowley on a record cover when they already seemed to live by his dicta. From their earliest successes they had been cast as a dirty, brutish counterpoint to the happy and lovable Beatles; their music was more aggressive and more obviously derived from the snarling grit of American blues. The month of *Sgt. Pepper's* release, three Stones (Mick Jagger, Keith Richards, and Brian Jones) were in London courtrooms on drugs charges, and by the end of 1967 their psychedelic equivalent of the Beatle album had been released, its title a sneering parody of the royal preface on British passports: *Their Satanic Majesties Request.* It was only a pun, but it was the first time the Prince of Darkness had been named on a major pop record.

Over the next couple of years the Rolling Stones became more associated than any other entertainers with a personal depravity that surpassed that of just hard-partying rock stars. There had been mavericks, bad boys, and tough guys in show business before, but the Stones took those prototypes to a deeper level of outrage. Much of this, certainly, was projected on them by critics and fans who wanted to ascribe to the group more significance than the members themselves wished. And some of their aura really came from their friends and hangers-on, who were already basking in the Stones' outlaw status and adding their own personal predilections into the mix. "There were a lot of Pre-Raphaelites running around in velvet with scarves tied to their knees . . . looking for the Holy Grail, the Lost Court of King Arthur, UFOs and ley lines," recalled Keith Richards in his 2010 memoir, *Life*.[5] Jaded aristocrats, bored Euro-trash, and striving Americans, the guitarist recalled, all showed off "the bullshit credentials of the period—the patter of mysticism, the lofty talk of alchemy and the secret arts, all basically employed in the service of leg-over."[6] It was the famous Rolling Stones, not their lesser-known supplicants, who took the heat for this.

That said, the musicians were infected with the intellectual fashions of the counterculture, and suffused as they were in drug experimentation, they made willing ventures into some of the growing body of occult literature then in currency—everything from the Taoist *Secret of the Golden Flower* (read by Mick Jagger while making *Their Satanic Majesties Request*) and collections of Celtic mythology to the American Charles Fort's compendium of reported natural aberrations, *The Book of the Damned* (1919), and Louis Pauwels's conspiracy-tinged *The Morning of the Magicians* (1960). All such work played to the prejudices of the young, the disaffected, the hip, and the stoned. They confirmed their views that the establishment was lying, middle-class morality was a sham, reality was subjective, and the world could be a magical place if you only knew where and how to look.

The Rolling Stones' next album, *Beggars Banquet*, took the implications of *Satanic Majesties* even further, with its hypnotic and tribal single "Sympathy for the Devil." This longtime favorite, which remains a Stones anthem to this day, originated with Mick Jagger's reading of Russian novelist Mikhail Bulgakov's allegorical *The Master and Margarita*. The literate and sensitive Jagger was given the book (written in 1939 but not published until the mid-sixties) by his then-girlfriend Marianne Faithfull. "He devoured it in one night and spit out 'Sympathy for the Devil,'" Faithfull remembered in her own autobiography of 1994. "The book's central character is Satan, but it has nothing to do with demonism or black magic. . . . Mick wrote a three-minute song synthesized out of this very complex book."[7] Now considered one of the great Russian novels, *The Master and Margarita* is a wild satire of life in the darkest days of the Stalinist USSR, with echoes of the Faust legend and appearances by Pontius Pilate and Saint Matthew.

With a working title of "The Devil Is My Name," "Sympathy for the Devil" was recorded by the Rolling Stones in the spring of 1968 (the sessions were filmed by Jean-Luc Goddard and incorporated into his eponymous film) and released in December. Jagger sang his classic first-person narrative of Satan's presence at crucial points in history, including the crucifixion of

Christ, the Russian Revolution, the Nazi blitzkrieg, and even the assassinations of John F. and Robert F. Kennedy, with the lyrics retouched to reflect the latter's death on June 6. It was a compelling song that, in a violent and tumultuous year, further stirred up an already fraught cultural mood. Yet, as Marianne Faithfull pointed out, Jagger's devilish act was completely affected. "The only reason that the Stones were not destroyed by the ideas they toyed with is that they never took them as seriously as their fans," she recalled. "Mick never, for one moment, believed he was Lucifer."[8] No, but plenty of others were far more credulous.

The Rolling Stones' link to the occult did not end with "Sympathy for the Devil." Keith Richards's partner, Anita Pallenberg, was a wickedly beautiful German model who, herself caught up in the vortex of drugs and debauchery in the band's orbit, was rumored to be a practitioner of the dark arts. Faithfull again: "Anita eventually took the goddess business one step further into witchcraft. There were moments, especially after Brian [Jones, the original Stone] died, where she went a little mad."[9] It didn't help that she was cast with Jagger in the film *Performance*, in which a London gangster (played by James Fox) changes identities with a decadent rock star (Jagger, naturally). Keith Richards considered the director, Donald Cammell, "a twister and a manipulator whose only real love in life was fucking other people up,"[10] but Pallenberg appeared to enjoy her nude scenes with Jagger and another member of their threesome, Michèle Breton. It made for a twisted atmosphere of jealousy and orgiastic dissipation that, whether Pallenberg really was or thought of herself as a sorceress, definitely made the rumors plausible.

Still the occult links deepened. The American underground filmmaker Kenneth Anger was in London and, through his connections with gallery owner and socialite Robert Fraser, approached the Rolling Stones to play in his latest project, *Lucifer Rising*. Anger was older than the Stones and their followers (he was born in 1927), a one-time Hollywood child actor, the author of the vitriolic tell-all *Hollywood Babylon*, and not least of all a devout student of Aleister Crowley. His low-budget shorts *Inauguration of the Pleasure Dome*, *Scorpio Rising*, and *Fireworks* were unintelligible cinematic collages of occult motifs, sadomasochism, pop appropriations, and gay male erotica. Anger described himself as a warlock and was deadly serious about his work; he corralled Mick Jagger into doing an abstract synthesizer soundtrack for one of his efforts, *Invocation of My Demon Brother*. He also needed money and the attention the presence of the world-famous rock group would lend to *Lucifer Rising*. "All the roles were to be carefully cast," Anger said later, "with Mick being Lucifer and Keith as Beelzebub . . . . The occult unit within the Stones was Keith and Anita, and Brian. You see, Brian was a witch, too. I'm convinced. He showed me his witch's tit . . . He said, 'In another time they would have burned me.' He was very happy about that."[11] But the Rolling Stones—as they did with so many—were only toying with Anger as long as he tickled their druggy fancy. Their real occupation was recording and performing their own music, and they saw earnest outsiders like Anger as disposable nuisances, trying to ride on their coattails and absorb some of their marketability. "Kenneth Anger they thought laughable," wrote Marianne Faithfull. "Mick and Keith were utterly contemptuous of his satanic hocus-pocus."[12]

The quintet's reputation grew yet blacker in 1969, when the deaths of two men were popularly attributed to them. Brian Jones was discovered drowned in his Sussex swimming pool on July 26. Though he had founded the Rolling Stones, and chosen their name from a Muddy Waters song, Jones had never been able to cope with their fame and the consequent sexual, alcoholic, and chemical license afforded them. He was, in fact, a very vulnerable personality and suffered bouts of asthma on top of his heavy drinking and drug use; his suspiciously convenient arrests for drug possession at the hands of a head-hunting Scotland Yard did little to help his state of mind. Jones was no more involved in the occult than anyone in the Stones or their circle (his witch's tit notwithstanding), but now the band appeared not just dangerous but potentially lethal. The band was definitely lethal for Meredith Hunter, a San Franciscan concertgoer who was killed by Hells Angels at the Stones' December 6 concert at the Altamont Speedway in California. Again, the cause of death was more banal than demonic— the weather was cold, the crowd was ugly, facilities were lacking, the show was late, the Angels were brutal, and hallucinogens were everywhere—but Hunter, stabbed while the Stones played "Under My Thumb," was another casualty for fans and foes to take in.

After the Altamont tragedy the Rolling Stones seemed to leave much of their recklessness, or in any case much of their sixties spiritual naïveté, behind them. With their next public appearances in 1972, they had entered a jet-set materialism and were no longer considered by their young fans to be minstrels of an imminent revolution. Their 1973 record *Goats Head Soup* did open with the seductive riff of "Dancing with Mr. D," which described graveyard trysts, fire and brimstone, and the whiff of voodoo, but by then such references from the Stones were not as inflammatory as they had once been. During this decade other rock 'n' roll acts had taken to spreading the occult message, and spreading it more widely, and more loudly, than ever.

One overlooked musician whose music made emphatic allusions to Aleister Crowley was the British rhythm 'n' blues keyboardist and vocalist Graham Bond. Unlike Mick Jagger or Keith Richards, Bond was no dabbler in the occult. He actually believed himself to be Crowley's illegitimate son—Crowley's acknowledged daughter died in childhood and he left no legal heirs—and his albums *Holy Magick* and *We Put Our Magick on You* listed songs with titles including "The Pentagram Ritual," "The Magician," and "The Judgement." Though Bond never scaled the peaks of fame and wealth as many of the contemporaries he influenced (his band the Graham Bond Organization became best known as the source of bassist Jack Bruce and drummer Ginger Baker in the superstar trio of Cream), his life and works are explicitly linked with the occult. Drug and career problems, combined with mental instability, drove Graham Bond to kill himself under the wheels of a London train in 1974.

In 1968 the former studio guitarist and Yardbirds member Jimmy Page formed his new quartet Led Zeppelin. Signed to the major label of Atlantic Records and abetted by the loyal and fiercely protective management of Peter Grant, Led Zeppelin quickly gathered a large following in the United Kingdom, Europe, and especially the United States, where its histrionic and very heavy brand of electric blues appealed to the restless post-*Sgt. Pepper* student cohort. Led Zeppelin bothered little with the typical promotional tactics of earlier rock 'n' rollers and its record and ticket sales suffered not at all, but what emerged from Page's infrequent interviews was his dedicated study of the occult. "You can't ignore evil if you study the supernatural as I do," he told a journalist in 1973. "I have many books on the subject and I've also attended a number of séances. I want to go on studying it."[13]

Throughout the seventies Led Zeppelin was at or near the apex of the rock world, and Page, as leader, guitarist, and producer of the group, was dominant in the band's occult reputation. Indeed the other players, Robert Plant, John Paul Jones, and John Bonham, had no affinity whatsoever for Page's tastes, but each became, in varying degrees, tarnished by association. In 1970 Page, now with ample flows of Zeppelin concert and royalty money coming in, had moved from collecting Aleister Crowley books and other artifacts to purchasing a one-time Crowley home, the Boleskine House, on the shores of Scotland's Loch Ness. That same year Page and engineer Terry

Manning inscribed the first vinyl pressings of the album *Led Zeppelin III* with Crowley's adjuration "Do what thou wilt / Shall Be the Whole of Law" on the runoff tracks, instead of the usual serial numbers.

In 1971 Led Zeppelin's fourth album was given no formal title but an identifying quartet of runic or alchemical symbols that were later displayed by all four band members in concert; Page's was an unreadable sigil resembling the word "ZoSo," which was eventually traced to the Renaissance Italian astrologer and mathematician Girolamo Cardano (c. 1501–1565) and two nineteenth-century texts from France, *Le Triple Vocabulaire Infernal* and *Le Dragon Rouge*. Plant's symbol of an encircled feather stood for the purportedly lost Pacific kingdom of Mu. The gatefold of this album was illustrated with an adaptation of the Hermit card from a well-known 1910 edition of the Tarot deck. In 1974 Page purchased a London occult book shop called The Equinox, in addition to architect William Burges's lavish neo-Gothic Tower House in the city's exclusive Kensington district. When Led Zeppelin founded a boutique record label Swan Song, also in 1974, launch party invitations with the heading "Do What Thou Wilt" were distributed, and strippers dressed as nuns were part of the festivities. The company's logo was a stylized rendering of the mythical winged Icarus or, by other interpretations, Lucifer, the fallen angel. In 1975 and 1977 Page performed concerts in a black stage costume embroidered with astrological symbols, the ZoSo sigil, and a full-length twisting dragon. In the 1976 Led Zeppelin film *The Song Remains the Same*, a solitary Page was shown on the wooded grounds of his English home; as he turned to the camera, his eyes were made to glow with an otherworldly light. Before Zeppelin's outdoor Knebworth gigs in 1979, Page investigated the occult antiques stored at the nearby mansion once home to Edward Bulwer-Lytton, Earl of Knebworth.

Trouble was brewing in the Led Zeppelin camp, however: singer Plant and his wife were seriously injured in a 1975 car accident, and Plant's young son died of an infection in 1977, shortly after John Bonham, Peter Grant, and two members of the group's road crew were arrested for assault backstage at an Oakland, California, concert. By that time Jimmy Page himself, like many rock stars of the period, was caught up in a serious cocaine and heroin habit. Page had also met Kenneth Anger at an auction of Aleister Crowley collectibles, where the rich guitar hero outbid the struggling cineaste, and Page had agreed to compose gratis a soundtrack for Anger's ongoing *Lucifer Rising* project. The two fell out, however, as

Anger complained about Page's delays in delivering usable music, while Page was annoyed that Anger had set up an editing room in the basement of his Tower House and was offering visitors unauthorized tours of the premises. Anger publicly broke with Page in 1976, telling journalists of Page's drug issues and threatening, "I'm all ready to throw a Kenneth Anger curse!"[14] Anger finally screened *Lucifer Rising* in 1980, with assorted shots of himself, Page, a heavily drugged Marianne Faithfull, and Mick Jagger's brother, Chris. The official soundtrack was credited to Bobby Beausoleil, an incarcerated murderer and member of the Charles Manson family.

Led Zeppelin formally disbanded in December 1980 after John Bonham drank himself to death in a binge at Page's Windsor home three months earlier, a year after another young friend of the band was found dead of an accidental overdose in Page's Sussex residence. In the band's last years, and for well beyond them, both fans and American antirock religious zealots claimed to hear subliminal "messages" in Led Zeppelin's famous "Stairway to Heaven" when the epic composition was played in reverse. Among the audible sounds therein, it was said, were the following phrases:

> *There is no escaping*
> *Whose path will make me sad, whose power is Satan*
> *He will give you 666*
> *Here's to my sweet Satan*

By then the tabloid press in Britain and rock publications in America had begun to print stories of "the Zeppelin curse" that had wrought such misfortune on the quartet. In addition to the "backward masking" rumors that attended "Stairway to Heaven"—which reached as far as a committee of the California state legislature in 1982—more conjectural whispers held that Page had actually sold his, Robert Plant's, and John Bonham's souls to the devil in exchange for Led Zeppelin's enormous popularity. John Paul Jones, the low-key musician's musician of the ensemble, refused to sign the infernal contract (so went the story) and thereby avoided the deaths and afflictions that struck the others. These tales reflected Led Zeppelin's enigmatic album covers, the band's loud, dramatic records and shows, Plant's mystical lyrics, and the players' notoriously profligate personal lives and violence-prone security backup, but they originated with Jimmy Page's admitted interest in the occult.

Yet as early as 1976 Page was backing away from the most speculative reports. "I do *not* worship the Devil," he asserted in a *Rolling Stone* interview that year. "But magic does intrigue me. Magic of all kinds." He went on to tell his interviewer, journalist Cameron Crowe, "I'm not about to deny any of the stories . . . I'm no fool. I know how much the mystique matters. Why should I blow it now?"[15] After the death of Plant's child and the "curse" myth that sprang up, Page was more adamant: "The whole concept of the band is *entertainment*," he told the UK music paper *Melody Maker*. "I don't see any link between that and 'karma,' and yet I've seen it written a few times about us, like 'Yet another incident in Zeppelin's karma.' . . . It's a horrible, tasteless thing to say."[16] Page has never denied his interest in Aleister Crowley and is believed to be a practicing Thelemite and still affiliated with Crowley's Ordo Templi Orientis (Order of the Temple of the East), but he told *Guitar World* magazine in 2003, "It's unfortunate that my studies of mysticism and Eastern and Western traditions of magic and tantricism have all come under the umbrella of Crowley. Yeah, sure, I read a lot of Crowley and was fascinated by his techniques and ideas. But I was reading across the board . . . . It wasn't unusual [in the sixties] to be interested in comparative religions and magic."[17] Long after Led Zeppelin's demise and entering retirement, Page has had to dispel the scurrilous curse and backward masking libels that arose during the seventies. "I don't want to get into too many backlashes from Christian fundamentalist groups," he was quoted in 1995. "I've given those people too much mileage already."[18] In 2000 he took legal action against a London magazine that published a story suggesting he had cast satanic spells over John Bonham as the drummer died; the story was retracted and Page was paid damages, which the millionaire musician and occultist donated to charity.

Allegations around Led Zeppelin came gradually during the group's life and into its formidable posthumous influence. But in 1969 the up-and-coming Zeppelin had shared bills in Los Angeles with another act that caused a much greater, if briefer, scandal with a flurry of controversial records and sensational concerts in the early years of the next decade: Alice Cooper. Initially a collective promoted by the master rock satirist Frank Zappa, the Alice Cooper band fused the raucous teenage energy of electric boogie music—simpler and less expertly played than Led Zeppelin's—with a ghoulish theatricality that was eventually labeled "shock rock." The singer was a young Vincent Furnier, a willing participant in the ploy, who soon became identified as Alice himself; the name, he maintained, was taken from a Ouija board session where he learned he was in fact the reincarnation of a seventeenth-century witch of that appellation. Cooper wore makeup and women's clothes on stage, performed with a live boa constrictor, destroyed baby dolls before audiences, appeared to hang and/or decapitate himself in climactic noose and/or guillotine rituals, sang songs titled "Dead Babies," "Halo of Flies," "Under My Wheels," "Only Women Bleed," "I Love the Dead," "The Black Widow," "Is It My Body," and the necrophiliac "Cold Ethyl," and put out albums called *Love It to Death*, *Killer*, *Welcome to My Nightmare*, and *Alice Cooper Goes to Hell*. A persistent folktale held that Cooper had won an onstage "gross-out" contest with Frank Zappa, which (depending on the storyteller) involved the public production and ingestion of bodily wastes. Parental groups and mainstream commentators were outraged, while the press lapped it up. In 1971 Albert Goldman, music critic for *Life* magazine, wrote that "the advance publicity for Alice Cooper almost turned my stomach . . . . It's a frightening embarrassment . . . . What gets everybody uptight is the sacrifice he makes of shame."[19] For a few short years, Alice Cooper was the ne plus ultra of rock 'n' roll ugliness: "We are the group that drove a stake through the heart of the love generation," he told eager reporters.[20]

Before long, though, Alice Cooper (the individual) began to downplay the shock rock label. He didn't disown his music or his stage routine, but he made it pretty clear that what he was doing was no more than a gimmick that had caught on with America's frustrated teenagers and their worried moms and dads. Cooper hobnobbed with old-time show business figures Groucho Marx and Bob Hope and was seen competing in very non-shocking celebrity golf tournaments. Behind the scenes, he was not a Satan-crazed drug addict but a minister's son from Phoenix, Arizona, and a functioning alcoholic. Casual observers naturally linked him to the cresting occult wave, given his garish spectacle and horrific lyrical themes, but insiders knew better. Journalist Bob Greene followed the Cooper band on an American tour and noted how unmoved the vocalist was by his own hype. "He was aware that much of America took his sick, blood-soaked image very seriously indeed, which made him all the more willing to laugh at himself," Greene wrote in his 1974 chronicle, *Billion Dollar Baby*. "Alice was proud of his intelligence and his sense of irony, and in the studio he did all he could to show that the job of playing the Alice Cooper role was just that—a job . . . . He was always eager to demonstrate once again that he was not mistaking himself for the dangerous wretch named Alice Cooper that was being sold to the public."[21]

During his reign as the king of shock rock, one of Alice Cooper's opening acts was the east coast American band Blue Öyster Cult. Unlike the headliner, the Cult did not go for blatant scenes of transvestitism or public execution; it had a similar heavy rock sound but with subtler material that retained some air of mystery. The group's lyrical themes were often tongue in cheek, as was the slightly ridiculous group name, but they were delivered with an intensity (laser beams and exploding flash pots were onstage staples) that made the Cult a popular draw in the mid-seventies. Much of this was down to the band's producer, manager, and co-songwriter Sandy Pearlman, a university graduate and occasional music critic who has been credited as the first to use the term "heavy metal" in describing aggressive guitar-based rock music. Keyboardist Allen Lanier himself formed a curious link between the crunching stadium rock of Blue Öyster Cult's genre and the cerebral bohemianism of his one-time partner, punk singer Patti Smith.

Following the Led Zeppelin model, BÖC devised a series of unfathomable album covers that implied occult significance: M. C. Escheresque graphics on its self-titled 1972 debut and the next year's *Tyranny and Mutation*, the menacing Luftwaffe jet fighter on 1974's *Secret Treaties*, and 1975's *On Your Feet or on Your Knees* picturing a sinister black limousine in front of an old church set against a storm-tossed sky. Each of these tableaux featured a cryptic logo that is said to stand for the scythe of Cronus, leader of the Titans of Greek mythology, and is the alchemical symbol for the heaviest of metals, lead. Like Jimmy Page's ZoSo, the BÖC design virtually became an occult trademark that millions of fans adopted onto their own clothes and other accessories. Use of the umlaut in "Öyster," pointless though it was, began a long trend of employing the intimidating Germanic accent in other heavy metal group names: Mötley Crüe, Motörhead, and so on. The band's songs further suggested a vaguely science-fiction or transgressive aesthetic, including favorite numbers like "Dominance and Submission," "Subhuman," "Tattoo Vampire," "Career of Evil," "Astronomy," "I Love the Night," "Nosferatu," "Flaming Telepaths," "E.T.I. (Extra Terrestrial Intelligence)," and the Tokyo-destroying monster riff of "Godzilla."

Blue Öyster Cult's biggest hit record became one of the best-known rock singles of its day—and one of the spookiest. Composed by guitarist Donald Roeser under his far cooler pseudonym Buck Dharma, "(Don't Fear) The Reaper" was a ghostly minor-key ballad of a lovers' suicide pact that hinted at the lurking presence of Death himself just outside the curtained window and the candlelit room. The morbid verses fit perfectly with the whispery arpeggios and remains, like Led Zeppelin's "Stairway to Heaven," an anthem of shadowed passions and gothic power. It was quoted in a variety of later cinematic and literary works, including Stephen King's end-of-the-world epic *The Stand* and a televised version of *The Executioner's Song,* Norman Mailer's nonfiction book about murderer Gary Gilmore. The album it highlighted, 1976's *Agents of Fortune*, again featured the Cronus logo and the arcane imagery of Tarot cards (as well as lyrics contributed by Patti Smith). For the legions of young rock 'n' rollers who learned the tunes on their guitars or who played the tracks on their bedroom stereos, "(Don't Fear) The Reaper" and other BÖC works were entries to the world of the occult—accessible yet indecipherable, catchy yet confounding.

Hard rock and heavy metal bands of the late sixties and throughout the seventies commonly referenced the occult, either directly in their music or as part of their general demeanor. A little-known British progressive rock group, Black Widow, made songs titled "Attack of the Demon," "Conjuration," and "Come to the Sabbat," while enacting sacrifices of nude females on stage. In 1969 the Chicago-based psychedelic folk act Coven made its own paeans to witchcraft and the black arts; through either a weird coincidence or the intervention of dark forces, its bassist was one Oz Osborne. Black Widow and Coven were perhaps too committed to their ideals to capture a wide audience, but later outfits appropriated occult trappings for fun and profit.

Gender-bending glam star David Bowie went through an Aleister Crowley fascination, aggravated by the extreme quantities of cocaine he consumed, and mentioned the occultist and the Golden Dawn in his 1971 song "Quicksand." The costumed quartet Kiss appeared in bizarre makeup as an ensemble of mysterious identities; bassist and vocalist Gene Simmons came as "The Demon" and revived classic theatrical trickery to breathe fire and spit fake blood in concert. Simmons also claimed to have invented the two-fingered heavy metal salute, which zealots detected as the sign of the devil but which the Demon explained was his way of waving back at his audiences while still gripping his bass guitar pick. In 1977 the savvy marketers in Kiss lent their names and likenesses to a Marvel comic series that was advertised as being printed in the real blood of the group's personnel. Australian rockers AC/DC scored a major hit with their 1979 album *Highway to Hell*, the cover of which portrayed guitarist Angus Young with horns and a devil's tail and singer Bon Scott with the occult symbol of a pentagram dangling from his necklace.

These small, offhand gestures of busy and ambitious working musicians, some of them chronically intoxicated, were all it took to inspire fans' excitement. Such was the size of the rock market in these years that audiences devised their own scary urban legends around players who neither needed much good publicity nor bothered to deny bad. The name Kiss, disclosed the hard core, was a secret acronym for the group's role as Knights In Satan's Service, while AC/DC stood for Anti-Christ/Down with Christ. The Demon and his fellow knights laughed all the way to the bank. "Complete and utter bullshit," Kiss guitarist Ace "Spaceman" Frehley wrote of the satanic allegations in a 2011 memoir, *No Regrets*. "I remember on some of our early tours, there were religious fanatics outside the shows burning our records, saying we were devil worshippers. Give me a fuckin' break!"[22] Meanwhile, AC/DC's Angus Young shrugged, "Just because you call an album 'Highway to Hell,' you get all kinds of grief. All we'd done was describe what it's like to be on the road for four years. When you're sleeping with the lead singer's socks three inches from your nose, believe me, that's pretty close to hell."[23]

But one rock act of the seventies was more identified with the occult than any other and indeed became the prototype for hundreds of occult-alluding bands that have formed ever since. The English quartet Black Sabbath codified the sound, look, and philosophy of an entire subgenre that could only have arisen during the decade. It was Black Sabbath that most explicitly introduced topics of mysticism, drug use, and despair into rock 'n' roll, and it was Black Sabbath that spread the unholy gospel of demonology through the whole pop music scene. In terms of sheer records and tickets sold, Sabbath was hardly the most successful group of the time, and by the end of the seventies the original lineup had disintegrated in personal acrimony, legal and financial woes, and the inevitable substance issues—an obvious target parodied in the hilarious "mockumentary" *This Is Spinal Tap*. But the band's influence on its own and later generations of rock listeners is unmatched. Neither the Beatles, nor the Rolling Stones, nor Led Zeppelin, nor Alice Cooper, nor Blue Öyster Cult popularized the occult as much as Black Sabbath.

Sabbath was formed in the decaying English industrial city of Birmingham in 1969. The members—singer Ozzy Osbourne, guitarist Tony Iommi, bassist Terry "Geezer" Butler, and drummer Bill Ward—were all barely out of their teens. Like thousands of artists scuffling around the local club circuits of provincial Britain, they were hopeful semiprofessional players of no blinding talent or originality who needed a career break more than a creative epiphany. By an amazing chance, they got both at once. Playing and rehearsing fairly derivative electric blues under the name Earth, Iommi brought to the band's practice session a simple three-note sequence based not on the standard I-IV-V sequence of blues progressions (the chords G, C, and D, for example) but on a dissonant, "wrong" pattern that incorporated a flattened fifth note of the major scale, in this case, G, an octave G, and the errant C-sharp. In other styles of songwriting, such an interval would have sounded merely off, but the heavily distorted and rhythmic rumble of rock played by Earth (in emulation of prominent bands Cream, the Jimi Hendrix Experience, and Led Zeppelin) made the tonal shift highly effective. It was compounded in weight by the manner in which Iommi detuned his electric guitar, slackening the strings to accommodate his fretting fingers, the tips of two having been severed in an accident at a sheet metal factory where he had worked. Before any words were put on the music, the fundamental sound of Black Sabbath had been established. "He came to rehearsal one day," Ozzy Osbourne remembered of Iommi's innovation in 2001, "and said, 'Isn't it funny how people pay money to watch horror films—why don't we start playing scary music?' And then he came up with that 'Black Sabbath' riff, which was the scariest riff I've ever heard in my life."[24]

Much has been made of Black Sabbath's standard device (some called it a formula) of using the flattened fifth note or chord in so many of its songs: the liturgical composers of medieval Europe warned of including this in choral or instrumental works, naming it *Diabolus in Musica*, or the Devil in Music. The term seems to have had more of a technical rather than religious meaning—a reminder to singers and players that some intervals on the scale produced discord rather than harmony—but in the case of Sabbath the grating tones of its guitar progressions were perfectly suited to the lyrics sung over them.

According to one legend, the film that prompted Iommi's suggestion to play "scary music" was the 1963 Boris Karloff movie *Black Sabbath*, an Italian-produced anthology of three tales where the aging *Frankenstein* actor was the chief attraction. But the movie itself was closer to the campy Hammer Films' output of the fifties and sixties than the intensely realistic horror cinema that appeared in the next few years. The real origins of Sabbath's occult leanings lay with Geezer Butler. Butler had received what he later called a "severe Catholic" upbringing and as a young man became interested in sorcery and witchcraft, which he read up on in the British magazine *Man, Myth, & Magic*, books by Aleister Crowley, and the penny-dreadful novels of British writer Dennis Wheatley, among them *The Devil Rides Out* and *To the Devil a Daughter*. Highly imaginative and suggestible, he worked elements of each into the verses he provided for the band. "I was seeing all kinds of things at the time, and not through drugs," he explained. "I'd moved into this flat that I'd painted black with inverted crosses everywhere. Ozzy gave me this sixteenth century book about magic that he'd stolen from somewhere. I put it in the cupboard because I wasn't sure about it. Later that night I woke up and saw this black shadow at the end of the bed . . . I ran to the airing cupboard to throw the book out, but the book had disappeared . . . . It scared me shitless."[25]

Between 1970's debut *Black Sabbath* and the final collection by the original configuration, 1978's *Never Say Die!*, Sabbath's music and public image offered a portrayal of demonism and the supernatural unparalleled in its medium. Not all the group's songs were about the occult; they also addressed drug abuse, paranoia, loneliness, space travel, and even the rock 'n' roll staple of young lust. But a significant portion of Black Sabbath material was openly concerned with cosmic evil that intervened in the affairs of men: terrifying tracks, including "Black Sabbath," "The Wizard," "N.I.B.," and "Warning"; the pacifist classics "War Pigs" and "Electric Funeral"; the surprisingly *pro*-Christian "After Forever"; "Children of the Grave," the haunting ballad "Changes," and the humanist "Under the Sun"; "Sabbath Bloody Sabbath," "Thrill of It All," and "Gypsy." Later incarnations of the band formed a parade of different vocalists, keyboardists, and drummers, but they still released "Heaven and Hell," "Lady Evil," and "Die Young." "It's a Satanic world," Geezer Butler was quoted in a dubious *Rolling Stone* article in 1971. "The devil's more in control now. People can't come together, there's no equality."[26]

Visually, the band members looked like they meant what they played. Their album covers showed a greenish cloaked woman near an English watermill at dusk (*Black Sabbath*), a sleeper with dreams infested by demons (*Sabbath Bloody Sabbath*), and a surreal nonreflective mirror (*Sabotage*). The inner sleeve of *Black Sabbath* presented an inverted cross. A winged devil served as the Black Sabbath corporate signature. The band's 1976 compilation album featured only red-and-white lettering against a black background: *We Sold Our Soul for Rock 'n' Roll*. All four original members were photographed together wearing crucifix necklaces, and Iommi customized the usual fretboard dots of his guitars with tiny crosses. An early TV clip saw them playing their immortal "Paranoid" superimposed against a nightmarish backdrop of an androgynous kohl-eyed face. Promotional pictures showed four unsmiling young men peering out from behind imposing masses of hair.

Critics of the time hated Black Sabbath. Influential American reviewer Lester Bangs wrote the band off as a "sub-Zeppelin kozmik behemoth,"[27] the *Village Voice*'s Robert Christgau called the band's first album "the worst of the counterculture on a plastic platter,"[28] and Parke Puterbaugh declared that "to attend one of their concerts was about as pleasurable an experience as a Gestapo interrogation."[29] Black Sabbath, the cognoscenti said, purveyed cheap "doom rock" to drug-addled teenagers already tripped out on the occult: very loud, very pretentious, and very dumb. Others reacted with alarm to Sabbath's overt emphasis on the devil and all his works. "The church went against us in a big way," recalled Tony Iommi in 1992. But the band's admirers may have been more problematic, the guitarist said. "One night, after finishing a show, we returned to the hotel and found the corridor leading to our rooms completely filled with people wearing black cloaks, sitting on the floor with candles in their hands, chanting, 'Ahhhhh.' So we climbed over them to get to our rooms, but we could still hear them chanting . . . . So we synchronized our watches, opened our doors at the same time, blew out the candles and sang 'Happy Birthday' to them. Pissed 'em off . . . . You wouldn't believe some of the letters we've received, and some of the people that have turned up."[30]

On the receiving end of all the condemnation were four working-class Britons whose formal educations had ended well before they became full-time rock musicians in their early twenties. They had found a winning approach that took them to fame and fortune in Britain, Europe, and North America, but they were not out to convert anybody to Satanism; they had not even converted themselves. Like Alice Cooper with his stage bloodbaths and Kiss bandmembers with their makeup and platform boots, the allegedly devilish Sabbath players all but conceded that they were only plying a pitch that paid off. "I've done interviews with Christian papers where, if I'm talking about how much I respect Jesus, they'll say, 'But you can't possibly respect Jesus! You wouldn't be in a rock band if you did!'"[31] Geezer Butler has remembered. "I mean, yes, we liked the *idea* of what's beyond, but as an interest," Iommi clarified. "Certainly in no way as the practice of such. And that's as far as it went, really."[32] For millions of Sabbath listeners, however, whether or not the group's members practiced what they seemed to preach was irrelevant. They made the occult an immediate presence in their headphones, on their T-shirts, and at their concert halls. There was no doubting Black Sabbath.

Occult-oriented acts and music, of course, were not the only trend in the rock 'n' roll of the sixties and seventies. There were folk and fusion, punk and reggae, the easy listening of Linda Ronstadt, and the sexy soul of Donna Summer. But the Rolling Stones' peak period was roughly between 1967 and 1973, the years of *Their Satanic Majesties Request*, "Sympathy for the Devil," and "Dancing with Mr. D." Led Zeppelin has sold nearly 300 million records since 1969, and "Stairway to Heaven," forward or backward, is considered the group's masterpiece. From 1972 to 1975 Alice Cooper was an inescapable media presence; ditto Kiss from 1975 to 1979. Blue Öyster Cult's "(Don't Fear) The Reaper" was a Top 10 U.S. hit in 1976. AC/DC's *Highway to Hell* was the long-lived quintet's first million-selling album. Over 20 million copies of *Sgt. Pepper's Lonely Hearts Club Band* have been purchased around the planet since 1967, representing 20 million thumbnail advertisements for Aleister Crowley received the world over. Black Sabbath was finally inducted into the Rock and Roll Hall of Fame in 2006. The group has sold 75 million albums worldwide. Its 2013 album *13* led off with the single "God Is Dead."

For the vast demographic of baby boomers aged from their early teens to their late twenties, the occult had been brought to them in their lingua franca of rock music. Much of its conveyance—by performers themselves young and questing erratically for personal or philosophical answers—had been expedient or accidental. But its reception—by people to whom rock spoke deep truths their elders had long withheld—transformed the spiritual outlook of a generation. And when members of that generation at last turned down their radios and put their records back in their sleeves, they found that not only was the occult available to them through pop songs, but that their elders too were undergoing a spiritual transformation of their own.

2

Bad Words

The sciences, each straining in its own direction, have hitherto harmed us little; but some day the piecing together of dissociated knowledge will open up such terrifying vistas of reality, and of our frightful position therein, that we shall either go mad from the revelation or flee from the deadly light into the peace and safety of a new dark age.
H. P. Lovecraft, "The Call of Cthulhu"

In 1966, Ira Marvin Levin's biggest successes as a writer seemed to be behind him. He had begun as a screenwriter for American television and was still involved with publishing and the theater, but his well received thriller novel *A Kiss Before Dying* dated back to 1953 and his hit Broadway play *No Time for Sergeants* was produced in 1955. His musical, *Drat! The Cat!*, had closed in New York after eight performances in 1965. Levin was thirty-seven years old and his wife, Gabrielle, was expecting his third child.

Then one day the native New Yorker attended a lecture that covered the topic of life cycles. "Everything from the stock market to our own internal cycles, all that stuff," Levin recollected in 1997. "Anyway, at some point in that lecture—I suppose when they were talking about birth and pregnancy—it struck me that it would be a very suspenseful situation for a novel if [its] heroine were pregnant and the reader knew something about the baby that she didn't know—that somehow she was carrying danger around inside her . . . . Also, by no small coincidence, my wife was pregnant at the time. I really was sort of . . . taking notes."[1]

Levin began to craft a novel wherein the "danger" carried by the expectant protagonist had been sired by none other than the devil himself. "Since the basic material—the premise of this young Catholic girl carrying Satan's child—was so unbelievable, the only way to make it believable was to move it very specifically into New York and the events of the day," he looked back. "The topical references, the plays and books and news events that Rosemary and Guy Woodhouse talk about were all very deliberate."[2] The inspiration for the story's setting of the Bramford Apartments came in part from New York's luxurious Dakota, but also from Levin's residence at the time, which, according to him, "had a laundry room kind of like the one in the book. I would never let my wife go down there alone."[3] The novel alluded to Barbra Streisand; the trendy hairstylist Vidal Sassoon; the 1965 visit to New York by Pope Paul VI and the citywide blackout of the same year; and the "Is God Dead?" issue of *Time*. "When, having decided for obvious reasons that the baby should be born on June 25th," the writer elaborated, "I checked back to see what had been happening on the night Rosemary would have to conceive, you know what I found: the Pope's visit, and the Mass on television. Talk about serendipity! From then on I felt the book was Meant to Be."[4] Levin titled it *Rosemary's Baby*.

Released in the spring of 1967—just before the Summer of Love that reverberated with the music of *Sgt. Pepper's Lonely Hearts Club Band*— *Rosemary's Baby* was a success in hardcover and won favorable reviews, although some critics thought Levin brought his tale to a too-obvious conclusion. "Ira Levin has urbanized the ghost story," praised Thomas J. Fleming in the *New York Times*, but he noted that Levin's "literal resolution of his story leaves the rueful feeling one might get from watching what seems to be a major-league game—and discovering, in the very last inning, that it was only good minor-league after all."[5] Such qualifiers did not prevent Levin's novel from becoming one of the most popular works of fiction of its time (some 6 million copies were eventually sold) and a milestone in the rising influence of the occult.

Rosemary's Baby described a modern married couple's move to a Manhattan apartment where they soon take the interest of their elderly, eccentric neighbors. The sudden vacancy itself is a lucky find for the pair. While first inspecting the premises, Rosemary Woodhouse chances on a scrap of writing left by the deceased previous occupant: *than merely the intriguing pastime I believed it to be. I can no longer associate myself—*

At first Rosemary and her husband, Guy, a hustling actor, regard the intrusions of Roman and Minnie Castevet with amusement, but Guy is more accommodating than the doubtful Rosemary. Her friend Hutch has warned her about the Bramford building and its history of unsavory tenants. "The Trench sisters," Hutch relates, "were two proper Victorian ladies who were occasional cannibals. They cooked and ate several young children, including a niece . . . . Adrian Marcato practiced witchcraft. He made quite a splash in the eighteen-nineties by announcing that he had succeeded in conjuring up the living Satan." Terry, a young female guest of the Castevets who has befriended Rosemary, is found dead by apparent suicide. "I *told* you she wouldn't be open-minded," a sleepy Rosemary hears distantly that night. "Time enough *later* to let her in on it . . . . All she has to be is young, healthy, and not a virgin."

After a subsequent dinner party at the Castevets, Rosemary becomes pregnant while lost in a bizarre erotic dream: "She opened her eyes and looked into yellow furnace-eyes, smelled sulphur and tannis root, felt wet breath on her mouth, heard lust-grunts and the breathing of onlookers." Guy, meanwhile, has won a choice part when another actor is suddenly stricken blind, as Rosemary begins a difficult trimester. Hutch falls into a sudden coma and dies. The Castevets and their strange circle are unusually involved in Rosemary's gestation and even recommend a doctor, but Rosemary is increasingly suspicious of their intentions and of what Guy may have negotiated with them to advance his career.

As her due date nears, Rosemary tries to escape the intrigues of her neighbors, but her emotional condition leaves her vulnerable to their and Guy's manipulation. When at last she delivers—at the Bramford, not a hospital—Guy and the Castevets' doctor tell her that the baby died at birth. Recovering at home from the ordeal under the watchful eyes of Minnie and her group, she hears a baby's cries from somewhere in the building. Rosemary escapes her captors to find her newborn is alive and being regarded reverently by the Castevets and a number of outsiders. The infant's eyes are "golden-yellow, all golden-yellow, with neither whites nor irises; all golden-yellow, with vertical black-slit pupils." "Satan is His Father, not Guy," Roman Castevet declares. "Satan is His Father and His name is Adrian! God is DEAD! *God is dead and Satan lives!*" By the end of the novel Rosemary is beginning to accept her child: "He couldn't be *all* bad, he just *couldn't*. Even if he was half Satan, wasn't he half *her* as well, [a] half decent, ordinary, sensible, human being?"

With *Rosemary's Baby* Ira Levin achieved both a fast-moving psychological drama—is Rosemary merely deluded in the strain of her pregnancy, or has she truly fallen into the conspiracy of a modern-day witch coven?—and a vivid depiction of twentieth century diabolism. It was the plausibility of the latter that would have the deepest reverberations in the next decade and for decades after. "Witchcraft and devil worship was the only explanation I could think of. I wanted to focus on one woman and her pregnancy," Levin recollected. "I wasn't thinking about any direct parallels to Goethe's *Faust* when I wrote the book, even though it's an obvious cultural reference . . . . I knew the devil was going to tempt Guy with whatever it was he wanted."[6] His cast of characters became the prototypes for the heroes, heroines, victims, and villains of many occult story lines in the future.

Roman and Minnie Castevet are not cobwebby medieval warlocks but seemingly banal big-city seniors (their bathroom reader is *Jokes for the John*). Guy is not a promethean alchemist but a ruthless New York thespian. Hutch is not a fanatical witch burner but a refined English writer and wit. Levin even characterizes the fictional Roman's Satanist father as a peer of Aleister Crowley. Most crucially, there is Rosemary herself, who is not an innocent damsel in distress but a sexually active lapsed (or lapsing) Catholic, at first uneasy with the Castevets' anticlericalism yet unwilling to show it: "I'm not offended. Really I wasn't." All these figures were recognizable to the readership of 1967. Here were smart, outwardly secular personalities who still believed—or who were forced to believe—in a very old kind of sacrilege. If the climactic description of a baby physically related to a supernatural creature was too much for some readers, others were too caught up in the machinations of the plot to be skeptical. With *Rosemary's Baby*, the occult had been fully reborn into the sophisticated contemporary world.

For the next few years the subjects raised by Levin's book gained more credence in North America and western Europe. This was already the time of the Rolling Stones' "Sympathy for the Devil," the Crowleyan explorations coyly admitted by Jimmy Page and David Bowie, and the first albums by Black Sabbath. Rock stars and the music business belonged to the young, though. The media of their cohort was not the only one to reflect the new vogue for witchcraft and the paranormal. In those pre-Internet days, the publishing industry was very large, very diverse, and (then as now) highly responsive to the currents of the moment. So in the wake of *Rosemary's Baby* came quick cash-ins at the bookstore between 1968 and 1971: the anthologies of short fiction *Hauntings: Tales of the Supernatural*, *A Walk with the Beast*, *Shapes of the Supernatural*, and *A Circle of Witches: An Anthology of Victorian Witchcraft Stories*. In the same stretch there were paperback collections of allegedly factual stories, for example, *The Devil's Own*, *Harvest of Fear*, and *The Blood Cults*. More substantial titles on the shelves as the decade turned were Kathryn Paulsen's *The Complete Book of Magic and Witchcraft*, Colin Wilson's encyclopaedic *The Occult*, Owen S. Rachleff's *The Occult Conceit: A New Look at Astrology, Witchcraft & Sorcery*, William Bernard Crow's *A Fascinating History of Magic, Witchcraft and Occultism*, and *Diary of a Witch*, by the celebrity sorceress Sibyl Leek. Novels included *The Mephisto Waltz*, by Fred Mustard Stewart, the unashamedly trashy offerings of Peter Saxon's *Satan's Child* ("The Whole town had damned Elspet Malcolm as a witch. But someone—human or thing—was exacting a terrible vengeance for her murder."), and Sandra Shulman's *The Daughters of Satan* ("Their beautiful bodies belonged to the devil."). Some publishers capitalized on the occult fashion by combining it with the old standby of sleaze, which by the late sixties was more liberally tolerated than ever, thus Louis T. Culling's *A Manual of Sex Magick* and Victor Dodson's *Devil Sex: The Erotic Lure of Witchcraft*. Specialized outlets and mail-order catalogs sprang up, including Weiser Press, the Universe Book Club, and the Mystic Arts Book Club

If many publishing houses were merely jumping on a bandwagon to put out anything with "Devil," "Witch," or "Magic" on the cover, others had found that some of their backlist authors had become part of the occult fashion. Paperbacks of J. R. R. Tolkien's *Lord of the Rings* trilogy had only been released in the United States in 1965—unauthorized at first, and well after the British hardcover editions of the fifties—but quickly became campus favorites. Tolkien's voluminous portrayal of Middle Earth and its inhabitants was embraced by the counterculture for bringing to life a preindustrial, non-Christian civilization of evil dragons, haunted forests, and powerful wizards. "Tell JRRT his following is no longer a cult," urged an American English professor in 1966. "It is a zeitgeist. He is determining the frame of mind of a whole university generation."[7] *The Lord of the Rings* took place in an environment where the things citizens of the sixties idealized in distant folklore, like monsters and magic, were aspects of day-to-day life. Led Zeppelin obliquely referenced Tolkien's runic kingdom in the songs "Ramble On," "Misty Mountain Hop," "No Quarter," and others, as did the Canadian hard-rock trio Rush with "Rivendell" and "The Necromancer." The gracious Oxford academic found the attention from young North Americans and Britons trying and resisted the role of guru to a fandom, but his books sold steadily in a climate where fantastic worlds had become nearly real.

Another writer whose works found a large audience in the occult revival was H. P. Lovecraft. The reclusive New Englander had died in 1937 after a mostly unsuccessful career writing short fiction for pulp magazines of the teens, twenties, and thirties, but gradually he acquired a posthumous following that grew steadily through the postwar era and that, by the late sixties, had become a significant market. Dismissed as a hack for many years, Lovecraft was now being reevaluated as the successor to Edgar Allan Poe as America's greatest author of supernatural tales: his stories took the genre into a realm of planetary horror where human characters found themselves inconsequential to a great race of evil beings from unknowable dimensions. Lovecraft seldom wrote of Christian demonology, nor did he create conventional ghost stories. His recurring theme was of the Cthulhu cult, an earthly underground derived from an extraterrestrial source, whose gods and demons passed indifferently through the lives of mortal men. "Theosophists have guessed at the awesome grandeur of the cosmic cycle wherein our world and human race form transient incidents," as he put it in "The Call of Cthulhu," first published in 1928. "They have hinted at strange survivals in terms which would freeze the blood if not masked by a bland optimism."

Such evocation of a universal force that dwelt in what Lovecraft called "the mad spaces between the stars" now found a receptive readership to whom voyages in both outer space (via rockets) and inner space (via psychotropic drugs) had become familiar. Numerous mass-market paperback anthologies of Lovecraft's stories were reissued by Ballantine Books in 1971, under the editorial supervision of his longtime correspondent and devotee August Derleth, and new stories by contemporary writers based around the complex Cthulhu mythos also appeared. "Behind the Wall of Sleep," from Black Sabbath's 1970 debut album, was a clear echo of his "Beyond the Wall of Sleep," from 1919, and an American rock group called H. P. Lovecraft released a few records around the same time. Later in the seventies a published version of Lovecraft's imaginary *Necronomicon* was issued, loosely based around various genuine ancient texts and alluding to Aleister Crowley and other real practitioners of black magic. Precisely because he had died before most of his readers had been born, and because of his consciously archaic prose style ("the monstrous burst of Walpurgis-rhythm in whose cosmic timbre would be concentrated all the primal, ultimate space-time seethings which lie behind the massed spheres of matter and sometimes break forth in measured reverberations that penetrate

faintly to every layer of entity . . .")[8], H. P. Lovecraft took on a porten-
tousness in the sixties and seventies that he had never been afforded in
his life. Ira Levin's *Rosemary's Baby* had had touches of humor and some
critics even thought it faintly satirical, but no such levity was attached to
Lovecraft. Along with J. R. R. Tolkien, he became an honorary inductee
into the new pantheon of the occult.

But the most famous and successful occult book of all—the one that
fixed the notions of Satanism and the unexplained in the public mind and
that continues to drive their acceptability today—was first conceived on
August 20, 1949, when a young student at Washington, DC's Georgetown
University read a *Washington Post* article headlined "Priest Frees Mt.
Rainier Boy Reported Held in Devil's Grip." The front-page piece began,
"In what is perhaps one of the most remarkable experiences of its kind in
recent religious history, a 14-year-old Mount Rainier boy has been freed by
a Catholic priest of possession by the devil, it was reported yesterday." "The
article impressed me," the student was to remember over twenty years on.
"For here at last, in this city, in my time was tangible evidence of transcendence. If there were demons, there were angels and probably a God and a
life everlasting."[9] The excited reader's name, of course, was William Peter
Blatty.

The Exorcist, Blatty's fictionalized version of the case, became an enormous bestseller upon its publication by Harper & Row in May 1971. It
was translated into numerous foreign languages, has been reissued in hardcover, paperback, and audio editions, and led to the blockbuster movie of
1973. Perched on the upper reaches of the sales charts for over a year after
its release, Blatty's book has sold an estimated 13 million copies and may be
the most important product to emerge from the occult wave of the sixties
and seventies. *The Exorcist* is widely considered to be the most frightening
novel of all time, and its origin in an actual episode of apparent demonic
possession, documented in an American city of the twentieth century, has
rendered it especially powerful.

But the 1949 story that so captivated William Peter Blatty, the details
of which he diligently uncovered after establishing a career as a novelist
and comedic screenwriter, differed considerably from the eventual *Exorcist*
narrative. Blatty, himself a Catholic, made contact with the Catholic priest
who had conducted the original exorcism, and he referred to the priest's
diary of the affair when constructing his own scenario. The account started
in early 1949, when the Lutheran family of the adolescent "Robbie" (the

boy's true identity has never been publicly revealed) turned to faith when their son began exhibiting bizarre behavior at home and in school, and as unexplained phenomena—scratching noises and heavy furniture moving of its own accord—began to occur in his presence. Robbie's parents initially sought the assistance of their pastor, who could not stop or account for his problems but who recommended they consult Catholic clergy.

Catholic officials were at first reluctant to become involved in a matter none of them had ever directly dealt with, the medieval associations of which had the potential to embarrass the church, but formal permission to conduct an exorcism was obtained and the very confidential process was set in motion. A small team of priests and lay assistants visited Robbie, now staying with his family at the home of relatives in St. Louis, Missouri. At times he appeared to be a healthy if quiet boy, but at night he was seized by traumatic nightmares and then broke out into violent fits of hyperactivity, sometimes accompanied by his harsh profanity, angry spitting, foul odors, and inexplicable movement of objects around him. Words, marks, and scratches appeared on Robbie's skin. Some cursory efforts were made to determine the exact nature of Robbie's condition, but most of the time the family and the priests relied on prayer and the traditional Catholic ritual of exorcism.

After several weeks of intervention, as Robbie veered from outward normality to wild bouts of cursing and rage, he was briefly placed in a St. Louis Jesuit hospital where the ministration continued. At last the boy—who had converted to Catholicism in the course of the ritual—underwent a final few minutes of screaming and contortions as he spoke in the voice of Saint Michael and commanded Satan to depart. Robbie then told the priests, "He's gone," and the exorcism was over.

Latter-day analysts who have read the 1949 diary and surrounding testimony have raised serious doubts about Robbie's affliction and the church's role in curing him. They underline how the youngster went in and out of his usual waking personality (reading, conversing, playing games, etc.) while "possessed"; how his family's spiritual beliefs preceded the onset of his illness; even Robbie's murky and possibly incestuous relationship with an aunt who died shortly before the symptoms appeared and whom he had attempted to contact through a Ouija board. Contrary to the first reports, Robbie did not live in Mount Rainier but another DC suburb, Cottage City. Above all, skeptics point to the church's necessarily subjective view of Robbie's condition, the overall credulity of witnesses, and the minimal

psychiatric and medical investigation of his health. Away from the influence of pastors and priests, a family of agnostics may have taken another
approach entirely to their son's disorder, and clinicians may have succeeded
with another approach in treating it. William Peter Blatty, however, trusted
the 1949 diary as the basis for his novel and considered it a "thoroughly
meticulous, reliable—even cautiously understated—eyewitness report of
paranormal phenomena."[10] The exorcist himself wrote Blatty, "I can assure
you of one thing: the case in which I was involved was the real thing. I had
no doubt about it then and I have no doubts about it now."[11]

By 1969, when he sat down to write *The Exorcist* at a retreat in Nevada
near Lake Tahoe, Blatty had made an eclectic career. After serving as a
first lieutenant in the U.S. Air Force's Psychological Warfare Department
from 1951 to 1954 and doing a stint with the U.S. Information Agency in
Beirut (he was of Lebanese descent), Blatty authored the novels *Which Way
to Mecca, Jack?* (1960), *John Goldfarb, Please Come Home!* (1963), *I, Billy
Shakespeare!* (1965), and *Twinkle, Twinkle, "Killer" Kane* (1966). He also
gained a foothold in Hollywood, writing screenplays for *A Shot in the Dark*
(1964), *Gunn* (1967), *The Great Bank Robbery* (1969), and a Julie Andrews
vehicle, *Darling Lili* (1970). But his specialty of comedies had become a
dead end. "I could not, as the saying goes, get arrested to write," he remembered in 2011. "And I said, what am I going to do? There is this novel I have
been thinking about writing since my junior year at Georgetown, and what
else have I got to do now? I'll do it. And I worked nine months."[12]

The setting of the book remained Washington, but to disguise any
connection with the 1949 event Blatty changed the possessed victim from
a boy to a girl and placed her as the daughter of a movie star, modeled on
the writer's friend, actress Shirley MacLaine. He also devised a subplot of
murder and created the character of Father Karras, an agonized Jesuit obviously based on Blatty himself; like Blatty, Father Karras is devastated by the
death of his mother, Mary (the author's mother, Mary Mouakad Blatty, had
died in 1967), who single-handedly raised him in the slums of New York.
The murdered Burke Dennings resembled J. Lee Thompson, the director
who had filmed the cinematic version of Blatty's *John Goldfarb*, and Father
Merrin, the exorcist, was inspired by the visionary Jesuit paleontologist
Teilhard de Chardin.

As had Ira Levin with *Rosemary's Baby*, Blatty situated his very modern
characters in a very modern milieu: dubious Father Karras, free-spirited
actress and mother Chris MacNeil, hard-nosed detective Lieutenant

Kinderman, gin-sodden filmmaker Dennings, and cheery American kid Regan "Rags" MacNeil. There are no traditional families in *The Exorcist*. Chris is divorced but confides in Regan's tutor, Sharon Spencer; her middle-aged housekeepers, the Engstroms, have a drug-addicted adult daughter. Chris is wealthy enough to afford expert medical care for Regan, and Karras is a qualified psychiatrist. There are mentions of hippies, the Beatles, the U.S. space program, and LSD. Blatty intended his novel to be about faith, redemption, and love, or what he thought of as "the mystery of goodness": "I have no recollection of intending to frighten anyone at any point in time," he said much later.[13] But *The Exorcist* went far beyond *Rosemary's Baby*, or any other previous work, in presenting the occult with more graphic and horrifying detail than ever before.

No small measure of *The Exorcist*'s impact was due to the groundbreaking grossness of its language and action. All media of these years were testing the boundaries of taste (Philip Roth's *Portnoy's Complaint*, Mario Puzo's *The Godfather*, Gore Vidal's *Myra Breckinridge*, and Jacqueline Susann's *Valley of the Dolls* being just four successful novels that did), but Blatty crashed headlong through them. So Regan appears at a household party "urinating gushingly"; has a convulsion of "masturbating frantically"; launches "a projectile stream of vomit" at Karras; and excretes "diarrhetically" during the exorcism. The demonic Regan cries "*Fuck* me!" and taunts Karras that his late mother is "sucking [another demon's] cock to the *bristles* . . . to the *root!*" Lieutenant Kinderman researches the ceremonies of Black Mass: "A statue of Christ was inserted deep into a girl's vagina while into her anus was inserted the Host, which the priest then crushed as he shouted blasphemies and sodomized the girl." Most notoriously, Regan violates herself with a crucifix and intones gutturally, "Let Jesus *fuck* you!" before holding her mother's face to her writhing pelvis. "Regan's vagina gushed blood onto sheets with her hymen, the tissues ripped." Blatty's explicit focus on sexual misdeeds, though drawn from factual sources, suggested his own Catholic guilt and parental anxiety (the writer was a father of two young daughters) as much as any external satanic evil. At any rate, in 1971 such material was in every sense sensational—this was way beyond the *Valley of the Dolls*.

The Exorcist's story of diabolical possession also embellished the 1949 case. Robbie never killed anyone, nor did he undergo the intensive medical and psychiatric attention that Regan is put through: sedation, X-rays, and an electroencephalograph, among other therapies. Robbie was never suspected of desecrating nearby churches (as is Regan, although it is never clear how she accomplishes this), nor were his personality and physical features ever completely taken over round the clock by a demonic entity. Some psychokinetic activity was reported around Robbie, but his bed did not levitate. He went through some extreme bodily strains, but unlike Regan, his head was never seen "turning slowly around on a motionless torso, rotating monstrously, inexorably, until at last it seemed facing backward."

A few detached readers of the book in 1971 found in it a parable of intergenerational conflict, but Blatty's more lasting achievement with *The Exorcist* was telling a profoundly frightening tale of almost no physical threat. Unlike Count Dracula, Frankenstein's monster, werewolves, or zombies, the demonic Regan poses little tangible danger to those around her; she is not a scary creature on the loose but a twelve-year-old child held down by restraining straps. Instead Regan is a sort of window into a vast and ancient force of such awesome malevolence that just the glimpse she offers is far creepier than any previous villain of supernatural literature. "I think the point is to make us despair; to reject our own humanity," speculates the wise Father Merrin of Regan's possession. "To see ourselves as ultimately bestial, as ultimately vile and putrescent." After the exorcism, Karras's Jesuit friend Father Dyer asks Chris (and Blatty asks the reader), "But if all the evil in the world makes you think there might be a devil, then how do you account for all the *good* in the world?" The novel's eeriest passage comes during Karras's realization that the gibberish Regan has voiced is actually speech coming from some faraway plane where every standard of comprehension is reversed, a nightmarish void of utter, imponderable negativity:

> *Nowonmai . . . I am no one. I am no one.*

The earliest reviews of *The Exorcist* acknowledged its lurid dialogue and descriptions but appreciated the excitement generated by Blatty's drama and the force of its religious implications. "I variously believed, discredited and respected *The Exorcist*," wrote Webster Schott in *Life*,[14] while Peter S. Prescott in *Newsweek*, said "The story . . . is also astonishingly obscene—astonishing because in this story obscenity is restored to its proper place and emphasis, not neurotically thrown away, but a screaming offense against nature."[15] *Time*'s R. Z. Sheppard was not impressed: "It is a pretentious, tasteless, abominably written, redundant pastiche of superficial theology, comic-book psychology, Grade C movie dialogue and Grade Z scatology."[16]

31

Blatty later said the novel nearly passed unnoticed until a choice publicity spot on Dick Cavett's au courant ABC talk show opened up. "They had lost a guest at the last minute and they were ready to go . . . Dick Cavett said well, Mr. Blatty, I haven't read your book, I said well, that's okay, so I'll tell you about it . . . I got to do a forty-one-minute monologue . . . . At the airport the next week, I picked up a copy of *Time* magazine, and I looked at the bestseller list—fiction—What? This is a mistake. It was Number Four. Two weeks later, it was Number One on the [New York] *Times* list, stayed at Number One for over four months. It was all an accident. I still didn't plan on frightening anyone."[17]

The huge popularity of *The Exorcist* confirmed that the occult had indeed come to the mainstream. Quickest to capitalize were other publishers, who put out Nat Freedland's journalistic *The Occult Explosion*, Peter Underwood's *Into the Occult*, Christopher McIntosh's *Eliphas Levi and the French Occult Revival*, and John P. Newport's *Demons, Demons, Demons: A Christian Guide Through the Murky Maze of the Occult* (all 1972), followed by John Thomas Sladek's *The New Apocrypha: A Guide to Strange Science and Occult Beliefs*, Peter Haining's *The Magicians: The Occult in Fact and Fiction*, Kent Philpott's *A Manual of Demonology and the Occult*, Nicky Cruz's *Satan on the Loose*, and Gordon Wellesley's *Sex and the Occult* (all 1973). Older titles and sets were reissued or reshipped, including Ace Book's The Exorcism series, which included Raymond Bayless's *Possessed by the Devil*, John Macklin's *Caravan of the Occult*, and Charles Lefebure's *Witness to Witchcraft*. After asking "Is God Dead?" six years earlier, in June 1972 *Time* put a hooded figure on its cover to illustrate that week's central article, "The Occult Revival." The massive-selling *Exorcist* paperback was released in July 1972 by Bantam Books, headquartered at New York's 666 Fifth Avenue.

Momentum grew. A sampling of titles from the next few years finds *Mediums, Mystics & the Occult*; *A Treasury of Witchcraft and Devilry*; *A to Z of the Occult*; *Demon Possession*; *Practical Demonology: Tactics for Demon Warfare*; *Power Through Witchcraft*; *Witchcraft and Black Magic*; *The Burning Demon of Lust*; Malachi Martin's *Hostage to the Devil: The Possession and Exorcism of Five Living Americans*; Francis King's *Satan and the Swastika: The Occult and the Nazi Party*; and Richard Wurmbrand's *Was Karl Marx a Satanist?* Occult novels were churned out by the hundreds: *The Strickland Demon*, *Demon Child*, *Demon Cat*, *Devil's Peak*, *Salem's Children*, *The Sentinel*, *The Mime*, *The Neighbors*, *The Godsend*, *Elizabeth*,

Lupe, and countless others, many with cover blurbs brazenly promising horror to rival *The Exorcist* or *Rosemary's Baby*. Occult periodicals appeared and disappeared. There was *Man, Myth & Magic*, the wide-ranging British magazine that featured historical articles of witch hunts and werewolf sightings, plus current reportage of pagan sects and laboratory research into psychic ability. Short occult and horror fiction was published in *Coven 13* and *The Haunt of Horror*. *Fate*, which had begun in the United States in the late forties, expanded its coverage from UFOs and rains of frogs to poltergeists and possessions; occasionally the *Fate* articles were scrupulous investigations that debunked specific occult claims. *Spirit World*, *Kindred Spirits*, *Psychic*, *Beyond Reality*, and *Occult* were lesser journals, and *Sexual Witchcraft* and associated titles put a satanic spin on otherwise ordinary soft-core pornography. Much later all this kind of material would migrate to the free-for-all of cyberspace, but in 1972 or 1975 it cluttered library shelves, magazine racks, and newsstands everywhere.

More serious and more subtle writing also appeared. Former actor Thomas Tryon's *The Other* was another 1971 publication that became a horror bestseller, and its plot of strange twin boys complemented the "evil child" theme that grew steadily in the aftermaths of *Rosemary's Baby* and *The Exorcist* (it was published by the Alfred A. Knopf house, where Blatty's manuscript had been read and rejected). Tryon did not write blood-and-thunder yarns of devil worship but more nuanced, and in some ways more unsettling, mysteries of family secrets and enduring superstitions. His *Harvest Home*, from 1973, was a character-rich novel of a young family's move to a rural community where primal fertility ceremonies were still practiced. Gradually, the protagonist discovers that the ceremonies require hidden sex rituals and human sacrifice. *Harvest Home* and *The Other* addressed the gray areas where paganism and psychic power overlapped with the occult, asking audiences to decide for themselves where the difference lay and how the difference mattered.

With the proliferation of fiction and especially nonfiction works on witchcraft, the paranormal, and alternative religions, specialized occult shops sprang up in cities across North America and Britain. Aside from selling books and magazines, such outlets also stocked items from jewelry, incense sticks, and candles to Tarot cards of various designs, rune stones, herbal medicines, and crystal balls. Los Angeles' Hermetic Workshop and Timeless Occult Shop, San Francisco's Metaphysical Center, St. Paul's Gnostica, Chicago's Occult Bookstore, Vancouver's Banyen Books, and

Brooklyn's Warlock Shop were only seven such emporiums that either began or boomed in the early seventies. They served as meeting places for like-minded readers looking to connect with common interests in palm readings, séances, astral projection, or deeper mystical explorations. Occult-related operations ran partly as regular small businesses with the usual concerns of inventory, overhead, advertising, and the like, but partly as centers of teaching and community for hitherto disparate groups of seekers and the curious. The Warlock Shop got some good publicity in 1971 when a local Catholic monsignor stated his opposition. "When that happened we sent out a 'Banned in Brooklyn' press release," remembered the store's proprietor, Herman Slater. "And we got written up by all the newspapers . . . . Of course, the nuns stopped coming in for their Rose of Jericho flowers, but it actually helped our business."[18]

The mainstream press scored yet another occult hit in 1973, with the Regnery firm's release of Flora Rheta Schreiber's *Sybil*. Strictly speaking, *Sybil* had nothing to do with magic or witchcraft, but its purportedly true account of a young woman's suffering under a severe infestation of multiple personalities appeared to be an authenticated companion to the fictional trauma suffered by Regan MacNeil in *The Exorcist*. Schreiber related Sybil's long therapeutic sessions with her psychoanalyst, Dr. Cornelia Wilbur, wherein some sixteen separate identities within her came forward, two of them male and one an infant. The author also told of the bizarre childhood abuse inflicted on the patient by her mother, in which she was given ice-water enemas, was vaginally penetrated with sharp objects, and underwent a regular "demonic ritual" where Sybil was forced to watch her mother defecate on neighbors' property. *Sybil* was a dark and chilling story of a psychological illness that verged on the unexplainable. William Peter Blatty himself had written that the tentative medical science of such afflictions was barely able to comprehend them: "In attempting to explain possession, one might as well say 'demon' as 'dual personality.' The concepts are equally occult."[19] Even the name "Sybil" carried a shiver—it was the name of female seers from Mediterranean mythology and also that of the contemporary self-styled English witch Sybil Leek. *Sybil* sold almost 7 million copies worldwide.

Many years afterward, though, it was found that Dr. Wilbur's treatment of Sybil (true name Shirley Mason), and Flora Rheta Schreiber's account of it, had been an exercise in self-deception. Journalist Debbie Nathan's *Sybil Exposed: The Extraordinary Story Behind the Famous Multiple Personality*

Case (2011) revealed that Wilbur, Mason, and Schreiber had together been actively or passively complicit in fabricating the tale of Mason's disorder. She was indeed Wilbur's patient and had a history of emotional distress, but the doctor had used highly questionable methods—including shock treatment and varieties of powerful drugs—to prompt her dubious confessions and recollections. Wilbur wanted to diagnose multiple personalities, Mason wanted to oblige her, and Schreiber wanted a commercial topic to write of. In the wake of *Sybil*, claims of "recovered memory" grew throughout psychological practice and even entered the criminal justice system as courtroom evidence of long-past abuses, but the sixteen separate personalities inside Shirley Mason had quite likely never existed.

The success of *Sybil*, however, showed that the standards of fact-checking and hard research in documenting "real" occult phenomena were often lax. Much of the occult-related nonfiction commissioned by publishers of the day was either recycled tabloid material or companions for the already credulous, as audiences demanded more occult books than could reasonably result from serious scholarship alone. After all, this was an area by its nature scarcely believable; for promotional purposes it was enough to say that something genuinely strange had once been genuinely witnessed somewhere. Looking too hard for alternative versions of the same event would spoil the fun.

This may have been what happened with Jay Anson's 1977 bestseller, *The Amityville Horror*. Issued by Prentice-Hall, the book chronicled the day-by-day terrors of George and Kathleen Lutz's move to a home on Long Island, New York, where a mass family slaying had occurred just over a year prior. In only four weeks' residence at 112 Ocean Avenue, Anson wrote, the couple and their children saw unnatural masses of houseflies cluster indoors; vile muck erupt from their plumbing; Kathleen's decorative crucifix somehow hung upside down; a hooded figure at the top of a staircase; an evil face appear burned into the back of their fireplace; and glimpses of the children's spectral "friend," a hellish pig named Jodie. They invited the blessings of a Catholic priest, who heard the words "Get out" uttered by a disembodied voice and who was driven from the premises in fear. The Lutz clan escaped shortly after. "The inverted crucifix in Kathy's closet, the recurrent flies, and odors of human excrement [found in the house] are all characteristic trademarks of demonic infestation," Anson concluded.[20] In the occult age, *The Amityville Horror* was not merely a haunted house story—here was a house apparently possessed by the devil. It sold over 6 million copies.

Yet as with *Sybil*, it emerged that the frightening revelations of *The Amityville Horror* had been, at the minimum, wildly exaggerated. The difference was that the emergence took only a few years. Twenty-three-year-old Ronnie DeFeo was certainly convicted of killing his parents and four siblings on November 13, 1974, in the house later occupied by the Lutz family, but everything since was a matter of dispute. Jay Anson, a journeyman reporter and TV scriptwriter with no previous book credits, died in 1980, but the Lutzes became involved in several lawsuits alleging they had come up with the Amityville story as a way of exploiting the DeFeo tragedy. From jail, DeFeo himself recanted his murder confessions (he originally said voices told him to turn a shotgun on his parents, two brothers, and two sisters) and claimed that his state-appointed lawyer, William Weber, had advised him to plead insanity for a shorter sentence and subsequent movie and book deals. "[Weber] said it would be 'The Godfather' and 'The Exodus,' I mean 'The Exorcist,' all in one," he testified while appealing his sentence in 1992. "The whole thing was a con, except for the crime."[21] Weber, for his part, attested in interviews that the Lutz couple were interested "in developing the demonism aspect of the case," which they did over a long night's conversation with the attorney.[22] "I don't remember the number of bottles of wine that we had," Weber said, "but it was certainly more than four."[23] George and Kathleen then brought their yarn to Anson, who shared with them the revenue from the book and its 1979 film adaptation—by one estimate it was no more than $300,000. Other investigators found that later occupants of the Amityville house said nothing disconcerting happened to them while there and that even Anson's meteorological descriptions in the book failed to correspond with recorded Long Island weather patterns in late 1975. Did *anything* untoward happen to George and Kathleen Lutz in Amityville? "People are disrespecting a true story," George Lutz maintained as late as 2005, shortly before his death. "It's my family's story, and it's hurtful."[24] By then the factual and fictional elements of *The Amityville Horror* had become a virtual franchise comprising several books and movies.

A third nonfiction series that gained wide attention in the seventies was American writer Jane Roberts's books covering her mediumistic dialogues with a being known as Seth. Seth was an "oversoul," Roberts claimed, "an energy personality essence no longer focused in physical reality." In contrast to the scares of *Sybil* or *The Amityville Horror*, Seth brought enlightenment: "The individual self must become aware of far more reality, it must allow its identity to expand to include previously unconscious knowledge. Your species is in a time of change."[25] Roberts documented her trance-induced conversations with Seth in a sequence of books, beginning with *How to Develop Your ESP Power* (1966), *The Seth Material* (1970), *Seth Speaks: The Eternal Validity of the Soul* (1972), *The Nature of Personal Reality: A Seth Book* (1974), *Adventures in Consciousness* (1975), *Psychic Politics* (1976), and *The Nature of the Psyche: A Seth Book* (1979). It was said that Roberts's voice and features changed when channeling Seth, and she also wrote of conversing with the (late) painter Paul Cézanne and the (late) psychologist William James using the same method. Seth and his teachings were not the dark occult of *The Exorcist*, but they were sorted into the occult section of many bookstores, and the Bantam edition of *Seth Speaks* even used a cover design that mirrored that of the Blatty bestseller. In Jane Roberts's case, it was not the message—which was received by many as a positive spiritual doctrine—but the medium that linked her to parapsychology and other occult practices. The various Seth transcripts have sold over 7 million copies.

Fictional books with occult themes—acknowledged fiction, that is—sold steadily throughout the seventies. Demons, witches, ghosts, and monsters were all viable subject matter. The hoary premise of vampirism was given a major resurrection with the 1976 publication of Anne Rice's *Interview with the Vampire*, which begat a long sequence of the novelist's works on the undead and other horror archetypes that eventually won Rice the unofficial title of "Queen of the Occult." *Interview with the Vampire*, like her other works, was actually less a reverent treatment of the genre's stock settings and personalities as it was a rethink of their psychological implications. What was it actually like to exist as a vampire? To subsist on human blood and never die? How did vampires sustain their own ancient community in a globalized, industrialized world? Did vampires feel love or lust? "How many vampires do you think have the stamina for immortality?" Rice's 400-year-old Armand asks. "Soon . . . this immortality becomes a penitential sentence in a madhouse of figures and forms that are hopelessly unintelligible and without value."[26] Rice's books invested occult stereotypes with a supercharged gothicism that converted a massive readership; *Interview with the Vampire* and her other titles have sold nearly 100 million copies.

Few authors reached that level of success, let alone surpassed it, but Stephen King did. Among the most widely read writers of all time, in company with Agatha Christie, Louis L'Amour, and Georges Simenon, King began his career as a horror novelist during the occult wave of the seventies and can be credited with completing the movement of the occult into its current central place in Western society. Though his work has now come to include memoir, criticism, suspense, science fiction, and fantasy, it is as a crafter of supernatural stories that he made his name and his most famous books. Before Stephen King, the occult was a growing but still discrete category of published fiction; after him it virtually became the industry itself. King did not so much bring the occult to the middle of the road as redirect the middle of the road to the occult. His is one of the most important accomplishments in contemporary literature.

King's first novel, *Carrie*, was released in hardcover by Doubleday in 1974 and was clearly intended as a competitor of *The Exorcist*: the cover blurb described it as "A Novel of a Girl Possessed of a Terrifying Power," while inside copy promised, "If *The Exorcist* made you shudder, *Carrie* will make you scream." The writer himself had little suspicion that his brief book, dealing with adolescent psychokinesis and maternal religious mania, was capitalizing on an increasingly profitable genre. "Up until that point, in the late fall and early winter of 1972," he recalled in 1980, "it had never crossed my mind to write a horror novel. It's odd because I had never actually sold anything *but* horror stories . . . . I was aware of publishing trends, was aware of the Tryon novel *The Other*, of *Rosemary's Baby*, and of the fact that the Blatty novel had been—no joke intended—a monster seller, but I never made the connection with my own work."[27] Soon enough, however, King's extraordinarily prolific output made him the foremost name in both mass-marketed fiction and commercially available occult material.

Carrie was followed by *Salem's Lot* (vampires) in 1975, *The Shining* (ghosts) in 1977, *The Stand* (apocalyptic plague) and *Night Shift* (short stories, mostly horror) in 1978, *The Dead Zone* (telepathy or clairvoyance) in 1979, *Firestarter* (psychokinesis) in 1980, and *Cujo* (killer dog) in 1981. There was no turning back. Aside from the simple name recognition King won with this run of bestsellers—a much greater bibliography of titles and word counts than Ira Levin or William Peter Blatty had produced in a similar period—he also took the occult deeper into the lives of ordinary places and characters. Levin and Blatty had turned witchcraft and demonology on modern cosmopolitans and showbiz types, rather than

European villagers from antiquity; King went to the next stage of turning his monsters on small-town working stiffs who watched television, drank beer, and drove pickup trucks. Levin and Blatty were clever writers whose best-known novels had strained for hipness (*Rosemary's Baby*) or spiritual significance (*The Exorcist*); King was a storyteller who drew as much scare power from everyday matters of alcoholism, family breakdown, and aging as from any paranormal elements he introduced. This was a meat-and-potatoes approach that earned him a huge audience among a public that usually avoided the more literary or elevated fiction his predecessors had sought to create. "Terror, that's Stephen King," Blatty conceded in a 2011 interview. "He's the master of terror."[28]

Like his cinematic equivalent Steven Spielberg (just nine months his elder), the 1947-born King had come to maturity in a media environment where the pulp fiction, comic books, B-movies, and TV shows of the fifties represented not just a particular phase or style of mass entertainment but more like Holy Writ, which could be updated and expanded but which would always be a foundational wellhead of creative ideas. King could thus repeatedly touch the nerves of a generation who at some level had always recognized and accepted the fantastic components of his plots. He didn't have to explain anything to them. And like Anne Rice with her secret clans of bloodsuckers, King often trafficked in clichés, but they were set against an eminently believable background: in his case, the folk vernacular and domestic detritus of recessional, post-Vietnam America. Such was his facility with prose that his novels and stories sometimes seemed like exercises in realizing far- or farther-fetched situations that an audience long accustomed to occult conceits could easily embrace. So, what if a Renaissance-era European vampire came to find victims not in Victorian Britain but present-day rural Maine? Answer: *Salem's Lot*. What if an isolated luxury hotel retained the psychic imprints of its most disreputable guests? Answer: *The Shining*. What if an astronaut returned from space bearing an invasion of alien life within his body? Answer: "I Am the Doorway." What if an industrial laundry machine took on a rampaging life of its own? Answer: "The Mangler." His prodigious writing at first stymied many reviewers, unprepared as they were to find King's kind of talent put to the service of such low thrills. "His own characters seldom serve any purpose save as ballast for his bizarre plots," ran a *New York Times* critique of *Night Shift*, "and because he has no greater ambition than to shock, his best stories have about as much thematic content as Gahan Wilson's macabre cartoons."[29]

To his credit, King was always quick to acknowledge his respect for earlier genre writers who had gone before him, including Shirley Jackson (*The Haunting of Hill House*), Richard Matheson (*Hell House*), Ray Bradbury (*Something Wicked This Way Comes*), and John D. MacDonald (the Travis McGee detective series). He also wrote admiringly of contemporaries like Harlan Ellison, Thomas Tryon, Ira Levin, and Robert Marasco's 1973 novel *Burnt Offerings*, which he cited as a formative influence on *The Shining*. But King himself became the major force in horror fiction of the seventies and beyond, boosting the presence of new names in the bookstore who were hyped by varying degrees of comparison to him—Chelsea Quinn Yarbro, Ramsey Campbell, T. E. D. Klein, Dean Koontz, James Herbert, and many others, as well as single titles like *The Glowing*, *The Howling*, and *The Burning*. From being one of thousands riding the occult wave, he started a tsunami of his own.

King entered a field where many of his scenarios had already been proven to work with a broad market. Children and young people with psychic or supernatural ability; abusive parents; broken homes; frank depictions of sexuality, vulgarity, and bodily function; repugnant, fathomless evil— all had been featured in *Rosemary's Baby*, *The Other*, *Harvest Home*, *The Exorcist*, *Sybil*, and *The Amityville Horror*. But, again, King broke those out of the occult substrata and into the realm of general household entertainment. Although he did have a faithful following, and attracted a few unstable aficionados, he did not inspire a league of hard-core devotees as had J. R. R. Tolkien, H. P. Lovecraft, or Jane Roberts, and nor did he trigger a renewed interest in Satanism or possession like that set off by Ira Levin or William Peter Blatty. Stephen King, instead, was the culmination of everything Tolkien, Lovecraft, Roberts, Levin, and Blatty had stimulated in the readers of the sixties and early seventies. Through him, the occult became a conventional trapping of pop culture. Through the occult, Stephen King became one of the most familiar American writers of the last fifty years. His books have sold nearly 400 million copies internationally.

Within the publishing business, then, the occult never really died out. It rather became so pervasive that it could no longer be defined as a specialized subject. While Black Masses, evil spirits, and poltergeists continued to bring customers to the Warlock Shop and the Metaphysical Center, they were also ringing up sales at pharmacies, airports, malls, and department stores. But never again would such matters have the emotional and social punch they packed in 1967 or 1971. Stephen King carried a wallop himself, but the deepest impressions were felt before him. Those first shudders set off by *Rosemary's Baby* and *The Exorcist* and their many, many imitations can still be seen and read as the books that confirmed the occult's primacy within a trade that was close to its economic peak, and among a population that was more literate than ever before or since: *après le Diable, le déluge.*

3

Sin Cinema

Good morning. You are one day closer to the end of the world.
—*The Omen* advertisement

After reading the first few pages of *Rosemary's Baby* in galley form, Roman Polanski remembered his initial reaction was "Hey, what is this, some kind of soap opera?"[1] He had arrived in Hollywood in early 1967 at the behest of the young Paramount Pictures executive Robert Evans, who wanted him to direct a movie of Ira Levin's as-yet unpublished novel. William Castle, an established producer and director of low-budget but profitable horror films like *House on Haunted Hill*, *Strait-Jacket*, *Mr. Sardonicus*, and *The Tingler*, had initially optioned the property with the intention of directing it himself, but he had been pushed aside by Paramount's management. A survivor of his native Poland's occupation by the Nazis, Polanski was thirty-three and had made a number of stylish suspense films in Europe—*Knife in the Water* (1961), *Repulsion* (1964), and *Cul-de-Sac* (1965)—and Evans felt his sophistication was a better match for Levin's material than the over-the-top campiness of Castle. Despite his early reservations, Polanski kept reading the yellow sheets of *Rosemary's Baby*. "By the time I was through my eyes were popping out of my head," he recalled. "When Bob Evans called the next morning and asked my opinion of the book, I gave it a rave review."[2]

In 1967 horror movies had become one of the movie industry's less respectable sidelines. The great run of black-and-white classics of Hollywood's Golden Age, like *Dracula*, *Frankenstein*, *The Invisible Man*, and *The Wolf Man*, had given way to a long line of commercial but crude B-pictures that recycled stock characters, plots, settings, and performers, from earlier works. Typecast actors Boris Karloff, Bela Lugosi, Peter Lorre,

Lon Chaney Jr., and Vincent Price labored away in interchangeable roles as vampires, werewolves, mummies, and mad scientists. In the fifties and early sixties, American independent producer Roger Corman and Britain's Hammer Films had cornered the market on gothic features that invariably delivered blood, revealing female clothes, and the requisite "chills," but these usually played as second-tier attractions and drive-in specials. Television had further reduced the staple horror premises to jokes in the prime-time comedy series *The Addams Family* and its shameless duplicate *The Munsters*. For every occasionally thoughtful and frightening film, like Jacques Tourneur's *Cat People* (1942) or *Curse of the Demon* (1957), there had been a hundred cheesy flicks with titles such as *Abbott and Costello Meet Frankenstein; Queen of Blood; Burn, Witch, Burn!; The Horror Chamber of Dr. Faustus; The Horror of Party Beach; The Curse of the Living Corpse; Billy the Kid vs. Dracula;* and *The Incredibly Strange Creatures Who Stopped Living and Became Mixed-Up Zombies!!?* In the parlance of 1967, horror was very definitely not happening.

But with Roman Polanski preparing a screenplay and settling in behind the camera, *Rosemary's Baby* promised to be different. Just as Ira Levin had transplanted the old themes of witchcraft and devil worship into the contemporary citified world, Polanski would impart a trendy psychological ambiguity to what traditional horror directors would have presented with corny shock effects and heavy-handed melodrama. Indeed, his previous work, *The Fearless Vampire Killers*, had explicitly parodied the standard Hollywood horror gimmicks. "For credibility's sake," Polanski stated in his 1984 memoir, "I decided that there would have to be a loophole: the possibility that Rosemary's supernatural experiences were figments of her imagination. The entire story, as seen through her eyes, could have been a chain of only superficially sinister coincidences, a product of her feverish fancies."[3] The result was an extension of Levin's urban believability: instead of looking like *Dracula* or *Frankenstein, Rosemary's Baby* would fit into the same cinematic category as innovative and admired releases like *Breathless* or *Bonnie and Clyde.*

Polanski planned to shoot his picture's exteriors in its environment of New York City, rather than a Los Angeles back lot, using the ornate Dakota Apartments across from Central Park as the model for Rosemary and Guy Woodhouse's Bramford. He also insisted on carefully blocking his interior scenes to suggest the is-this-really-happening uncertainty of Rosemary's predicament. "In trying to convey this subjective immediacy, I often staged long, complicated scenes using short focal lenses that called for extreme precision in the placing of both cameras and actors . . . . Ideally the lens should be at the same distance from the subject as the eye of the notional observer."[4] There were no thunderstorms or rattling chains in the director's vision, no cheap scares. "My devotion to authentic detail was growing with every picture I made," he said.[5]

In casting *Rosemary's Baby*, Polanski also bucked the genre's conventions. Rather than selecting players with established reputations as horror stars, he called on experienced character actors Ruth Gordon, Ralph Bellamy, and Sidney Blackmer to portray the middle-aged members of the New York witch coven (one exception was the cameo by Elisha Cook Jr., who had appeared in *House on Haunted Hill*). For the young couple at the center of the tale he wanted healthy, wholesome people to heighten its relevance to the youth movement: Warren Beatty, Robert Redford, and an up-and-coming Jack Nicholson were considered for the role of Guy, but Polanski chose John Cassavetes, himself an actor and filmmaker with a noncon-formist streak. Mia Farrow, then married to Frank Sinatra, was picked as Rosemary. "There are so many things in Rosemary that are so typical of Mia," Ira Levin later remarked. "Her humor, her sensitivity, her Roman Catholic childhood . . . . I've always thought John Cassavetes was miscast, because you always knew he was up to no good."[6] Polanski and Cassavetes would frequently clash on the set (Polanski wanted to stick to the script and Levin's original dialogue, while Cassavetes wanted to improvise), but the director got on well with Farrow. "He had an infectious enthusiasm that few could resist, and a real knowledge of what would work professionally," she remembered.[7] Polanski too was pleased with his star's talent, although he had originally pictured the all-American Tuesday Weld as Rosemary and had privately hoped that a studio boss might recommend for the role his own actress wife, Sharon Tate.

Despite the friction between Polanski and Cassavetes, and Frank Sinatra's delivery of divorce papers to Mia Farrow on the set, the filming of *Rosemary's Baby* during the last half of 1967 went smoothly. Levin's novel had been released to good notices and strong sales, and Polanski's film was a faithful adaptation of it. A minimum of stunts and special effects meant the production was unimpeded by complex technical shots. Its final budget came in at a reasonable $2.3 million, somewhat over the original esti-mates but approved by Robert Evans, who supported Polanski. "Roman, just go back on the set and do it your way," the producer told him when his methods caused consternation among the older executives. "I'll take responsibility."[8]

It was Polanski's attention to domestic realism—the apparent ordinariness of the Bramford Apartments and their occupants—that gives the movie its lingering power. His first impression of Levin's novel as "a soap opera" was to be the one that informed its scene-by-scene escalation of suspense. As the Woodhouse couple, Farrow and Cassavetes really do appear to be just ambitious newlyweds in the big city, looking forward to their growing family and his ascending career; Sidney Blackmer and Ruth Gordon really do seem in the beginning to be no more than nosey neighbors, idiosyncratic but harmless; and Ralph Bellamy's avuncular Dr. Sapirstein really does come across as a caring, trustworthy obstetrician with only the expectant mother's best interests in mind. The Bramford Apartments are virtually a character unto themselves, designed and shot to look like no more than desirable rental space and well-appointed love nest. Slowly and skillfully, Polanski's neatly limned tableau of household coziness and conjugal bliss becomes inverted into a mood of diabolic menace.

The most surreal part of the movie was the dreamy, hallucinogenic sequence in which Rosemary is impregnated by Satan as a gathering of naked, dumpy devil worshippers chant in the background. A long-standing but discredited rumor holds that Polanski called on an eccentric San Franciscan who had started his own religion to advise him on the take and to appear in costume as the briefly glimpsed figure of Satan himself—the advisor, supposedly, was Anton LaVey of the Church of Satan. In fact, LaVey did not participate at all in the photography. "After finishing that scene," Farrow recounted, "the actor climbed off me and said politely, in all seriousness, 'Miss Farrow, I just want to say, it's a real pleasure to have worked with you.'"[9] When the entire production wrapped, an emotionally distraught Farrow sought refuge in Transcendental Meditation and journeyed to India in February 1968, where she studied under the Maharishi Mahesh Yogi with members of the Beatles and the Beach Boys.

Rosemary's Baby was released in June 1968, with a potent ad campaign that showed a baby buggy silhouetted in an unearthly green light, with the tagline "Pray for Rosemary's Baby." The film was a box-office hit and drew appreciative reviews; as with Levin's original novel, the write-ups acknowledged the inherent fantasy of the plot but praised the plausibility of its execution. "Only a director with wit could have made the witchcraft credible," noted the esteemed Stanley Kauffmann in the *New Republic*. "Only a director with real cinematic gifts could have made a sequence like the one where Rosemary barricades herself in the apartment or the childbirth scene."[10] The movie's presentations of nudity and blasphemy were forward for 1968 (the same season as the equally provocative *The Graduate* and *I Am Curious [Yellow]*), which spurred protests from Catholic groups and thus more good publicity. Ruth Gordon eventually received an Academy Award for Supporting Actress for her portrayal of the conniving Minnie Castevet, and Polanski's adapted screenplay won an Academy nomination.

Yet with *Rosemary's Baby*, Polanski had done more than to make Satanism merely "realistic." Aided by the celebrity of Mia Farrow—ex-Mrs. Sinatra, seeker of enlightenment, and pal of Beatles—he had made the occult *fashionable*, something to be discussed in the same hip circles that argued over New York real estate, European cinema, Broadway theater, sexual morality, and maternity advice. The irony was that neither the picture's lead actress nor its director took the occult as seriously as the millions of moviegoers who responded to it. Mia Farrow, raised a Catholic, was gradually shedding her received beliefs in the cultural tumult of the sixties and her disintegrating marriage. "My religion, as it had been presented to me and as I had interpreted it, was no longer helpful, satisfying, or even acceptable to me," she recalled in her 1997 autobiography, *What Falls Away*. "With the help of the books I had brought with me, along with a few I found at the ashram, I began to redefine my relationship with Christianity, Catholicism, and Being."[11] And Roman Polanski later wrote: "Being an agnostic . . . I no more believed in Satan as evil incarnate than I believed in a personal god; the whole idea conflicted with my rational view of the world."[12] Anton LaVey, meanwhile, who never tried to dispel the legend of his role in the movie and who probably encouraged it, described *Rosemary's Baby* as "the best paid commercial for Satanism since the Inquisition."[13]

In the first few years after *Rosemary's Baby*, Hollywood moved to capitalize on its appeal—but what exactly was its appeal? Certainly, the occult was now a commercial subject, yet just how commercial depended on the filmmakers' interpretation of it. In 1968 Britain's Hammer Films put out *The Devil Rides Out* (titled *The Devil's Bride* in the United States), based on the book by Dennis Wheatley, the novelist who had so influenced lyricist Geezer Butler of Black Sabbath. *The Devil Rides Out* was a decent effort from screenwriter Richard Matheson and Hammer's principal director Terence Fisher. It starred Christopher Lee in an unusual (for him) part as the good guy and future James Bond villain Charles Gray as an Aleister

Crowley-like Satanist. The film's stagy portrait of secret rites among the English upper crust, however, complete with a costume devil at their center, had little of *Rosemary's Baby*'s mod subtlety. More exploitative were 1970's *Bloodsuckers* (a.k.a. *Incense for the Damned*), about a Greek sect of vampirism; 1971's *The Blood on Satan's Claw*, about witchcraft in seventeenth-century England; *The Brotherhood of Satan*, about a contemporary rural American witch cult; and 1972's *Demons of the Mind*, about possession and incest; and *Blood Sabbath*, about a young man caught up in an all-girl witch coven ("They were evil, they were sadistic, they were drop dead gorgeous!"). To varying degrees these films offered spooky moods and effective frights, but to a large extent they were merely redressing old horror with a new veneer of occult exposition—pentagrams, covert ceremonies, mysterious religions—as well as more open presentations of sex and gore. None found major success.

Other films of the early seventies fared better in incorporating the occult into their story lines. Maverick English cineaste Ken Russell's *The Devils*, from 1971, retold Aldous Huxley's critical history *The Devils of Loudun* in his trademark flamboyant fashion. With Vanessa Redgrave and Oliver Reed, *The Devils* was Russell's violent and wildly eroticized take on an episode of alleged demonic possession in a convent of nuns in seventeenth-century France; the real devils, Russell and Huxley suggested, were extreme sexual repression and political intrigue. *The Mephisto Waltz*, also from 1971, was adapted from Fred Mustard Stewart's 1969 novel and saw Alan Alda as a musician battling with the ritual soul-stealing of Curt Jurgens. Like *Rosemary's Baby*, this was an adult consideration of a topic that had been more often treated as drive-in fodder, replicating the attractive young couple (Alda and Jacqueline Bisset) unknowingly caught up in a satanic conspiracy. Director Robert Mulligan's 1972 adaptation of Thomas Tryon's *The Other* similarly captured the book's understated tone and disturbing plot of childhood psychological aberration in a Connecticut farm community. That same year Shirley MacLaine starred in *The Possession of Joel Delaney*, based on Ramona Stewart's 1970 novel, as—once again—the disbelieving, educated urbanite faced with an unexplainable phenomena, in this case the soul of a murderous Puerto Rican voodoo victim taking over the body and actions of her younger brother (played by Perry King). Stewart's book and MacLaine's movie were smart and relatively decorous treatments of occult themes, slowly discounting the expected "rational explanations" of the era (schizophrenia, illicit drugs) before coming to terms with the irrational truths behind the mayhem. MacLaine's appearance in *The Possession of Joel Delaney* came after she dropped out of another project with a similar subject, when an author and screenwriter friend of hers could not get a satisfactory deal to have her take the lead in the film of his own novel, whose main character she had inspired. Instead, William Peter Blatty went on to produce *The Exorcist* without her.

Blatty's securing of authority over Warner Brothers' treatment of *The Exorcist* was the first of several key creative moves that made that picture one of the highest grossing and most influential in cinematic history. *The Exorcist* not only made tens of millions of dollars on its initial release but propelled the occult boom to its greatest commercial heights, inspiring dozens of filmic imitations, hundreds of books, countless parodies, and its own passel of sequels and prequels. Its impact resonated throughout the decade and is still felt today. By 1972 Blatty was wealthy from the royalties of his novel and had years of experience in the movie industry, and he was well positioned to take control of the production after unflattering or underhanded bids from showbiz biggies Lord Lew Grade and Paul Monash. In granting himself supervision over the elements that went into bringing *The Exorcist* from print to screen—a capacity seldom attained in Hollywood by mere writers—Blatty ensured his landmark story became a movie of legendary proportions. Even midway through the shooting of *The Exorcist*, he observed, "I've witnessed the making of a film that not only is faithful to the novel but, on certain levels is better."[14]

Blatty's most important decision was to hire William Friedkin to direct. He had previously sought out for the job heavyweights Stanley Kubrick, Arthur Penn, and Mike Nichols, each of whom turned him down, but after screening Friedkin's 1971 hit crime drama, *The French Connection*, Blatty recognized the qualities he wanted for his own film: "The pace! The excitement! The look of documentary realism!"[15] In that heyday of the American auteur, *The Exorcist*'s studio of Warner Brothers afforded the director as much or more artistic license as the producer, and thus Blatty had to hand Friedkin the last word on the picture's scene-by-scene construction. It paid off. The eventual posters for the film emphasized its combined authorship: "William Peter Blatty's *The Exorcist* . . . Directed by William Friedkin."

Thirty-four-year-old Friedkin, who had trained as a documentarian and was hot off an Academy Award for Best Director for *The French Connection*, had firm ideas from the start. He rejected Blatty's draft screenplay (full of subplots and comic relief, it would have run four hours if filmed) and asked for a shorter, punchier blueprint that retained the most memorable scenes of the novel but pared away the red herrings and interior monologues. Friedkin also brought in two important members of his *French Connection* team, cinematographer Owen Roizman and associate editor Norman Gay. In both Friedkin's films, Roizman used a gritty color palette to achieve a bleak, naturalistic lighting scheme; in both Friedkin's films the editing constantly pushed the story ahead without pausing for setup or resolution. Quick, seemingly random clips of action and conversation jumped across the screen, leaving viewers unable to quibble with the mechanics of the plot. "One of the things I was conscious of doing while editing *The Exorcist*," Friedkin later explained, "was to keep it moving and not stop in one place anywhere, where the audience could say, 'Oh, wait a minute fella . . . '"[16] The raw visuals and headlong momentum of *The Exorcist* made it what the director called "a realistic look at inexplicable events."[17]

Casting the film was also crucial to its verisimilitude. Though Jane Fonda had turned down the part of Chris MacNeil, the final lineup of Ellen Burstyn, performer-playwright Jason Miller, stage veterans Lee J. Cobb and Jack MacGowran, and Ingmar Bergman player Max von Sydow—fine but not hugely famous actors—took the project to yet another level of believability. The role of the possessed Regan went to twelve-year-old Linda Blair, whose spontaneity in rehearsals with Burstyn impressed Friedkin and who was credible as both a bubbly adolescent and, under Dick Smith's grisly makeup, a victim of demonic possession. Prepared with improvisations and script conferences among the cast, the director found more of the you-are-there immediacy that made an inherently outrageous story seem like a slice of life.

The Exorcist began shooting in August 1972. The production soon bogged down with a number of accidents and offstage tragedies, which were later played up in the film's initial publicity handouts: Max von Sydow's brother died, Jack MacGowran died, Jason Miller's son was injured, crewmen were hurt, sets burnt down, and so on. These events were really attributable to the normal upsets and attrition that take place over any long and occasionally delayed production schedule, but they made good copy as evidence of a diabolical curse placed on the picture. For a few of Linda Blair's scenes as a possessed child, the young actress was replaced by adult stunt doubles Eileen Dietz and Linda Rae Hager, and her final demonic voice was dubbed by old pro Mercedes McCambridge, who reliably delivered lines like

That's much too vulgar a display of power, Karras!

and

Stick your cock up her ass, you motherfucking, worthless cocksucker!

in an appropriately gravelly voice. "There has not been a human being who does not have a dark side," McCambridge shrugged of her obscene contributions. "That's why it was so easy to do *The Exorcist* . . . to play the devil, I was honest enough to admit there's a devil in me, probably as heinous as Lucifer himself."[18] In a couple of infamous shots, an animated dummy of Blair was used to depict her head rotating almost 360 degrees, a gimmick Blatty objected to ("Supernatural doesn't mean impossible," he complained to Friedkin[19]) but which became two of *The Exorcist's* best-remembered images.

During the film's editing stage in the fall of 1973, Friedkin mercilessly cut its running time down from 140 to 122 minutes, which meant dispensing with the author-producer's deepest theological messages. "In editing *The Exorcist*, every attempt is being made to play down the metaphysics and play up the horror," the director commented.[20] Blatty felt such excisions— most notably of a questing dialogue between Jason Miller and Max von Sydow as Fathers Karras and Merrin, just before the climactic exorcism— diluted the spiritual importance of the story. "Here we had an explicit articulation of the theme that gave the film clarity and a definite moral weight," Blatty wrote afterward in *The Exorcist: From Novel to Film*. "Clarity because it focused the story on Karras and his problem of faith; and moral weight because it put the obscene and repellent elements of the film into the context of evil's primary attack on mankind: namely, the inducement of despair."[21] Friedkin objected to such material for slowing the urgency of the narrative and was probably correct, but the lasting result was to change *The Exorcist* from a wordy meditation on belief to a terrifying masterpiece of the occult.

As we look back on the picture forty years after its debut on December 26, 1973, some obvious datedness stands out. Its quietly ominous prologue at Father Merrin's archaeological dig in northern Iraq recalls that country's uneasy peace with America at the time while ruled by a brutal Ba'athist regime (the first voices heard in the movie are Muslim calls to prayer). The personal honorability of its Catholic priests, left alone to care for a psychologically disturbed youngster, is never in doubt. The film's setting in Washington, DC, in the middle of Watergate gave its presentations of guilt and corruption an unexpectedly human relevance, and its release less than twelve months after the *Roe v. Wade* Supreme Court decision, which legalized abortion in the United States, likewise made its haunted mothers and problem children somehow more germane. *The Exorcist*'s credits were designed in the same red-on-black motif used in *Time*'s "Is God Dead?" cover, a color pattern that became widely used in countless titles for conveying anything to do with demonology, witchcraft, or Satanism.

Though prepared by Blatty's best-selling novel and the already existing cultural fascination with the occult, the public of 1973 and 1974 was still shocked and horrified by the film: words and actions that were upsetting enough on the page became certifiably appalling when put on celluloid. The mainstream press, including both *Time* and *Newsweek* magazines, ran feature stories on *The Exorcist* "phenomenon," which saw long lineups outside movie houses and fainting, nausea, miscarriages, heart attacks, and other crises inside them. Catholic clergy reported a rush of solicitations from people who imagined themselves possessed. A handful of suicides and psychotic episodes were attributed to recent viewings of the film. The split-second frames of a demonic face in Father Karras's dream sequence, cleverly extracted by Friedkin from test shots of Eileen Dietz in ghoulish face paint, were said to have brought on epileptic seizures. Some religious leaders condemned it for apparently showing Satan victorious; others praised it for highlighting the true ugliness of evil. (Almost no one remarked that the real possessor of Regan MacNeil, as Blatty construed it, was likely not Satan himself but Pazuzu, an ancient Assyrian demon.) The movie raked in over $66 million in the first year of its screening, which made it one of this most lucrative ever made; adjusted for inflation, it is still among the highest-earning pictures of all time. Some critics reluctantly acknowledged *The Exorcist*'s brute filmic force: "This is the most scary picture I've seen in years—the *only* scary picture I've seen in years," wrote Stanley Kauffmann. "*The Exorcist* makes no sense, [but] if you want to be shaken, it will scare the hell out of you."[22] "I am not sure exactly what reasons people will have for seeing this movie; surely enjoyment won't be one, because what we get here aren't the delicious chills of a Vincent Price thriller, but raw and painful experience," noted Roger Ebert. "Are people so numb they need movies of this intensity in order to feel anything at all?"[23]

There was also a backlash. Vincent Canby in the *New York Times* called *The Exorcist* "a chunk of occultist claptrap,"[24] and pointed out that, among its thronging spectators, "not five out the 100 people seem to give a hang about the instruction being received. They're getting their kicks out of seeing a small girl tortured and torn, quite literally."[25] For all its quasi-pornographic set pieces, a few interpreters took *The Exorcist* to be conservative wish-fulfillment in the wake of Woodstock and the Summer of Love, putting a foul-mouthed, disobedient adolescent through a punishing physical ordeal and having her emerge docile and respectful of her mother and God. Some dismissed the filmmakers' claims to be reaching for religious depth. "'The Exorcist' is the kind of movie you get when you leave religion to screenwriters and businessmen," declared a Catholic priest, Father Eugene C. Kennedy. "In a country that can find a spiritual message in 'Jonathan Livingston Seagull,' that thinks Rod McKuen is deep, sees another Harry Truman in Gerald Ford, and has suddenly made Barry Goldwater into an elder statesman, the success of 'The Exorcist' may not be so surprising after all."[26]

Much of the controversy centered on the film's graphic scenes of urination, vomiting, sexual desecration, and extreme profanity, most of it performed by a child, which many said rated an X rather than R classification by the Motion Picture Association of America (MPAA)—the X, of course, would have severely limited the size of its potential audience. "The film contains brutal shocks, almost indescribable obscenities," wrote Roger Ebert in his 1974 review. "That it received an R rating and not the X is stupefying."[27] In fact, *The Exorcist* was a big-budget production released by a major American studio, featuring respected actors and made by an Oscar-winning director, and therefore had a sway over the MPAA ratings board that a cheap foreign exploitation movie did not. Like the contemporaneous shock rock of Alice Cooper and Kiss, the record-breaking popularity of the movie provided yet more evidence for opponents that society was sinking into a cesspool of vulgarity and immorality. In the arenas of free speech, censorship, community standards, and cinematic offensiveness, *The Exorcist* broke down barriers that have never been repaired.

The movie's influence spread. *The Exorcist* was nominated for several Academy Awards in 1974, including Best Picture, Best Director, Best Adapted Screenplay, Best Supporting Actor for Jason Miller, and Best Supporting Actress for Linda Blair, and won for Blatty's screenplay and Chris Newman's Sound Design. By then it had already entered the pop lexicon, with a parody in *Mad* magazine ("The Ecch-orcist"), jokey references on *The Bob Newhart Show* and, in time, *Saturday Night Live* (guest host Richard Pryor as a very nervous priest), the satirical series *Soap*, and elsewhere on television. Musicians were affected too. In 1974 R 'n' B guitarist Curtis Mayfield released an album and eponymous single, *Sweet Exorcist*, and Mike Oldfield's distinctive "Tubular Bells," from the movie's soundtrack, became a hit record and advanced Oldfield's career as a pioneering composer in the expanding New Age genre. Both Blatty's novel and Friedkin's film had turned on the very potent plot point of Father Karras hearing Regan's recorded unintelligible speech become demonic language when played back in reverse, which very likely contributed to the "back masking" rumors that grew around Led Zeppelin's "Stairway to Heaven" and other rock anthems. Members of Black Sabbath spoke of watching the picture multiple times and, in a triumphant pinnacle of the occult boom, a teenage Linda Blair was photographed with the band backstage at a 1976 concert in New Haven, Connecticut, giggling sweetly while held aloft in the tattooed arms of Ozzy Osbourne. Perhaps Satan had won after all.

If there had been any lingering reservations about the commercial attractiveness of the occult, *The Exorcist*'s spectacular profits erased them. Indeed, the film's most immediate effect was to transform the entire topic into blatant cash-in fodder, having less to do with the Prince of Darkness than the Almighty Dollar. Whatever the private sentiments held by the makers of *The Exorcist, Rosemary's Baby, The Devils, The Brotherhood of Satan, The Possession of Joel Delaney*, or *Blood Sabbath*, which had ranged from sincere faith to agnosticism to opportunism, the occult's overriding imperative in Hollywood now became pure greed. And whereas the fringe artist Kenneth Anger was at least genuinely committed to the themes of his avant-garde films *Lucifer Rising* and *Invocation of My Demon Brother*, many of the producers of more mainstream pictures were unabashed schlockmeisters. Complemented by synergistic appeals in pop music and publishing (a fresh *Exorcist* paperback was reprinted with a cover banner, "See the movie—it's the most electrifying thing that will ever happen to you!"), the movie industry hurried to capitalize on what was undeniably the social trend of the decade.

Over the remainder of the seventies the inventions of *The Exorcist* turned into the clichés of dozens of American and foreign movies. There were the mysterious forces that were directed at or through a child or young adult: *Beyond the Door, It's Alive, Devil Times Five, The Brood, Alice, Sweet Alice* a.k.a. *Communion, Audrey Rose, The Chosen* a.k.a. *Holocaust 2000*,

Cathy's Curse a.k.a. *Cauchemars*, *The Child*, *To the Devil—A Daughter*, *The Omen*, *Carrie*, Brian DePalma's 1976 adaptation of Stephen King's debut novel, and Stanley Kubrick's 1980 film of King's *The Shining*. There was the involvement of the church: *Abby*, *The Tempter*, *The Sentinel*, *The Omen*, *Alice, Sweet Alice*, *The Amityville Horror*, and *To the Devil—A Daughter*. There was the invocation of biblical or other ancient doctrine to impart a cosmic, millennial gravitas to the story: *The Omen*, *The Manitou*, *The Chosen*, *The Sentinel*, and *The Devil's Rain*. There was the exploitation of nudity and gory violence to portray the supposed perversities of demonism: *Suspiria*, *The House of Exorcism* a.k.a. *Lisa and the Devil*, *Abby*, *The Tempter*, *The Satanic Rites of Dracula*, *Satan's Cheerleaders*, *Satan's Slave*, *Help Me, I'm Possessed!*, and numerous U.S. and European hard- and soft-core pornographic features, including *Nuda per Satana*, *L'Ossessa*, *Satánico Pandemonium*, and *The Devil in Miss Jones*. Even the article "The" in titles seemed meant to convey a coldly Lovecraftian realism: *The Omen*, *The Manitou*, *The Sentinel*, *The Fury*, *The Chosen*, *The Child*, *The Brood*, *The Devil's Rain*, *The Amityville Horror*, and *The Reincarnation of Peter Proud*. Above all, the common thread running through most of these films was their stubbornly serious treatment of the supernatural. There was little that was campy or tongue-in-cheek here. Within their particular dumb or derivative premises, they kept a straight face and maintained that the occult was no joke.

Television, someone once said, is the sincerest form of flattery. Just as the big screen was inundated with devilish material after *Rosemary's Baby* and *The Exorcist*, the living room's electronic hearth was also made to glow with occult-related programming over the same period. An early entry into the field was the series *Dark Shadows*, a gothic soap opera of vampirism and family intrigue that aired on America's ABC network from 1966 to 1971. A pair of feature TV movies, *House of Dark Shadows* and *Night of Dark Shadows*, followed; Canadian actor Jonathan Frid, as the cadaverous and undead Barnabas Collins, became an unlikely sex symbol. There was also *Rod Serling's Night Gallery*, a horror-based anthology show introduced by the former *Twilight Zone* host and head writer. Serling was actually dissatisfied with the constraints imposed on him by his corporate superiors (referring to a routine detective series of the time, he complained that they wanted "*Mannix* in a shroud"[28]), and unlike the *Twilight Zone* episodes he had made some ten years previously, *Night Gallery* bore little of his humanist stamp. Nevertheless, the best stories from the program were smart and usually ended with a macabre twist, as with "The Lone Survivor" and "Clean Kills and Other Trophies," and the adaptations of H. P. Lovecraft's "Cool Air" and "Pickman's Model." *Night Gallery* was on NBC from 1969 to 1973.

A third occult television drama that later acquired cult status was *The Night Stalker*, in which hard-boiled newspaperman Carl Kolchak (Darren McGavin) investigated a different unexplainable case each week. Starting with a TV movie and a sequel, *The Night Strangler*, Kolchak hunted down a variety of horror figures (werewolves, zombies, demons, etc.) in the context of a modern urban underworld; like its cinematic equivalents of the era, *The Night Stalker* dispensed with the Old World or medieval trappings of traditional genre yarns and reset them in the same reality that contained street crime, office towers, and telephones. In the pilot film Kolchak catches a thirsty vampire in the act of stealing blood bags from a laboratory cooler. Chris Carter, who went on to create the popular *X-Files* series twenty years later, cited *The Night Stalker* as an influence. Its brief run on ABC lasted over 1974 and 1975.

Several made-for-TV movies of the seventies—in the years when made-for-TV was a distinct medium—reflected occult concerns, and some of these offered real scares. *The Norliss Tapes*, from 1973, was a creation of *The Night Stalker*'s Dan Curtis, and its comparable plot found a fearless reporter seeking out a covert vampire network. The very creepy *Don't Be Afraid of the Dark* was shown that same year and featured Kim Darby as a young wife harassed by small goblin-like creatures in her home; like Rosemary Woodhouse and the Bramford Apartments' witch coven, only Darby knew that the creatures existed and that they had malevolent designs on her. *Satan's School for Girls* also premiered in 1973, dealing with witchcraft among the students of an all-girl academy. A two-part dramatization of Flora Rheta Schreiber's book *Sybil* won high ratings in 1976, with Sally Field in the title role and Joanne Woodward as her doctor. *Sybil* emphasized the most unsettling qualities of the multiple-personality case (childhood trauma and disembodied intelligences), and *Exorcist* fans would recognize the supporting role acted by Gina Petrushka, who had appeared in William Friedkin's film. *The Possessed*, from 1977, was more clearly inspired by *The Exorcist*: James Farentino portrayed a priest dealing with a possession outbreak at a girls' school and contained an effective scene of a female victim spitting nails at him. *The Spell* (1977) and *The Initiation of Sarah* (1978) each lifted the *Carrie* theme of a young woman's psychic retaliation against her tormentors, while 1978's *Devil Dog: The Hound of Hell* was, not surprisingly, about a demonic canine. Also in 1978 came *The Dark Secret of Harvest Home*, a not-bad television treatment of Thomas Tryon's earlier novel *Harvest Home*, starring the formidable Bette Davis as a rural elder who turned out to be leading a murderous, matriarchal fertility cult. Stephen King's vampires-in-a-small-town tale, *Salem's Lot*, was made into a miniseries in 1979.

None of these TV series and films, to be sure, offered in-depth examinations of occult issues. Several were merely rip-offs of successful theatrical productions, with PG rather than R glimpses of sex or violence and which could be watched for free in the comfort of home rather than for a few bucks down at the local bijou. But in a decade where there were only three nationwide broadcast companies in America and when most households received no more than a dozen TV channels, and before the widespread introduction of home video equipment, the relative amount of occult programming in the United States during the seventies is striking. In millions of ordinary homes, the subjects of possession, supernatural beings or abilities, and dark, explicitly anti-Christian forces became familiar entertainments. The occult may have been a show business fad, but it had also mutated into a fixture of popular culture and folk belief.

Indeed, the pervasiveness of Satanism in the cinema of the decade (let alone in the rock music and the books) made for a continual reinforcement of its credibility. In only one or two movies, the notions of devil worship or demonic power would have remained pretty outlandish, but the scores of pictures that were exhibited and aired made such devices all the more common and thus acceptable. The *Rosemary's Baby* and *Exorcist* models that were copied in nearly every other picture were predicated on the protagonists' initial skepticism being slowly and frightfully supplanted by conviction: "This is no dream, this is happening!" exclaims Mia Farrow's Rosemary while being ravished by Satan, while Ellen Burstyn's Chris MacNeil asks a panel of medical experts who have recommended the rite of exorcism as a shock treatment to save Regan, "You're telling me that I should take my daughter to a witch doctor. Is that it?" The repeated point was that the occult only *seemed* to be an outmoded superstition. By constantly setting up science and rationalism as straw men to be demolished by undeniable paranormal occurrence, producers and directors secured the willing suspension of disbelief among a huge viewership.

The occult figured in films of divergent moods and styles, even in those from genres outside horror: the 1973 James Bond adventure *Live and Let Die* (voodoo and Tarot cards); Nicolas Roeg's thriller *Don't Look Now* (psychic visions); and the mystery of *The Wicker Man* (Celtic paganism). Sometimes the settings were conventional, as in *The Legend of Hell House* from 1973 (disparate group faces frights inside a mysterious old mansion), and others bordered on the preposterous, as in *The Car*, from 1977 (evil, driverless limousine runs people over). The most successful occult movies in the wake of *The Exorcist* were imitative enough to ride on the commercial coattails of previous blockbusters and original enough to set new standards of filmic and even religious ingenuity.

Released in 1974, *It's Alive* was a low-budget effort that came with high-value marketing, including an evocative marquee poster that showed an inhuman claw emerging from a bassinet and featuring the memorable come-ons, "There's only one thing wrong with the Davis baby . . . " and "The one film you should not see alone." Director Larry Cohen kept the monstrous killer infant mostly unseen for maximum suspense, and the story line referred to the highly current matters of abortion, widespread environmental pollution, and the perils of modern medicine. What brought people into the theaters was the prospect of seeing the title villain in action (it was a special-effect puppet designed by makeup whiz Rick Baker, who had assisted Dick Smith on *The Exorcist*), but what remained with them after the credits was the sobering thought of how the real unborn might be contaminated by the chemicals that pervaded everyday life in twentieth-century America.

Race with the Devil, from 1975, starred Peter Fonda and Warren Oates as vacationing motorcycle buffs who, with their spouses, stumbled upon a sacrificial satanic cult in the rural United States. The theme of naïve city slickers menaced by depraved backwoods types had echoes of previous films *Deliverance*, *Straw Dogs*, and even *The Brotherhood of Satan*, and may have reflected the decade's increasing distinction between tolerant, open metropolis and repressed, reactionary heartland. But *Race with the Devil* also seemed to refer to the official corruption revealed by Watergate, as when the heroes called on the intervention of local police, who themselves turn out to be part of the unholy conspiracy. The movie's highlight, of course, was the exciting chase scenes that put an occult angle on vehicular action, and its downbeat surprise ending emphasized the negative outlook that characterized so many other works on contemporary witchery: even the well-meaning and the resourceful were no match for the might of Satan.

By the time of the 1979 premiere of *The Amityville Horror*, the exaggerations and outright fictions of Jay Anson's purportedly "true" book on which it was based had already come to light, but the movie was still a box-office smash. With James Brolin (who had starred in *The Car*) and Margot Kidder (who had acted in *The Reincarnation of Peter Proud*) as the unsuspecting George and Kathy Lutz, and with a hyperventilating Rod Steiger as a hapless Catholic priest, *The Amityville Horror* told an essentially made-up story with a believable delivery. Like the published account, the cinematic version had all the elements that had by then been codified as mandatory in portraits of occult horror: children in danger, religious desecration, stomach-churning substances, and the lingering presence of prehistoric evil (the Amityville house was said to be situated on what had been an ancient Indian enclosure of the diseased and the dying). Some observers suggested that the book and the movie were really parables of home ownership and its hazards in an age of rising inflation and interest rates—in *Danse Macabre*, his verbose 1981 study of the genre, Stephen King wrote that "the movie might as well have been subtitled *The Horror of the Shrinking Bank Account*."[29] Was the Lutzes' home a portal to hell, or just a fixer-upper money pit? The surface terrors of the narrative, however, were scary enough.

By far the biggest occult movie after 1975, though, was *The Omen*. Like *The Amityville Horror*, this also neatly combined the category's requisite ingredients of satanic shock: a malevolent youngster; bloody violence (including decapitation and impalement); the intervention of Catholic clergy; and heavy theological implications. *The Omen* boasted an A-level cast, led by Hollywood greats Gregory Peck (*Gentleman's Agreement, To Kill a Mockingbird*) and Lee Remick (*Days of Wine and Roses*), and picturesque location scenes in Britain and Rome. One of the first preplanned summer blockbusters that were mass-marketed by movie studios in emulation of Steven Spielberg's *Jaws*, *The Omen* was launched in hundreds of North American theaters in June 1976 and became Twentieth Century Fox's most profitable release of the year, pulling in nearly $200 million in the United States, a huge return on its initial budget of just under $3 million. "I remember reading [the script] and thinking, this is going to be a commercial success," recalled Gregory Peck, "but I didn't know it would be that kind of blockbuster . . . I really thought it would be a good paperback thriller. The success is almost obscene."[30]

The picture's religious premise was what really set it apart, and this aspect would have a social reverberation for many years. *The Omen* was not about a single coven of devil worshippers, or isolated cases of demonic possession or haunted houses, but about the Antichrist, an evil ruler whose coming was foretold in the biblical Book of Revelation. According to Saint John of Patmos, the nominal author of Revelation, the Antichrist would emerge before the end of the world, when he would hold dominion over mankind: "And there was given unto him a mouth speaking great things and blasphemies; and power was given unto him to continue forty and two months." *The Omen* posited that the Antichrist, like Rosemary's baby, would have to grow up from a normal human childhood before assuming the vast and wicked authority he would wield for the short time preceding Armageddon and the return of Jesus Christ. Thus, the film shows little Damien (Harvey Stephens) adopted into the home of the U.S. ambassador to the United Kingdom (Peck), even as horrific deaths, accidents, and other mischief occur in his presence. As his identity as the future Antichrist becomes clear, the drama builds on the question of whether or not he can be destroyed before growing to maturity and entry into the political arena. *The Omen*'s publicity played on the solemn scriptural authenticity of its story line: "Remember . . . You have been warned" and "If something frightening happens to you today, think about it. It may be *The Omen*."

For many lay viewers, the movie was the first time they had been made to consider the Book of Revelation, if they had heard of it at all, as being applicable to modern life. But *The Omen*'s screenwriter David Seltzer had actually made up his own biblical-sounding lines in conjunction with the vague imagery of Revelation to suggest a specific vision of planetary destruction that was found nowhere in the real Bible: "From the eternal sea he rises / Creating armies on either shore / Turning man against his brother / 'Til man exists no more." Most biblical experts, then and now, have interpreted the Book of Revelation not as a prediction of distant events but an allegorical indictment of Roman imperialism in the early Christian era. Revelation's beastly number 666, which in *The Omen* is ascribed to the boy Damien, is believed to have originally been a reference to *Neron Kaisar*, that is, Emperor Nero, translated into the Hebrew and Aramaic numerical codes; some specialists have even claimed the more accurate translation is 616. Through the centuries many Christians had designated various enemies as 666 or the Antichrist (Protestant reformer Martin Luther thought it stood for the institution of the papacy itself), and Aleister Crowley had proudly taken the figure as his own alias, along with "the Great Beast." A handful of very speculative rock listeners had even seen 666 in the ZoSo sigil of Led Zeppelin's Jimmy Page. Unusually, David Seltzer wrote the novelized movie tie-in for *The Omen*—most such paperbacks were the work of outside hired guns—which repeated the film's religious contrivances and which became a major bestseller on its own. By the late seventies the subjects of the Antichrist, 666, and the impending Apocalypse had entered everyday parlance among millions of people with no formal background in theology or history. After the movie's great revenues, Seltzer himself conceded, "I did it strictly for the money . . . I just wish I'd had this kind of success with something I personally found more meaningful . . . I do find it horrifying to find how many people actually believe all this silliness."[31]

"Silliness," though, had been made very believable. The gripping realism with which filmmakers had treated the occult was so impressive that demonstrable facts could hardly contest their embellishments. Though practicing witches of many sects certainly held gatherings across North America and around the world, the very few that were linked with criminal activity were soon uncovered by law enforcement. The many troubled individuals who approached church or psychiatric officials with claims that they suffered from diabolical possession were delusional, their illnesses often triggered by the prevalence of possession tales in popular media. The very rare certified instances of unexplainable mental ability or domestic oddity were never as frightening or as destructive as cinematic special effects made out. Global turmoil that seemed to bear out cosmic warnings from old religious texts was really just the continued shifting of geopolitical reality (*The Omen*'s author, David Seltzer, went on to write the screenplay for a 1979 environmental horror movie, *Prophecy*), and the cosmic warnings themselves were symbolic allusions to then-current affairs rather than to anything that might come to pass two millennia later. The movies and television that inspired such imaginings had been so artistically ingenious and phenomenally commercial they shaped everyday opinion about God, the devil, and the supernatural.

They still do. The most celebrated occult films became trademarked as the founding documents of whole series based on the original characters and plots, every new entry increasingly inferior to the first. John Boorman's

Exorcist II: The Heretic came out in 1977 and was an enormous critical and box-office flop, but William Peter Blatty rallied to direct *Exorcist III* in 1990, and two competing pictures, *Exorcist IV: The Beginning* and *Dominion: Prequel to The Exorcist* came out in 2004 and 2005, respectively. The 1973 *Exorcist* was reissued in 1998 with digital enhancements and restored scenes that clarified the spiritual messages William Friedkin had first cut over Blatty's objections. *Rosemary's Baby* was followed by a made-for-TV sequel, *Look What's Happened to Rosemary's Baby*, in 1976 and a television remake in 2014. *It's Alive* begat *It's Alive II* (1978), *It's Alive III: Island of the Alive* (1987), and a 2008 remake. *Beyond the Door* led to *Beyond the Door II* in 1977 and *Beyond the Door III* in 1989. *Damien: Omen II* was made in 1978 as the title character entered his teens (he discovers a small 666 inscribed on his scalp), after which came *Omen III: The Final Conflict* in 1981, which saw Damien Thorn grow up into an American diplomat. *Omen IV: The Awakening* was a TV adaptation from 1991, while a full-fledged remake, *The Omen*, was debuted on June 6, 2006, and featured Mia Farrow as Damien's nanny. *The Amityville Horror* spawned *Amityville II: The Possession* (1982), *Amityville 3-D* (1983), *Amityville 4: The Evil Escapes* (1989), *The Amityville Curse* (1990), *Amityville '92: It's About Time* (1992), *Amityville: A New Generation* (1993), *Amityville: Dollhouse* (1996), a remade *Amityville Horror* (2005), and a TV movie, *Amityville: The Final Testament* (2010). *The Exorcist* was even revived as a Los Angeles stage play in 2012. In short, the legends told by these movies—and they were legends, with little or no foundation in known truths or reputable scholarship—became postmodern cultural traditions, handed down from generation to generation since their inception at the zenith of the occult era.

But even at that zenith, the youngest generation had been included in the fun.

4

Little Devils

Ah! Join *me, fiends! Ol'* Uncle Creepy *was just in the midst of turning over a* new leaf . . . . *As you can see, I got a bit* carried away! *And so will* you *when you see the* ghoulish goodies *I'm offering up this month! But don't take* my *word . . . . Rush on and* read 'em yourself!
—Uncle Creepy

In 1971 Laura Levine was a young copywriter who had just moved from San Francisco to New York City, where she was hired at the Dancer, Fitzgerald, Sample advertising agency. Her creative director, Tony Jaffe, soon gave her the choice job of scripting a campaign for a line of children's breakfast foods. "General Mills had come up with a new cereal, to be produced in two different flavors—one chocolate and the other strawberry," she recalls today. "At the time Cap'n Crunch was very popular and Tony wanted to do funny commercials à la Cap'n Crunch. My assignment was to come up with two cereal characters that would lend themselves to funny commercials . . . there was never a directive (from Tony or General Mills) to make them horror characters."[1] Yet among the several entries Levine submitted were a pair based on the two most famous horror characters of all, and they were the ones ultimately selected by the client. General Mills' new "monster cereals," Count Chocula and Franken Berry, were on the supermarket shelves by Halloween of that year. The packaging and all-important TV commercials were designed by art director Bob Tollis, while Levine wrote the spots and the characters were voiced by actors James Dukas, doing a Bela Lugosi impersonation for Chocula, and Robert McFadden, doing Boris Karloff for Franken Berry. "The basic joke," according to Levine, "was simply that these two supposed horror characters were in fact scared of their own shadows."[2] General Mills later introduced Boo Berry (a disembodied spirit who sounded like Peter Lorre) and Fruit Brute (a howling werewolf). In 1972 the rival firm Ralston put out a competing cereal of strange-shaped nuggets, which were sold under the name Freakies. So it had come to this. Vampires, monsters, ghosts, lycanthropes, mutations: the counterculture had landed directly on the national kitchen table, and tykes across America consumed the occult with their toast, juice, and milk.

Rock music's surging popularity, as well as that of horror novels and movies centered around children, confirmed that the culture of the late sixties and early seventies was preoccupied with youth. This was the adolescence of the baby boom. No generation in history was so prosperous and no generation's favor had been as devoutly courted as theirs. In the United States the voting age had been lowered from twenty-one to eighteen in 1970, and the demands of student protesters had made front-page news and altered political agendas around the world. The boomers' younger siblings were proportionately fewer, but their needs too were accommodated by the state and their tastes were catered to by the market. Naturally, the interests of middle-aged and young adults were filtered down and made palatable for kids. Count Chocula, Franken Berry, Boo Berry, Fruit Brute, and Freakies were just a few examples of how the occult was making the transition.

At some level this was already a society that was showing a decided ambivalence toward the young. Their "innocence" was everywhere in doubt, symbolically in *The Exorcist* and *The Omen*, more directly in non-horror films like *Paper Moon* (Tatum O'Neal's Depression-era con artist), *Taxi Driver* (Jodie Foster's teen prostitute), and *The Bad News Bears* (foul-mouthed little leaguers, led by O'Neal, again). In the seventies the teenaged *Exorcist* actress Linda Blair carved out a specialized career playing traumatized adolescents, in the 1974 TV movie *Born Innocent* (where she was subject to a reformatory rape) and as a kidnapped girl who falls in love with her captor (Martin Sheen) in 1975's *Sweet Hostage*. The cartoonish, heavy metal bloodletting of Alice Cooper and Kiss was made for a teenybopper audience, with songs like Cooper's "I'm Eighteen" and "Teenage Lament '74" and Kiss's "Christine Sixteen." Kiss dolls, decals, trading cards, lunchboxes, and other merchandise—featuring Gene Simmons's fire-breathing Demon front and center—were sought after in schoolyards across North America. Kids who hadn't been allowed to get into theatrical showings of *Rosemary's Baby* or *It's Alive* could still stay up to watch *Don't Be Afraid of the Dark*, *The Possessed*, *Night Gallery*, or *The Night Stalker* on television. The motorcycle stuntman born Robert Knievel rode and jumped his way into the hearts of bike-riding boys throughout the seventies, under his permanent nickname of Evel. Things had changed since Tom Sawyer and the Little Rascals.

Of course, the music and other entertainment aimed at juveniles did not convey serious occult ideas, much less promote Satan worship or blood sacrifice. Many of the themes propounded in the comic books and board games of this time had been fixtures of Halloween festivities and sleepover ghost stories for generations. What was different, however, was the range of media by which the themes were transmitted, and the presumption that teens and preteens could embrace monsters, devils, sorcerers, and other macabre figures as readily as they had embraced stuffed animals, superheroes, cowboys, and doll houses. The parents and grandparents of these youngsters had never encountered the grotesque and the sinister so often and in so many places—from Saturday morning to summer vacation.

And in the toy shop. Among Barbie, GI Joe, Sea-Monkeys, Smash-up Derbies, and their accessories in the seventies were many amusements based at least peripherally on horror gimmicks. After querying officials from over eight hundred toy companies at a 1970 trade fair, the Associated Press reported that occult products would be the industry's key movers in the next years; it was an accurate forecast. Between 1969 and 1975 the Hot Wheels die-cast car line issued vehicles named the Demon (hot rod), the Sand Witch (dune buggy), and the Evil Weevil (souped-up Volkswagen). Vincent Price appeared in TV ads for Milton Bradley's Shrunken Head Apples, a do-it-yourself kit for making hideous gnarled faces from dried fruit. In 1974 Pickwick Records marketed the *Sounds of Terror!* sound effects album to the grade-school set, with bloodcurdling tracks like "The Headless Horseman," "The Nightmare of Lost Souls," "Count Dracula and the Vampires of Death," and "The Exorcism." Toddlers could spend hours with Romper Room's Weebles Haunted House. The monster dioramas of the Aurora plastic model firm had sold steadily from the mid-sixties on, with Dracula, the Wolfman, Frankenstein, and skeletal pirates sharing shelf space with tanks, planes, and drag racers. There was the Creepy Creatures line of jigsaw puzzles, of Dracula, Frankenstein, and a two-sided Dr. Jekyll and Mr. Hyde. Bristol-Myers released a Monster brand of chewable vitamins in the early seventies. A Monster Gift Pak of the ubiquitous GAF Viewmaster 3-D toy was available. Monster makeup, monster action figures, and monster masks all did reliable business. Kids had always been thrilled by monsters, but during the occult boom the variety of monster items on sale became, well, monstrous.

Children's publishing also adapted itself to the trend. Again, witches, ghosts, and haunted houses had been central to juvenile fiction for more than a century, but by the sixties and seventies the industry, like its adult counterpart, was moving to reflect the cross-generational fascination with all things scarifying and to place the occult not in a realm of far-off fairy tales but in the here and now. Early readers might hide under the covers after 1968's *The Crack in the Wall and Other Terribly Weird Tales*, by George Mendoza and illustrated by Mercer Mayer, featuring the delightfully eerie stories and pictures of "The Devil's Pocket," "The Crack in the Wall," and "The Skunk in the Pond." They could also enjoy the adventures of Dorrie, a series begun by writer-illustrator Patricia Coombs in 1976 with *Dorrie and the Halloween Plot*, about a little witch who apprenticed in spells and broomstick riding at the feet of her witch mother. Older children would be ready for novels like Mollie Hunter's *The Haunted Mountain* (1972), Phyllis Reynolds Naylor's *Witch's Sister* (1975), and John Bellairs's supernatural-tinged narratives *The House with a Clock in Its Walls* (1973), *The Figure in the Shadows* (1975), and *The Letter, the Witch, and the Ring* (1976). Diana Wynne Jones launched a long career as a popular author of children's fantasy and mystery with her imaginative *The Ogre Downstairs* (1974), *Eight Days of Luke* (1975), *Cart and Cwidder* (1975), and *Power of Three* (1976). Katherine Paterson's poignant *Bridge to Terabithia*, wherein two youngsters construct an elaborate imaginary kingdom known only to themselves, was awarded the prestigious Newbery Medal for children's literature in 1977.

Modern witchcraft figured prominently in Zilpha Keatley Snyder's *The Headless Cupid* from 1971, in which a family's new stepsister turns out to be practicing magic and their new house may be haunted. The writer's classic *The Witches of Worm*, about a troubled girl's adoption of a demonic cat, won the Newbery in 1973. The occult themes of both books, and their realistic portrayals of childhood's unhappiest emotions, aroused parental controversy and were challenged in some North American school libraries, but they were strong sellers. Though *The Witches of Worm*, *The Headless Cupid*, and the other kids' titles did not approach the grown-up, graphic shocks of *The Exorcist* or *The Other*, stories for young readers had plainly come a long way. The cackling crones of Hansel and Gretel and Snow

White had been replaced by characters and situations recognizable from adolescents' daily lives.

Movies and TV of the sixties and seventies likewise brought the contemporary occult down to a junior level. The Disney studio had produced the theatrical or televised films *The Strange Monster of Strawberry Cove* (1971), *Mystery in Dracula's Castle* (1973), *Escape to Witch Mountain* (1975), *The Ghost of Cypress Swamp* (1977), and the southern gothic ghost story *Child of Glass* (1978), all with the recurring, reassuring premise of good little people outwitting bad big people. *Escape to Witch Mountain*, featuring two children with psychic powers, was a box-office hit and was followed by a sequel, *Return to Witch Mountain*, in 1978. That same year the wizards, elves, and dragons of J. R. R. Tolkien's *The Lord of the Rings* made it to the big screen in an animated version. Debuted in late 1969, the milestone educational program *Sesame Street* introduced an entire cast of friendly monster muppets, among them Herry Monster, Grover, Cookie Monster, Oscar the Grouch, and the Dracula-inspired Count von Count, who taught preschoolers about numbers. Whether the shows were frightening or funny, children were absorbing the idea of alternative dimensions where magic was plausible, where strange creatures existed alongside human beings, and where horror began at home.

The most influential occult-related TV series of the era, however, was *Scooby-Doo, Where Are You!*, which ran on Saturday mornings on CBS from 1969 to 1971 and established the goofy Great Dane and his human pals as some of the longest-lived cartoon characters ever. Ironically, the running principle of the episodes—the ironclad predictability of them, in fact—was that the paranormal phenomena encountered by Scooby, Shaggy, Fred, Daphne, and Velma always turned out to be hoaxes concocted by devious humans for some greedy purpose. At the climax of each story the "supernatural" villain would always be unmasked or otherwise exposed and say something like "It would have been a perfect plan, too, if it wasn't for those meddling kids and their dog." Yet if the point was that the unknown could be rationally explained, given resourcefulness, courage, and enough Scooby snacks, the enjoyment of *Scooby-Doo* derived from how creepy the unknown initially appeared.

Scooby-Doo was the product of Bill Hanna and Joe Barbera's Hanna-Barbera company, which had built its reputation on TV as makers of half-hour weekly cartoon series, including *The Flintstones* and *The Jetsons*. The output necessitated by such schedules was made possible by Hanna-

Barbera's specialty of "limited animation"—the constant recycling of the same economized drawings and actions, as distinguished from the lavish, lifelike artwork that had gone into the classic Disney or Warner Brothers cartoons of decades past, not to mention Hanna and Barbera's own Tom and Jerry shorts for MGM. With tentative titles *Mysteries Five* or *Who's S-S-Scared?*, the program was developed by Hanna-Barbera writers Joe Ruby and Ken Spears, with Scooby and the other cast designed by artist Iwao Takamoto, under the encouragement of CBS children's programming director Fred Silverman. Silverman, who went on to become a dominant executive presence in American television into the seventies and beyond, was the one to suggest the final name *Scooby-Doo*, after the scat singing that closed Frank Sinatra's 1966 song "Strangers in the Night." The early impetus behind the program was to compete with *The Archies* in presenting the regular adventures of another gaggle of happy, healthy teenagers and highlight them with soft-rock musical interludes. Scooby's friends were pretty hip for kids' shows in 1969: Daphne wore miniskirts, Shaggy was a goateed beatnik (inspired by Maynard G. Krebs from the earlier *The Many Loves of Dobie Gillis*), and they drove around in their customized van, the Mystery Machine. Bill Hanna later surmised, "One of the biggest reasons for *Scooby-Doo*'s great appeal, I think, was that the show in certain ways captured the sound as well as the look of the period in all its flower power."[3] The cause of Shaggy's insatiable appetite, the precise nature of the relationship between Fred and Daphne, and the peculiar reviving properties of Scooby snacks later aroused much speculation.

If the basic plot (and much of the animation) of each episode was rigorously repackaged over and over, *Scooby-Doo*'s writers showed ingenuity in devising new frights every time. Vampires, werewolves, ghosts, evil scientists, a frozen caveman, and monsters of various descriptions were encountered by the Mystery Machine's occupants, with requisite cliffhangers, comic relief, and chase scenes before the final revelations. Though every ghoul and goblin was ultimately debunked, it was their apparent plausibility that intrigued young viewers and kept them coming back every Saturday. The entertainment value derived from the scares more than the scams. *Scooby-Doo, Where Are You!* spun off into a whole franchise of TV sequels and other products that are still produced today, first with *The New Scooby-Doo Movies* in 1973, where the gang solved mysteries with the aid of familiar seventies-era guest stars like the Harlem Globetrotters, Jonathan Winters, Tim Conway, Dick Van Dyke, and Sonny and Cher. Numerous imitations of the series sprang up on CBS and rival networks, with wholesome youth, wacky sidekicks, and harmless monsters bumbling through mildly occult scenarios: *Funky Phantom* (1971), Canadian TV's *Hilarious House of Frightenstein* (1971), *Goober and the Ghost Chasers* (1973–1975), *Buford and the Galloping Ghost* (1979), *Clue Club* (1976–1977), *Drak Pack* (1980), and the live-action *Monster Squad* (1976).

While preteens were enthralled, some adults wondered if television had become too bizarre for growing minds, as critic Bill Greeley wrote in a *Variety* article from 1973: "Weird creatures abound, but they are mutants of the old monsters and freaks that saturated the schedule before the public caught on . . . . It's not children's programming. It's sort of shrunken adult programming."[4] By this time many North American TV stations ran *Creature Feature* or *Shock Theater* matinees that brought the old cinematic horrors of Hollywood and Japan—*King Kong, Godzilla, Rodan, Dracula, The Mummy, The Wolf Man, The Beast from 20,000 Fathoms*, et al.—to after-school living rooms, often sponsored by sugary fare like Freakies and the General Mills line of monster cereals. The ads, the toys, the movies, and *Scooby-Doo* and its rip-offs and reruns all imparted a G-rated surrealism that kids living through the occult wave could not help but ingest. Eventually, Stephen King's 1981 novel *Cujo* incorporated a subplot of Red Razberry Zingers, a Franken Berry-like breakfast treat that was advertised on Saturday morning TV, whose scarlet dye additive unintentionally provoked from its little consumers red vomit.

By far the greatest range of occult material for children, and some of the darkest, was found in the older medium of comic books. Comics had first been printed in America in the 1930s, when the original icons of the genre Superman and Batman were created, and by the early fifties the field had expanded to include science fiction, crime, romance, and mystery titles, churned out by a thriving industry of publishing houses. A politically charged national "outrage" over the disturbing content of some, however—for instance, the infamous EC periodicals *Tales from the Crypt, The Vault of Horror*, and *Shock SuspenStories*—resulted in a widespread collapse of the business in the middle of the Eisenhower decade. Parents, educators, churches, and legislators pressured the publishers for allegedly fostering juvenile delinquency, and frightened comic producers and distributors purged their rosters of all but the tamest humor lines or the most upright superheroes. A self-regulating Comics Code was drawn up by the leading comic firms in 1954, and all issues had to meet its standards before shipment to the newsstands of the United States: "Approved by the Comics Code Authority," promised the little stamp on the covers.

It was not until 1971, as Count Chocula and *The Headless Cupid* premiered and as *Scooby-Doo, Where Are You!* scored high ratings, that the Comics Code was relaxed somewhat and a wave of horror titles reappeared in corner stores. The change reflected both the evolving notions of acceptability in the culture generally and the fact that some publishers had been simply bypassing the Comic Code's stipulations to successfully put out sequential art in the form of black-and-white magazines, made available alongside "real" magazines rather than comic book spinning racks. The pictures and storylines of mainstream comic companies DC and Marvel, catching up with the underground press and the irreverence of the independent *Mad* magazine, had been gradually growing in sophistication from the late sixties, addressing topical matters like racism and drug use; the Comics Code now permitted the formerly taboo inclusion of vampires, zombies, werewolves, and other occult staples so long as they were "handled in the classic tradition [of] high-caliber literary works."[5] So began a renaissance of American comic books, whose preoccupation with the ghastly and the uncanny mirrored that of society at large.

A few horror-based comic series had survived the original dictates of the Comics Code. Innocuous cartoons, including Gold Key's *The Little Monsters* and Harvey's *Spooky, Casper the Friendly Ghost*, and *Wendy the Good Little Witch*, had already been around for years in 1971, as had Gold Key's more realistic *Boris Karloff's Tales of Mystery*. A syndicated comic strip, Russ Myers's *Broom-Hilda*, told daily gags about a cantankerous, cigar-smoking witch and her oddball familiars; it first ran in American newspapers in 1970. DC Comics' *The House of Secrets*, *The Witching Hour*, and *The Unexpected* had come out in 1968 and 1969, while the publisher's *House of Mystery* dated back in various incarnations to the fifties. Its chief competitor Marvel had *Tower of Shadows* ("Tales to Blow Your Mind!") and *Chamber of Darkness*. But as American ghettoes and Asian jungles burned, and as idealistic political leaders were gunned down by assassins, it was a fair guess that the sensibilities of the comics' young audience had matured. So, then, did the comics themselves.

There was a feast of occult issues on sale from 1971 on. Some publications came and went within a year or two, while others lasted for most of the decade before falling victim to new trends and new technologies. DC produced *Ghosts* (1971–1982), the innovative crossovers *Weird War*

Tales (1971–1983) and *Weird Western Tales* (1972–1980), along with *Weird Mystery Tales* (1972–1975), *Secrets of Haunted House* (1975–1982), and *Secrets of Sinister House* (1972–1974). "Carmine [Infantino, publisher] decided that 'Weird' sold anything," remembered editor Joe Orlando of DC's rush of new series in the seventies.[6] Marvel released *Werewolf by Night* (1972–1978), *Ghost Rider* (1973–1983), *Man-Thing* (1974–1975), *Frankenstein* (1973–1975), *The Tomb of Dracula* (1972–1979), and—an inflammatory title incredible to think of now—*Son of Satan* (1975–1977). The smaller Charlton enterprise had *The Monster Hunters* (1975–1979), *Haunted* (1971–1984), and *Midnight Tales* (1972–1976), as well as a previous title, *The Many Ghosts of Doctor Graves* (1967–1982). Gold Key added *The Occult Files of Doctor Spektor* (1973–1977) and *Grimm's Ghost Stories* (1972–1982). Some comics, such as *Ghosts* and *Midnight Tales*, were anthologies, with three or four stand-alone stories per edition (occasionally with a one-page all-text piece), while the likes of *Frankenstein* and *The Monster Hunters* boasted recurring characters involved in different exploits every issue. *The House of Mystery* and its ilk typically had several tales introduced by a fearsome regular "host," as had the fifties' EC comics that had aroused so much adult opprobrium.

Warren Publications was one of the businesses that had avoided the restrictiveness of the Comics Code by printing black-and-white comics in the larger magazine size, thus making them technically not comics at all. Its trio of titles, *Creepy* (1964–1983), *Eerie* (1966–1983), and *Vampirella* (1969–1983), were among the most stylish in the field and were also noteworthy for more explicit pictures of violence and nudity than their Marvel and DC challengers. Warren writer Bruce Jones recalled the excitement in the comics community in those years: "Dozens of titles still flourished, chances were constantly being taken, and new things were always being tried."[7] The stories of *Creepy* and *Eerie* were presented by the grotesque Uncle Creepy and Cousin Eerie, who nevertheless addressed "Dear Reader" with unctuous charm (and offered the reader subscription deals and fan club memberships), just like *Tales from the Crypt*'s old Crypt Keeper. *Vampirella*, on the other hand, was an inspired creation who combined the scariness of the traditional fanged creature with the sexiness of the Playboy Bunny: a statuesque brunette in high-heeled boots and a barely-there red chemise, the stunning "Vampi" became one of comics' most memorable females and was a tribute to her artists' anatomical draftsmanship.

Were occult comics any good? Were they better or worse than the dominant superhero series? Many of their illustrations and stories were undoubtedly formulaic; the mass manufacture and distribution of so many monthly titles meant that publishers relied on a routine assembly line of editors, writers, pencil renderers, inkers, colorists, and letterers, working under constant deadlines, making endless variations on a cycle of well-worn plot devices. Comic books were an industry. Even their covers adhered to tried-and-true templates, like the full-busted maiden menaced by some looming horror, or the hovering death's head looking down on an oblivious future victim. Inside, there was the usual yarn of the nice person murdered by the nasty person and then the nice person's ghost or rotting corpse coming back to seek revenge on his or her killer. There was the sadistic person who, in the inevitable twist, was gruesomely undone by some surprise form of his own sadism. And there was always the dismissive skeptic who came face to face with the supernatural object of his dismissal:

Mother of mercy! It can't be! You're not real—!

Yet, like Hollywood in the Golden Age of the studio system, there was still a possibility that individual flashes of inspiration or exceptional talents—an Orson Welles, a John Ford, an Alfred Hitchcock—could rise above the medium's inherent constraints.

Horror comics seldom offered occult material more substantial than *Scooby-Doo, Where Are You!,* but at their best their images and narratives were powerful examples of graphic art and pop fiction. They made the grim sociological implications of *Rosemary's Baby* or *The Omen* accessible to readers too young to understand them in their original form. They could even be very scary; once in a while some genuinely unsettling drawings and dialogue emerged from the factory. Consider "The Demon Within," from a 1972 *House of Mystery,* which told of a little boy who could turn himself into a terrifying monster and frighten his parents and big sister— all in fun, of course, until his family decides enough is enough and the lad is shown in the last panel placid, well-behaved . . . and lobotomized. *Weird War Tales* took the blood 'n' guts sagas of ordinary combat comics and gave them a malefic antiwar spin; *Frankenstein* made Mary Shelley's monster vulnerable on the mean streets of contemporary urban America. Possession and diabolism made their way into the comics, as in "The Ghost Who Possessed Lisa" from a 1975 number of *Ghosts,* and the all-text "Spirit That Seized a Soul" from the same issue. Even lightweight teen titles got in on the occult movement, with *Josie and the Pussycats'* "Hooded Horror of Haunted Hill!" and "Vengeance from the Crypt" (Josie herself becomes possessed) in 1972. Classic horror writers were sometimes given a comic book treatment: with H. P. Lovecraft's "The Terrible Old Man" in a *Tower of Shadows* from 1971 and "The Haunter of the Dark" drawn for Marvel's *Journey into Mystery* in 1973, and *Creepy*'s adaptation of Edgar Allan Poe's "The Imp of the Perverse" from 1976. Some of the most vaunted illustrators of the twentieth century provided horror comic art in these years—Frank Frazetta, Richard Corben, Joe Kubert, Bernie Wrightson, John Severin, and many others. Neal Adams's unhinged rooftop sniper and his victims, from *Creepy*'s 1975 "Thrillkill" (story by Jim Stenstrum), virtually erupted off the page, just as you could almost feel the blood dripping from Russ Heath's patricidal "The Shadow of the Axe" in a subsequent issue (story by Dave Sim). Val Mayerik's panels for "Fury of the Night-Creature" in an edition of Marvel's *Frankenstein* were like film-noir stills; José González's 1972 full-length painting of Vampirella was a masterpiece of erotic fetishism. The occult comic books of the sixties and seventies were marketed to kids, but for better or worse their words and visuals helped turn kids into adults.

When children put down their copies of *Weird Mystery Tales*, *Midnight Tales*, or *Creepy*, they found further frights awaiting them in the paneled rec room. Board games by the hundred were marketed every year in the sixties and seventies, based on fleeting fads, on hit TV shows—and, here too, on a sanitized version of the occult. So preadolescents spent rainy afternoons and birthday parties moving their pieces around in the Game of Dracula, Haunted House, Scream Inn, Galloping Ghost!, Superstition, Creature Castle, Creature Features, Voice of the Mummy, a Barnabas Collins/*Dark Shadows* game, Haunted Mansion, Ghost Train, and Green Ghost, with its novel glow-in-the-dark effects. Except in their superficial packaging and premises, these were not much different from scores of other games from the period (Life, Operate, Sorry, Battleship, and so on), but they revealed a generational attraction to vampires, monsters, and ghosts that manufacturers were happy to encourage.

Ouija boards were another matter. In 1966 the major American game company Parker Brothers had purchased for $975,000 the rights to make Ouija boards from the Fuld family, whose ancestors William and Isaac had patented their "Mystic Oracle Talking Board" in the late 1800s. The spiritual revival of the nineteenth century—which the twentieth century's occult boom echoed in many ways—had seen an infatuation with mysticism across Europe and North America, and the French planchette device was a popular diversion in enlightened circles. Planchettes themselves derived from various folk means of foretelling the future or communicating with spirits and had been used since antiquity. Some planchettes used pencils, while others moved a heart-shaped wood block toward letters or words printed on a wooden tablet; the principle, as always, was that unseen forces would direct the device as a group of communicants rested their fingers on it. It was Americans, typically, who found a way to produce and sell such items in quantity, and several different talking boards were marketed by the turn of the century. The famous name supposedly was an Egyptian phrase meaning "good luck," but it is more likely that the Fuld brothers just combined the French and German words for yes: Ouija. Once acquired by Parker Brothers (which, by coincidence or not, had a factory in the historically bewitched city of Salem, Massachusetts), Ouija boards sold in the millions over the rest of the sixties and throughout the next decade. In a telling demonstration of how the spiritual concerns of one era had superseded the material concerns of forty years before, within the first twelve months of Parker Brothers' deal, the numbers of Ouija boards retailed even surpassed those for Monopoly.

Ouija boards, though, were not exactly games, even if Parker Brothers certainly never claimed they were anything else. Both teenagers and adults used them in all seriousness as a way to make contact with ghosts or other beings absent from the visible plane of reality. Many late-night gatherings of young people in the sixties and seventies experimented with some form of channeling the fabled "other side" within the confines of a darkened room while parents were absent. In countless Ouija board sessions, mysterious arrangements of letters and numbers revealed themselves, mysterious answers came to posed questions, and someone would later swear that a friend of a friend heard about somebody else's mysterious Ouija board party that ended in madness and/or murder. Jane Roberts, the medium who wrote the well-known Seth series of books, claimed that some of her dialogues were accomplished with a Ouija board, and it was a mainstay of Alice Cooper's publicity handouts that the shock rocker's name had come from a Ouija visitation from a seventeenth-century witch. In 1949 the Washington, DC, boy known as Robbie Mannheim had used a Ouija board to communicate with his recently deceased aunt Harriet, and William Peter Blatty retained this element of his story when taking it as the inspiration for *The Exorcist*. In Blatty's novel and William Friedkin's film,

Regan MacNeil's descent into demonic possession is prefigured by interaction with the unseen Captain Howdy through a Ouija board. "The occult is something different," warns the psychic Mary Jo Perrin in the book of *The Exorcist*. "I think dabbling with that can be dangerous. And that includes fooling around with a Ouija board."

Skeptics raised the obvious objection that Ouija board directions, when they produced intelligible language, were either unconsciously steered by whatever group of participants had their fingers on the pointer or were deliberately manipulated by a single jokester or fraud in the session. The phenomenon was termed "idiomotor action." Any assembly of teenage suburbanites in 1975 would have brought their own preconceptions, inner tensions, and inadvertent body language to a Ouija board, resulting in the "messages" that were solemnly reported back in homeroom on Monday morning. Candlelit ceremonies, séances, and Ouija board sittings, ultimately, were for the young and young-minded of those years an occult variant of their most important commodities in the affluent postwar society: leisure, socialization, and entertainment.

It was another game, however, that had the most impact on young people's amusements during the occult boom. Unlike Ouija boards, this one made no pretense of offering a conduit to the spirit world; unlike comic books or TV programs, this kind of recreation asked its audience members to supply their own story lines; unlike rock music, the vast majority of its enthusiasts were sober, bookish white males. Yet by the end of the seventies Dungeons & Dragons—D&D, to aficionados—was one of the most popular pastimes among high school and college students, and its wide-ranging networks of ongoing leagues and tournaments confirmed the absorption of occult motifs into public consciousness. What would have been perceived as a perverted fixation with sorcery and violence fifty years prior had become, with D&D, merely the inventive fun of the nice boys next door. At least, so the boys said.

Complex strategy games based on imaginary scenarios were not new when Ernest Gary Gygax and Don Kaye's Tactical Studies Rules (TSR) first commercially released Dungeons & Dragons in 1974. But Gygax and his gaming partner, David Arneson, had come up with several significant modifications on the model, which they had first tried with their 1971 prototype, Chainmail (they had floated and rejected the names Swords and Spells and Magic and Monsters before settling on Dungeons & Dragons). First, rather than attempt to accurately re-create medieval or other historic conflicts,

Gygax and Arneson introduced fantasy figures borrowed from the fiction of Robert E. Howard (*Conan the Barbarian*) and H. P. Lovecraft, and especially from Tolkien's *The Hobbit* and *The Lord of the Rings*: wizards, elves, dwarves, orcs, and of course dragons. Second, they created a much greater set of variables to determine the course of play and possible outcomes, with four-, six-, eight-, ten-, twelve-, and twenty-sided dice that could be tossed. These were even used to define the very attributes of each player's character—not simply generic "men" but individuals with differing qualities of strength, dexterity, and wisdom. Before D&D, the thirty-six-year-old Gygax had worked as an insurance agent in Lake Geneva, Wisconsin, and he understood that chance and odds were not based on single rolls of the dice but on many separate factors that could sometimes counterbalance each other. These would be noted on ledger sheets that players maintained as they consulted the D&D rule book—an actual book, not the two-sheet pamphlet that came with Scrabble or Frustration.

Finally, Dungeons & Dragons allowed players to essentially make up their own sequence of events as the game progressed, according to the parameters established by a supervising "Dungeon Master." What this meant was that, unlike the relatively narrow scopes of traditional board games, the average Dungeons & Dragons competition was more like an epic, unpredictable saga from Middle Earth or Cimmeria unfolding in real time. "I played D&D for the first time in 1978," recalled Warren Spector, who later went on to run the digital production of Disney Interactive Studios. "I had heard that there was this wild game that allowed you to tell your own stories as you played. You mean I don't just throw dice and move around a board and win? I can really become the hero of my own adventure? That, I think, was the magic of it."[8]

Sales of D&D steadily increased after its emergence. In 1974, 1000 copies were purchased, based on its reputation within a niche of hard-core gamers; by 1975 the number rose to 3000, and doubled every six months thereafter, until by the early eighties annual revenues for D&D broke $20 million. Gygax continued to revise his creation, putting out Advanced Dungeons & Dragons in 1978, and an extensive subindustry of rule books, figurines, and other paraphernalia grew. Rival companies moved to make their own simplified versions of D&D, using conventional boards and rules: Dungeon Dice, Dungeon, Swords and Shields, The Sorcerer's Cave, Divine Right, and a game based on the 1978 film of *The Lord of the Rings*.

But the magic was not only in the cleverness of the game itself, or in its swelling leagues of followers. Throughout its first decade and well into its second, parents and educators raised alarms about D&D. Partly it was its seemingly addictive nature that worried them, as socially awkward kids convened indoors for hours on end to drink pop, eat potato chips, and sit at tables rolling dice. Partly it was the way it required gamers to act out their characters, be they human or halfling; Dungeons & Dragons was to be categorized as a "role-playing" game as chess or cards never were. Most of all, though, its occult elements set off adult concerns. Here was a hobby set in a labyrinthine universe of trolls, warlocks, and supernatural powers, taken up by sensitive youths in the hundreds of thousands. Evil forces and cruel deaths were regular features of D&D levels, and players vicariously destroyed strange creatures and each other in bloody clashes as they explored dangerous villages, forests, and castles. It sounded suspicious.

In August 1979 a young student at Michigan State University named James Dallas Egbert was reported to have disappeared in the school's underground network of heating and plumbing corridors. William Dear, a private investigator, was called in by the boy's parents to track him down. Upon locating Egbert shortly thereafter, Dear acknowledged to the press that an obsession with Dungeons & Dragons had played a part in Egbert's sudden vanishing act, as if he had been trying to live out a D&D adventure in a dark, gloomy physical reality. The publicity surrounding the case and its tragic denouement—Egbert committed suicide the following year—tarred D&D as a game with potentially sinister, even fatal, effects on its adolescent devotees. *Mazes & Monsters*, a 1981 novel by Rona Jaffe, was a fictionalized account of the Egbert case, and later books and movies also capitalized on the controversy, as D&D's reach continued to widen. In fact, it turned out that Egbert was a very troubled person who had problems with drugs and his sexual identity, who may have never even played the game at all, and whose wanderings in the bowels of the MSU campus had nothing to do with D&D. But the reputation stuck, and there was now yet another type of social crisis that seemed to stem, ultimately, from the occult.

Children and teenagers, of course, may have been the ones most inclined to accept the fundamental propositions of the occult. Dungeons, dragons, Ouija boards, *The House of Mystery*, *The Witches of Worm*, and all the other products and entertainments they consumed in the sixties and seventies had an advantage of being made for a clientele whose core sense of disbelief was much newer and easier to suspend—the occult never had a more impressionable audience. Yet even when it came watered down and cleaned up, even when it was made as silly as Broom-Hilda or as safe as *Scooby-Doo, Where Are You!*, it still ran in parallel to the adult intellectual fashions of the same time. Kids believed, but grown-ups could still be persuaded. Kids may have been naturally credulous, but their credulity didn't end when they turned eighteen.

Obviously, then, the occult mania had permeated every demographic group and had been manifested in just about every cultural medium. Obviously, it had eager backers in Hollywood, Madison Avenue, Publishers' Row, and Top 40 radio. Obviously, the occult could sell just about any kind of consumer product to any consumer market. Obviously, the occult could once in a while make for sensational amusement, brilliant art, and great stories. But there was something to complicate the matter: what if some of the stories were true?

5

Stranger Than Science

Strange things are happening on our planet, and ignoring them will not remedy the situation. Sticking our heads in the sands of three-dimensional reality cannot hide the mysteries we must eventually confront. We cannot escape from the cosmic interface.
—D. Scott Rogo, *The Haunted Universe*

While young people and cosmopolitans across Europe and North America were developing an ever-greater fascination with weird religions, mystical powers, and black magic, a large segment of the public remained immune to such fancies. These were the members of Richard Nixon's "silent majority"—the conservative, sensible men and women who had no time for and no inclination toward the occult. Ghosts and devils were all well and good for the hippies and hipsters in Los Angeles, New York, and London, but they held little interest for the solid citizens of the heartland. The rugged, sparsely populated mountains of Northern California, for example, may have been just a few hours' drive from psychedelia's capital of San Francisco, but they were culturally and politically in another realm. Yet it was there that the occult—or some organic form of it—made an unexpected breakthrough into the lives and thoughts of Middle America.

On the early afternoon of October 20, 1967, two men from Washington State were riding horseback in California's Six Rivers National Forest, a wilderness area far from any human settlement, when they turned northward up the partly dried bed of Bluff Creek. Roger Patterson and Bob Gimlin both carried shotguns, and Patterson was equipped with a 16-millimeter movie camera. They later recounted that as they rounded some piled-up deadfalls of logs, they came upon a large creature squatting near the bank of the waterway. Their horses panicked and reared up, and Patterson was thrown to the ground and temporarily pinned by his horse, which had fallen on him. When in a few seconds he was freed, Patterson scrambled for his camera, called for Gimlin to stand by with his weapon, and began to track the unidentifiable animal as it rose up and strode quickly into the forest on two legs. He managed to get a few seconds of footage before his magazine ran out.

The short film taken by Roger Patterson in 1967 has been called the second-most examined piece of nonprofessional cinema in history, after Abraham Zapruder's brief sequence capturing the assassination of John F. Kennedy almost four years previously. Patterson's silent, grainy shots appear at first view to have all the flaws of every inexpert home movie from the era: the initial blurry frames as the handheld camera is activated, an unfocused background as the operator seeks his best vantage, and then eventually the subject. But in this case the jumbled snatch of film documents not a wedding or a birthday party but a hulking, bipedal primate that had never before been captured by photography. Its existence had long been dismissed as native mythology or backwoods legend; yet in an age of television, nuclear power, and space exploration, Roger Patterson had possibly produced incontrovertible evidence that the monster Bigfoot lived and walked in the contemporary world.

In the film, the beast is some distance away and merely moves off from the onlookers, turning to regard them for an instant before entering the woods. Patterson and Gimlin later said they chose not to pursue it as their horses had bolted and they had used up their film in any case. But soon the footage was licensed by the men and was widely shown in news clips and television programs. The very amateurishness of the film, showing Patterson's desperate rush to find and focus on his target through the viewfinder in what little time he had, gave it an unnerving authenticity no Hollywood feature could ever duplicate. Its clearest handful of images were enlarged and made into intriguing still pictures of the hairy figure momentarily looking at the viewers, wearing an expression of (depending on how long and how closely you peered at it) fright, anger, or simple shyness. More eyewitness accounts and physical clues emerged, from a variety of sources. The publishing, movie, and other industries covered the issue in their own fashions. What had formerly been a quaint strand of regional folklore became an international topic of scientific study, a controversial affront to urban rationalism, and not incidentally a hot commercial property.

Through the rest of the sixties and for most of the seventies, Bigfoot was a phenomenon. But there were other equally unusual beings, mental abilities, geographical areas, and interpretations of history that captured the popular imagination during the same period. Unlike demonic possession, witchcraft, or the Antichrist, these matters bore no relation to morality or religious dogma. While *Rosemary's Baby* and *The Exorcist* may have left their deepest impressions on devout Catholics, the puzzles of Bigfoot, parapsychology, the Bermuda Triangle, and *Chariots of the Gods?* were open to both the faithful and the atheist. Moreover, Bigfoot and his brethren were touted as facts, not fiction: they appealed to hardheaded reason, not the willing suspension of disbelief. They had to be investigated by experienced explorers, scholars, and scientists, rather than spaced-out teenagers or conflicted priests. Yet they too played into the era's general mood of uncertainty and dislocation that amplified, and was amplified by, the occult.

The apparent conquest of nature and the first forays into the stars had left millions of people with an empty, unspoken longing for some remaining mystery to the cosmos; even the race to the moon had been run and won by the impersonal apparatus of the state, with its unflappable teams of crew-cut test pilots and number-crunching engineers. The social divides over Vietnam, feminism, and civil rights had provoked grave doubts about the honesty of government, the reliability of the press, and indeed the viability of "the System" itself. Even the deaths of JFK, Robert Kennedy, and Martin Luther King Jr. seemed to reveal a fundamental chaos under the everyday façades of stability and predictability. Was the world really such a comprehensible place? Surely science and technology had not solved every last riddle of observable reality? Surely mankind had not exhausted the unknowable? Thus the occult came to include not just Satanism, backward masking, and Dungeons & Dragons, but a whole other field of natural marvels that were just as strange and that, in their own ways, could be just as disturbing.

Stories of Bigfoot in the western United States and Canada had long predated the Patterson film of 1967. The aboriginals of what is now British Columbia told white settlers of the Sasquatch, a hairy giant who lived high in the mountains, and reports of occasional sightings and other contacts— including attacks and abductions—had trickled in from British Columbia, Washington, Oregon, and California through the nineteenth and twentieth centuries; one had been noted by future U.S. president Theodore Roosevelt in 1893. With the scaling of Mount Everest in the 1950s, North Americans also learned of the Abominable Snowman, or Yeti, a comparable large primate said to live in the Himalayan reaches of Nepal and Tibet. A turning point came in August 1958, when a set of oversize humanoid footprints were discovered near a construction site in Humboldt County, California, and a local newspaper coined the name "Bigfoot" to characterize the unknown man or animal that had made them. Into the early sixties a wealthy Texan named Tom Slick had funded searches for both the Yeti and Bigfoot, led by the Irish big-game hunter Peter Byrne, but no living or dead specimens were found.

Once the Patterson footage came out to extensive publicity, Bigfoot became big. At first it was unclear whether the label referred to an elusive individual who somehow kept turning up in lots of different places, like Santa Claus, or to an actual species, hitherto unclassified, with a small population whose members were scattered across the forests and mountain ranges of the Pacific Northwest. Some of the advocates for Bigfoot's existence were serious men who carefully accumulated footprint casts, the testimony of witnesses, and biological analyses of what exactly the creature might be in an evolutionary sense—the literate and scrupulous Peter Byrne and the University of Washington anthropologist Grover Krantz fell into this category. Others were eccentrics and obsessives who lived and worked in the same wild environment as Bigfoot and perhaps envied the monster's solitary withdrawal from the cacophony of industrialized society. All of them found an eager audience. Bigfoot definitely made good copy, whether treated as filler for the silly season or, as was increasingly the case through the seventies, as a genuine mystery.

Bigfoot got some early attention in the pages of the long-running men's adventure magazine *Argosy*, which ran pictures from the Patterson film in February 1968; *Argosy* specialized in macho true-life drama of the outdoors, and what it called "America's Abominable Snowman" was an ideal subject for its readership. A raft of Bigfoot books came out: John Green's *On the Track of the Sasquatch* (1968), John Napier's *Bigfoot: The Yeti and Sasquatch in Myth and Reality* (1972), Don Hunter and Réne Dahinden's *Sasquatch* (1973), Peter Byrne's *The Search for Bigfoot: Monster, Myth or Man?* (1975), Robert and Frances Guenette's *Bigfoot: The Mysterious Monster* (1975), M. E. Knerr's *Sasquatch: Monster of the Northwest Woods* (1977), and John Green's *Sasquatch: The Apes Among Us* (1978).

Movies and television also got in on the Bigfoot fad. Some offered fairly straightforward nonfiction studies, like the 1974 TV documentary

Monsters! Mysteries or Myths?, narrated by Rod Serling, whose resonant tones had been inextricably linked with the paranormal since hosting *The Twilight Zone* and *Night Gallery*. Other pictures were far more exploitative, based on "reenactments" of dubious accuracy, or promoted as true stories, since no one would go to the trouble of conclusively disproving them: *Bigfoot* (1970), *The Legend of Boggy Creek* (1972), *Shriek of the Mutilated* (1974), *Creature from Black Lake* (1976), *The Legend of Bigfoot* (1976), *Return to Boggy Creek* (1977), a TV movie, *Snowbeast* (1977), and *The Capture of Bigfoot* (1979). A number of films simply recycled interviews with the same Bigfoot researchers, retold the same sighting stories, and replayed Roger Patterson's Bluff Creek footage. In 1977 the toy maker Milton Bradley issued Bigfoot: The Giant Snow Monster board game, and in 1976 and 1977 the popular TV series *The Six Million Dollar Man* featured a multi-episode story line of the bionic agent Steve Austin battling Bigfoot. A Bigfoot action figure based on the show's version of the monster was later sold.

The ubiquitous presence of Bigfoot in the media of the seventies no doubt explained many of the supposed sightings of the monster that were recorded in those years. Bears, tree stumps, other human beings, and, above all, excited imaginations were the likely truths behind all those glimpses of what were first perceived as Bigfoot. But a small number of cases could not be so easily written off. Here and there, in British Columbia, Washington, or Oregon, ordinary loggers, hikers, fishermen, or prospectors came forward with odd, eerily similar descriptions of a huge, apelike form they had seen ambling through the bushes or near a roadside, at dusk or at dawn, as they were going about their own jobs or domestic affairs. These claimants were usually not Bigfoot buffs or even believers. If they had been hoaxed by somebody in a gorilla costume, that somebody must have waited a long time in an isolated area to put himself on display as well as in danger of being shot, in districts where many adults owned high-powered guns and used them as everyday tools. Seldom did the stories introduce any note of danger or aggression on the part of the Bigfoot. Seldom, really, was there that much to tell. The flatness of the episodes, as they were reluctantly admitted to by men and women of sound mind and good character, made them all the more plausible. As Peter Byrne reminded, "If one is going to be so bold as to say that one has actually encountered a Bigfoot, surely one is not going to spoil a good story with a dull and unconvincing account of a shy giant that simply turned and walked away and did nothing. This is not what the modern audience wants at all. This is not the stuff of which legends are made."[1]

Bigfoot, or something that might have resembled Bigfoot, was often spotted through the seventies. In 1975 the U.S. Army Corps of Engineers, a department of the American federal government, officially recognized the Sasquatch as an indigenous species in its *Washington Environmental Atlas*: "Legendary or actual, Sasquatch excites a great popular interest in Washington."[2] Bigfoot-like beings were also alleged to have been seen elsewhere in the United States, including in Florida, Texas, and Missouri. But there had been other, even more bizarre creatures witnessed across the continent in the occult era. The sea serpent "Ogopogo" was filmed with a Super-8 camera in British Columbia's Lake Okanagan in 1968, while another water monster was photographed in New York's Lake Champlain in July 1977. "I knew what a sturgeon was," recalled Sandra Mansi, who took the 1977 shot. "They're absolutely huge. But they're not that big. And then the head came up, and then the neck came up, and then I could see the back . . . I wasn't afraid—it was more, 'Oh, my God.'"[3] Research uncovered Native tales and pioneer accounts suggesting the animals had long histories in their waters; Lake Champlain's "Champ" had supposedly been noticed as early as 1609. Like Bigfoot, they became a selling point for local tourism and a draw for would-be monster hunters.

In 1966 and 1967 there was a flurry of news stories from around Point Pleasant, West Virginia, in the Ohio Valley, about the Mothman. The Mothman was said to be a ten-foot-tall flying humanoid with huge, bat-like wings that had been seen by many people, always at night. In one instance it had even chased a car and its terrified occupants. Local resident Linda Scarberry described the Mothman: "To me it just looks like a man with wings. It has a body-shape form with . . . wings on its back that come around it. It has muscular legs like a man and fiery-red eyes that glow when the lights hit it . . . I couldn't see its head or arms. I don't know if the eyes are even in a head."[4] Paranormal specialist John Keel authored two books covering the events, *Strange Creatures from Time and Space* (1970) and *The Mothman Prophecies* (1975), based on his on-site interviews and findings, although like others in his narrow field he brought his own preconceptions to the mystery: "The moment I met [a witness], I knew she was telling the truth," he affirmed.[5] Keel tied the Mothman sightings to the collapse of Point Pleasant's Silver Bridge on December 17, 1967, in which forty-six persons died, including some Mothman witnesses.

The venerable Loch Ness monster was also back in the press during the occult years. First documented by the Irish saint Columba in AD 565 and the subject of frequent accounts in the next centuries, the monster had generally been considered to be, as Bigfoot had, a single quasi-immortal creature. But by the seventies hard science had trained its eyes on the phenomenon, and there was speculation that whatever lurked in Loch Ness might have been a small population of an erstwhile hidden genus, perhaps a kind of plesiosaur that had survived the mass extinction that terminated the Cretaceous era of the dinosaurs. Led Zeppelin's Jimmy Page, who owned and occasionally stayed in Aleister Crowley's former property the Boleskine House overlooking the water, was one of many who found the thesis credible.

Significantly, perhaps, "Nessie," "Champ," and "Ogopogo" were each inhabitants of long, deep lakes—possibly trapped there after the last ice age—lending another factor of rational consistency to their purported existence. Equipped with advanced sonar and underwater photography equipment, a team led by MIT alumnus and Academy of Applied Research president Robert Rines scoured the Scottish loch for solid proof of the monster, and on August 8, 1972, a close-up photo of a submerged reptilian flipper was taken. Three years later, Rines and his crew produced another murky image of a large marine body moving through the dark loch.

Bigfoot, the Yeti, the Mothman, Ogopogo, Champ, and Nessie belonged to the novel discipline of cryptozoology, the study of unconfirmed or unrecognized animals (the neologism was attributed to French scientist Bernard Heuvelmans in the late fifties). Proponents of the science argued that they looked for not only weird beasts of legend but new subspecies of established organisms, of which they indeed found several. They could also link their quests to the nascent ecological movement, as they lobbied to protect and preserve the near-extinct lines whose trails they followed. Byrne again: "The Bigfeet [sic] are not a threat to man in any way and in the long run, if they could be left alone, if people could just accept them and let it go at that, the best policy would be to leave them alone."[6]

Others considered cryptozoology to be a branch of Forteana, the anecdotal collections of unusual facts compiled by Charles Hoy Fort. Fort, who died in 1932, had published his influential *The Book of the Damned* in 1919, which was followed by *New Lands* (1923), *Lo!* (1931), and *Wild Talents* (1932), featuring short but proven (or at least independently observed) entries about disappearances, poltergeists, rains of frogs or fish, and bizarre living creatures. These he had gathered through persistent review of obscure newspapers, scientific journals, and press releases from around the globe. Popular appetite for Fort's books and the *Fortean Times* journal had been revived with the rise of the counterculture. His position that human knowledge was an arbitrary construct, from which the abnormal and the contrary had been deliberately excluded, won an appreciative young audience during the occult years. "Every science is a mutilated octopus; only the maimed is what we call understandable," Fort had written.[7] However defined, cryptozoology and Forteana may likewise have appealed to the expanding political fringes of the late sixties and early seventies, as each carried an implication of secrecy and censorship that had been already demonstrated in the embarrassing revelations of Vietnam and Watergate. If authorities had lied about body counts and dirty tricks, were they also covering up giant hominids, winged nocturnal bogeymen, and sea monsters?

Obscure life-forms were not the only unknowns that haunted the culture of the period. This was also a heyday of parapsychology, the science of latent or dormant capacities within human beings: precognition, telekinesis, telepathy, and other potentials that seemed to exist in a vague, rarely realized overlap of mind and spirit. Here too the evidence extended from the conscientious and controlled to the flaky and fraudulent. And here too parapsychologists held that their explorations were apart from any religious doctrine—or maybe they represented the clinical bases of what had previously been described in religious language. In William Peter Blatty's *The Exorcist*, the early symptoms of Regan MacNeil's demonic possession are diagnosed as various "natural" pathologies of a heightened consciousness. "Boy, miracles sure don't come easy with you, do they?" her mother asks the skeptical Jesuit psychiatrist Father Karras. The possibility that reason could confirm revelation, that magic might have a basis in materialism, was the hook that drew in many who otherwise had no affinity for the occult. Tom Wolfe's definitional 1976 essay, "The 'Me' Generation and the Third Great Awakening," detected the soul behind the scholarship: "The ESP or 'psychic phenomena' movement began to grow very rapidly in the new religious atmosphere,"[8] he wrote. Parapsychology made the miraculous palatable to the secular.

"Mind reading" and "visions" had been displayed in parlor games and theatrical exhibitions for decades, the term "extrasensory perception" (ESP) had been used since as far back as 1934, and folk wisdom had long related tales of persons gifted with "second sight." By various names, all sorts of strange mental powers had been catalogued through history. Celebrated psychics included Edgar Cayce, the "Sleeping Prophet" (1877–1945), a mild-mannered American Protestant who was said to detect illnesses, perceive distant actions and locations, and even solve faraway crimes while in self-induced trance states; he went on to pronounce on the fate of mankind and the lost history of Atlantis. More recently, there was Jeane Dixon, a Washington, DC, clairvoyant who made a career out of her accurate 1956 forecast of the assassination of the president elected in 1960. By the sixties such unique figures as Cayce and Dixon were being grouped into a broader systemic understanding that strove to quantify their seemingly special talents as untapped potential in every human brain.

In late 1969 the members of the American Association for the Advancement of Science voted to accept into its organization the Parapsychological Association (PA), a smaller group of academics and professional psychic investigators. The famed anthropologist Margaret Mead made an outspoken defense of the PA's application, saying, "The whole history of scientific advance is full of scientists investigating phenomena that the establishment did not believe were there. The PA uses standard scientific devices such as statistics, blinds, double blinds, and placeboes. I submit that we vote in favor of this association's work."[9] A crucial milestone had been reached: ESP and other previously paranormal topics were at last allowed into the arena of sanctioned science. For some time thereafter, in universities, laboratories, and government offices around the world (and even outside the world), researchers conducted clinical trials to determine whether mind could indeed ascend over matter.

Some of the trials were compelled not purely by scientific curiosity but by the Cold War. The publication in 1970 of Sheila Ostrander's *Psychic Discoveries Behind the Iron Curtain* revealed that the Soviet Union and its satellites were themselves pursuing serious explorations of parapsychology, and soon enough the U.S. military and intelligence communities were looking into the strategic value of telepathy and its relatives. In June 1972 the Stanford Research Institute (SRI) initiated experiments in ESP or what it referred to as remote viewing, explained as "one of a broad class of abilities of certain individuals to access, by means of mental processes, and describe information sources blocked from ordinary perception and generally accepted as secure against access."[10] Later that year the Central Intelligence Agency released $50,000 to the SRI to share what it learned, continuing to fund the research until 1975 when the operation came under congressional criticism. Meanwhile, other branches of the American armed forces made their own top-secret forays into psychic weaponry—like the U.S. Army's Project Gondola Wish (later titled Project Grill Flame), launched in September 1977—to test the tactical viability of mind reading and mind control in battle with their Russian enemy. And in 1971 U.S. astronaut Edgar Mitchell, while aboard the Apollo 14 lunar module on its way to the moon, had tried his own unofficial ESP "transmissions," based on the standard Zener symbol cards typically used in such assessments, to colleagues on Earth to see if his thoughts could be received over thousands of miles of the infinite.

Most parapsychology, however, was less rigorous. As with the hucksters and cranks who sought to bask in the glories of Bigfoot and the Loch Ness monster, the sensational notion of unknown mental forces drew people who had already decided that such forces were real and, coincidentally, that they possessed them for themselves. Some became moderately famous. There was Ted Serios, a hard-drinking, ne'er-do-well Chicagoan who could allegedly project "thought pictures" onto Polaroid film, which sometimes did seem to show blurred images of the objects he imagined while holding a camera to his head. He was first publicized in 1967, in parapsychologist Jule Eisenbud's *The World of Ted Serios: "Thoughtographic" Studies of an Extraordinary Mind*. There was Dutch-born Peter Hurkos, the celebrity psychic sleuth who was often consulted by European and American police in murder cases (including the Tate-LaBianca slayings in 1969) and by private citizens in disappearances; he also made regular public appearances at nightclubs and theaters, divining secrets from audience members for show. Best known was Uri Geller, an Israeli who claimed the ability to move objects, stop or start wristwatches, and even bend cutlery by mind power alone. Geller went to America and his unusual talents were tested by the Stanford Research Institute in 1972; like Peter Hurkos, he also performed his feats as paid entertainment live and on TV.

The staunchest parapsychologists were adamant that they were not occultists, but the renown of Ted Serios, Peter Hurkos, and Uri Geller was unmistakably part of the same trend that included demonism, witchcraft, and cryptozoology: for most of the public the distinction between magic, monsters, and mind power was academic. Certainly, the media treated parapsychology with the same credulity as it regarded sea serpents, possession, or the Antichrist. Here again numerous quickie documentary films were assembled to ride the wave, among them *Encounter with the Unknown* (1973) and *The Amazing World of Psychic Phenomena* (1976). The syndicated TV series *In Search Of . . .* began running in 1976. The series was narrated by Leonard Nimoy of *Star Trek* before that program was revived into a lucrative movie and television franchise. Nimoy's voice was instantly connected by most viewers with the weird and the alien, much as Rod Serling's had been. *In Search Of . . .* featured weekly overviews of UFOs, Bigfoot, and various tangents of parapsychology, distilling each subject into a half-hour montage of interviews and ostensibly authentic footage of the phenomenon in question, all tied together by Nimoy's Vulcanized omniscience.

Publishing, too, was all over parapsychology. The many books issued on its mysteries included Jess Stearn's *Adventures into the Psychic* (1969), Evelyn Monahan and Terry Bakken's *Put Your Psychic Powers to Work: A Practical Guide to Parapsychology* (1973), Peter Tompkins's biological speculations in *The Secret Life of Plants* (1973), *The Art and Practice of Astral Projection* by someone named Ophiel (1974), Jeffrey Mishlove's *The Roots of Consciousness* (1975), and John Randall's *Parapsychology and the Nature of Life* (1977). Stephen King, who made psychokinesis the starting point for his 1974 debut novel *Carrie* and put parapsychology into *The Shining*, *Firestarter*, and other horror stories, later admitted, "It seems to me that the writer who deals with psychic phenomena in his or her fiction has a responsibility to deal with such phenomena respectfully but not in a state of utter, worshipful belief."[11] King and other novelists moved quickly to give their stories a gloss of authenticity by incorporating (and often exaggerating) into them the latest findings in parapsychology.

Some nonfiction authors built durable careers as full-time exponents of all things unusual or (possibly) inexplicable, including John Keel (*The Mothman Prophecies*, *The Eighth Tower*, *Our Haunted Planet*), Ivan T. Sanderson (*Abominable Snowmen*, *Investigating the Unexplained*, *Invisible Residents*), Raymond Bayless (*The Enigma of the Poltergeist*, *Experiences of a Psychical Researcher*, *Voices from Beyond*), Martin Ebon (*They Knew the Unknown*, *The Devil's Bride: Exorcism Past and Present*, *The Evidence for Life after Death*), and D. Scott Rogo (*An Experience of Phantoms*, *Exploring Psychic Phenomena*, *The Haunted Universe*). In a sense these writers were modern-day Charles Forts, who laboriously gathered dozens or hundreds of supernatural anecdotes and reported them with straight-faced amazement. To their subjects they brought an infectious enthusiasm in tandem with a kind of wounded dignity, as they recognized the critical scorn with which their theories were frequently received. In *The Haunted Universe* (1977), D. Scott Rogo insisted, "One thing is certain—this book is not being written for entertainment or to make a fast buck by polluting the already overstocked book market on pop parapsychology and do-it-yourself miracles. I'm writing it with the firm conviction that many things exist around us that we are only beginning to become aware of and which conventional science and even conventional parapsychology are ignoring or overlooking."[12] And John Keel in *The Mothman Prophecies* took the same stance: "In recent years we have seen a worldwide revival of interest in psychic phenomena and the supernatural. Stern no-nonsense scientists now drag their beards to Loch Ness to search for the monster, while others comb the woods of the Northwest seeking the Sasquatch . . . . But gradually all these men are being drawn closer and closer to ontology; to an examination of the question that lies beyond the simplistic, 'Can these things be?' The real question is, 'Why are there these things?'"[13]

Beyond parapsychology lay the wider but similarly occult arena of what was often categorized as "The Unknown." In this there was no more gripping matter than that of the Bermuda Triangle. The Triangle had been given its geometric designation in a 1964 *Argosy* article, and its visibility was raised further by a piece in the same magazine by Ivan T. Sanderson that appeared in August 1968, "The Spreading Mystery of the Bermuda Triangle." It represented a synthesis of every disappearance, UFO, ghost, abduction, sea monster, and even Satanism story that crowded the libraries and airwaves of the sixties and seventies, only this time there was an undeniable streak of truth running through them: numerous ships and aircraft *had* been lost in a vast expanse of the mid-Atlantic roughly triangulated by Florida, Puerto Rico, and Bermuda. A cultural mania for several years, the Bermuda Triangle made for a small industry of books, films, newspaper and magazine articles, and even a Bermuda Triangle board game of 1977.

The Triangle had already been discussed in John Wallace Spencer's 1969 work *Limbo of the Lost* and elsewhere, but it was the publication of Charles Berlitz's *The Bermuda Triangle* in 1974 that fixed the issue in the popular mind—the book was a number one bestseller and 10 million copies were purchased worldwide. "The strange doings are described with relish," acknowledged reviewer John Moorhead in the *Christian Science Monitor*, "but Berlitz leaves this reader feeling unconvinced and slightly manipulated."[14] "*Triangle* takes off from established facts, then proceeds to lace its theses with a hodgepodge of half-truths, unsubstantiated reports, and unsubstantial science," echoed *Time* magazine.[15] Berlitz, the American-born grandson of the famous French linguist and language teacher Maximilian Berlitz, first became interested in the Triangle as a major in the U.S. Army Reserve after World War II, when he had served in the Intelligence, Counterintelligence, and Special Warfare division; he was also an experienced scuba diver and knew the waters off the Florida coast firsthand.

Following the huge success of *The Bermuda Triangle*, Berlitz wrote *Without a Trace: New Information from the Triangle* in 1977. By then his competition included Adi-Kent Thomas Jeffrey's *The Bermuda Triangle*, George Johnson and Dan Tanner's *The Bible and the Bermuda Triangle*, Richard Winer's *The Devil's Triangle*, Alan Landsburg's *Secrets of the Bermuda Triangle* (Landsburg was also a producer of *In Search Of . . .*), and even Jay Gourley's *The Great Lakes Triangle* (which described another comparably dangerous region). The area also starred in the movies *Satan's Triangle* (1975), *Beyond the Bermuda Triangle* (1975), *Mysteries from Beyond the Triangle* (1976), *The Bermuda Triangle* (1978), and *Secrets of the Bermuda Triangle* (1979), and had cameos in *Close Encounters of the Third Kind* (1977) and *Airport '77*.

While there were any number of aerial or marine disappearances that had taken place in or around the Bermuda Triangle, only a few were regularly invoked as the most mysterious, beginning with the legendary Flight 19 in 1945. On the afternoon of December 5 of that year, five TBM Avenger torpedo bombers flew east out of Fort Lauderdale, Florida, on a training exercise. These were the same make of massive single-engine planes that had sunk Japanese shipping in the Pacific War, one of which had been piloted by future U.S. president George H. W. Bush. Each aircraft of the group but one carried a pilot, a radio man, and a gunner (one crewman was absent). While on the second leg of their routine circuit, the flight leader, Lieutenant Charles Taylor, lost his bearings and a series of anxious communications were received from the flight:

> *We must have got lost after that last turn . . .*
>
> *I'm sure I'm in the Keys, but I don't know how far down . . .*
>
> *We are not sure where we are . . . It looks like we are entering white water . . .*
>
> *We're completely lost . . .*

Taylor reported that his compasses were malfunctioning, and, in the stormy autumn weather, he had somehow determined the mission had strayed over the Gulf of Mexico rather than its true location off the eastern Florida coast. As the planes ran low on fuel, two Martin Mariner flying boats were dispatched to search for Flight 19, but one of these soon disappeared from radar scopes and was seen to explode in midair. The five Avengers and their fliers were never found, and no debris or human remains from them ever materialized. (In 1991 five crashed Avengers were found on the ocean floor off Fort Lauderdale, but the planes' serial numbers did not match those of Flight 19.)

Other craft had gone missing in the Bermuda Triangle. Last reported at Barbados, the USS *Cyclops* freighter disappeared in March 1918. A British passenger plane, the *Star Tiger*, was lost northeast of Bermuda in 1948, the same year an American DC-3 airliner failed to arrive in Miami from Puerto Rico; no trace of either was discovered. The tanker *Marine Sulphur Queen* had vanished in 1963, as had a racing yacht, the *Revonoc*, in 1967. There were many more such episodes over the years. Among the explanations advanced by Charles Berlitz and others was that they had been captured by flying saucers, sucked into an underwater vortex, caught in a time-space warp, or taken to the lost continent of Atlantis. Berlitz had written *The Mystery of Atlantis* in 1969, and his *The Bermuda Triangle* and *Without a Trace* made respectful reference to Edgar Cayce's Atlantis prophecies. "The onetime existence of Atlantis and the present day existence of the Bermuda Triangle are two of the ocean's outstanding mysteries," he wrote in *Without a Trace*. "The explanation of one may lead to the solution of the other."[16]

Though it had been identified only since the sixties, the more diligent Triangle delvers retroactively incorporated into its history accounts from as far back as the voyages of Columbus and his travels through the Sargasso Sea, a peculiarly calm patch of ocean whose boundaries extended into the Triangle. "The Bermuda Triangle has been an area of danger, mystery, and often doom ever since the early European discovery of the West Indies," Berlitz declared.[17] Over this time there was a wide selection of sea and air vessels reported missing, or whose surviving crews had bizarre tales to report, to choose from. Together the loss of so many ships, planes—and people—made for a startling compendium of unsolved mysteries that many writers and filmmakers took as a starting point for an imaginative spectrum of Bermuda Triangle conjectures.

But even at the height of the Triangle trend, doubters were dispelling the entire concept. Many noted that the area around Florida and the Bahamas was home to a huge amount of air and sea traffic and that the number of disappearances there was no more than a statistical average. Weather in that vicinity was capricious and prone to sudden violence. Strong ocean currents would disperse most wreckage far from its supposed location, and deep underwater trenches made more debris inaccessible. Different factors, from human error and structural failure to storms and simple misadventure, would account for the great majority of Triangle losses, if researched on a case-by-case basis. The Bermuda Triangle itself was seen as particularly vague in its definitions, according to which advocate had put together which reports—some puzzles, like that of the ship *Mary Celeste*, found unaccountably abandoned off Portugal in 1872, had occurred far from the Triangle's borders. The U.S. Coast Guard was obliged to issue a standard disclaimer to inquiries from worried pilots, seafarers, and the general public: "It has been our experience that the combined forces of nature and unpredictability of mankind outdo even the most farfetched science fiction many times each year."[18]

If there was one paranormal subject that surpassed the Bermuda Triangle in mass appeal during the seventies, it was the "ancient astronaut" hypothesis made by Erich von Däniken in his *Chariots of the Gods?: Unsolved Mysteries of the Past*, first published in German in 1968 and released in an English translation by Putnam in 1970. His *Gods from Outer Space* came out in 1971, followed by *The Gold of the Gods* in 1973 and a pictorial volume, *In Search of Ancient Gods*, the next year. Von Däniken became famous as a lecturer on his claims, and by 1974 it was estimated that his books had sold 6.5 million copies. A TV documentary based on his writings, *In Search of Ancient Astronauts*, was broadcast in 1973. Naturally, there came many books and movies that borrowed from von Däniken: 1975's *The Outer Space Connection* was produced by Alan Landsburg and narrated by Rod Serling (the title took off from previous hits like William Friedkin's *The French Connection* and the karate flick *The Chinese Connection*); R. L. Dione's subtly named *God Drives a Flying Saucer* (first published in 1969 but reissued in 1973); W. Raymond Drake's *Gods or Spacemen of the Ancient Past?* (1975); Robert Temple's *The Sirius Mysteries* (1976); Rupert Furneaux's *Ancient Mysteries* (1977); and Zecharia Sitchin's *The 12th Planet* (1976) and *The Stairway to Heaven* (1980). In 1973 Oscar Dystel of Bantam Books remarked on the *Chariots of the Gods?* phenomenon: "We can't find any pattern of sales. Hippies are buying it, college students, middle America, your uncle and aunt, the sophisticated and the unsophisticated. People seem to be looking for something, and these books provide that something."[19]

Briefly, *Chariots* and its sequels and rivals stated that ancient civilizations had been visited and significantly influenced by extraterrestrials, who had left many clues behind. Some remained as physical artifacts, like the pyramids of Egypt and Central America, the Nazca lines of Peru, and the statues of Easter Island, as well as smaller objects unearthed by archaeologists around the world. More evidence was found in the earliest art, religion, oral histories, and sacred texts of many societies, which could be interpreted as primitive peoples' depiction of space vehicles and other high technology usually thought to have been impossible for them to have conceived, let alone make or use. In short, there was clear proof of an alternative history of humankind that could completely alter the understanding of humanity's origins and its traditional faiths. "Time will show whether our own age is seriously interested in discovering such fantastic, awe-inspiring secrets," von Däniken wrote in *The Gold of the Gods*. "Is it prepared to decipher an age-old work even if it means bringing to light truths that might turn our neat but dubious world picture upside down? Do not the high priests of all religions ultimately abhor revelations about prehistory that might replace *belief* in the creation by *knowledge* of the Creation? Is man really prepared to admit that the history of his origin was entirely different from the one which is instilled into him in the form of a pious fairy story?"[20]

As Oscar Dystel realized, von Däniken had touched the same cultural nerve that had responded to Bigfoot, parapsychology, and the Bermuda Triangle. *Chariots of the Gods?* was very much in the sphere of the occult. Here was an explanation of reality that conspicuously broke with the version proffered by mainstream science, history, and creeds. The distrust of the state and the church that had grown in the postwar decades now had potent arguments in its favor, in the form of strange but striking abnormalities that could be neither accommodated nor ignored by conventional thought. How *could* the stone-age tribesmen of Easter Island have erected such massive monuments without any outside assistance? Why *would* pre-Columbian South American natives design giant patterns in the desert that could make sense only if viewed from the air, many centuries before the invention of aircraft? What *was* the biblical prophet Ezekiel describing in 592 BC when he gave witness to "a great cloud with brightness around it and fire flashing forth continually, and in the middle of the fire, something like gleaming amber. In the middle of it was something like four living creatures . . . . In the middle of the living creatures there was something that looked like burning coals of fire, like torches moving to and fro among the living creatures."? These and related questions were open-ended enough to be tied into the continued suppositions around Atlantis, UFOs, and many other topics; even Led Zeppelin's Robert Plant had adopted a symbol from the lost Pacific kingdom of Mu as his personal trademark. Was it all starting to make sense? Had Erich von Däniken come across the underlying secrets of the human species?

Most detached reviewers thought not. The librarians' journal *Choice* admitted that *Chariots of the Gods?* "undoubtedly deserves a place of honor besides J. Churchward's *The Lost Continent of Mu* and related texts on the lost continent of Atlantis, but it cannot be recommended, in all conscience, for an academic library."[21] The *New York Times* said the book's prose was "Early Terrible . . . . It puts the reader's brain into a mixmaster of facts, speculations, rhetorical questions and a mishmash of archeological and mythological materials."[22] Many critics noted that *Chariots* was premised on an elementary logical fallacy: since we aren't sure about X (what happened thousands of years ago), it can only be explained by Y (there must have been interplanetary contact). It also emerged that von Däniken had no training as an archaeologist or historian—he was a hotel manager in Switzerland—and was a convicted embezzler. If nothing else, his books did alert their audience to exotic curiosities in other lands, and did present some very basic introductions to Egyptian, Mayan, and Polynesian antiquity, before taking off on his own very subjective interpretations. Despite, or because of, their rejection by established scholarship, the assertions of *Chariots of the Gods?* became common currency for many years and millions of people have found them persuasive.

Indeed, by the mid-seventies the allure of von Däniken and his peers had become so broad that old-fashioned reason and empiricism were forced to mount a counterattack. On April 30, 1976, in Buffalo, New York, a group of American teachers, writers, and researchers announced the formation of the Committee for the Scientific Investigation of Claims of the Paranormal (CSICOP). Comprising more than thirty members, CSICOP included astronomer Carl Sagan, psychologist B. F. Skinner, magic performer James "the Amazing" Randi (who had done some of Alice Cooper's stage effects), and authors Isaac Asimov, Martin Gardner, and L. Sprague de Camp (the last of whom had written the standard biography of H. P. Lovecraft). "It is vital that individuals develop some understanding of the effective criteria for judging [paranormal] claims," said the committee's cochairman, philosophy professor Paul Kurtz. "There is always the danger that once irrationality grows, it will spill over into other areas. There is no guarantee that a society so infected by unreason will be resistant to even the most virulent programs of dangerous ideological sects."[23]

CSICOP's mandate was not to automatically dismiss every posited paranormal phenomenon. "We wish to make it clear that the purpose of the Committee is not to reject on *a priori* grounds, antecedent to inquiry, any or all such claims," Kurtz elaborated, "but rather to examine them openly, completely, objectively and carefully."[24] CSICOP investigators bore no resemblance to the stereotypical snooty scientists so disdained by Charles Fort, but they also distanced themselves from the "pseudoscience" that assumed anything not proven false must therefore be true. "Many people have developed minds that are not only open, but gaping," said L. Sprague de Camp.[25] In 1977 CSICOP lodged a formal complaint with the U.S. Federal Communications Commission over the NBC television showings of *Exploring the Unknown*, and it also protested *In Search Of . . .* and *The Outer Space Connection*, all for the documentaries' conceits of factual and scientific exactitude. By then the committee and its sympathizers had scored some important victories.

Chariots of the Gods? was an early target. "If I undertook a thorough analysis of one of von Däniken's books, the result would be a book several times the size of the original," de Camp pointed out. "Von Däniken's books are solid masses of misstatements, errors and wild guesses presented as facts, unsupported by anything remotely resembling scientific data."[26] A critical anthology, *Some Trust in Chariots: Sixteen Views on Erich von Däniken's Chariots of the Gods,* was published in 1973. Two years later author Lawrence Kusche's *The Bermuda Triangle Mystery: Solved* came out. Kusche was a librarian and licensed pilot who went into the most famous Triangle disappearances and found nearly all of them to be attributable to mistakes, bad luck, and weather, rather than paranormal causes. "The legend of the Bermuda Triangle is a manufactured mystery," he concluded. "It began because of careless research and was elaborated upon finds perpetuated by writers who either purposely or unknowingly made use of misconceptions, faulty reasoning and sensationalism. It was repeated so many times that it began to take on an aura of truth."[27] Of the lost Flight

19 of 1945, the U.S. Navy's Board of Inquiry had ultimately decided, "The disappearance was caused by temporary mental confusion resulting from faulty judgment on the part of the flight leader and instructor of Flight 19, Lt. Charles C. Taylor, in permitting himself to lose knowledge of his general position relative to the peninsula of Florida."[28] The explosion of the Martin Mariner search plane that had flown to find Flight 19 could be blamed on that aircraft's extreme flammability, which was notorious among aviators. The U.S. Coast Guard also clarified, "The U.S. Board of Geographic Names does not recognize the Bermuda Triangle as an official name and does not maintain an official file on the area."[29]

Uri Geller and the psychics came in for debunking as well. CSICOP examiners cautioned that the true test of any special mental ability was that it could be observed by independent viewers under laboratory conditions, as well as routinely replicated by the supposed psychics themselves. Geller, Peter Hurkos, and Ted Serios did not meet these standards. James Randi bluntly called Geller a fake, selling clever magic tricks as genuine psychic talents, an accusation borne out on a 1973 *Tonight Show* broadcast where Geller's powers had conspicuously little effect. Serios's thought photography likewise looked to have come with the aid of pocketed films he kept discreetly on his person. There were plenty of performances where the cutlery did not move, the predictions were wrong, and the thoughtographs didn't come out. Spoon bending and mind reading were part of any competent magician's stable of effects, Randi said, except that Geller, Hurkos, and Serios (and too many of their spectators) were trumpeting them as innate gifts rather than neatly executed stunts. He added that the study of Geller by the Stanford Research Institute was woefully uncontrolled. "Wherever there is any possibility of . . . chicanery being an element in any experimental process," Randi warned, "an experienced conjuror must be called in. And not just any conjuror, but one whose specialty is just that particular brand of chicanery."[30] Randi's harshly skeptical book, *The Magic of Uri Geller*, was on the shelves in 1975.

Cryptozoology was never as fully discredited as parapsychology, but important revelations nonetheless turned up. The Mothman that had been sighted around Point Pleasant, West Virginia, was considered by experts to have been either a sandhill crane or a large owl: seen in darkness, either would have been no more than winged shapes, roughly man size, with eyes that reflected back any light. No further Mothman evidence was found, although John Keel wrote of sinister, foreign-seeming individuals who had been intimidating witnesses in the area. Ogopogo, Champ, and the Loch Ness monster have never been shown to exist; only a handful of indistinct photographs of them have ever been taken, and in 1994 the famous 1934 "surgeon's photo" of a silhouetted neck and head emerging from the loch was revealed to have been faked with a model submarine, in a deathbed confession by one of the accomplices. Doubters added that Lake Okanagan, Lake Champlain, and Loch Ness did not have sufficient aquatic life to sustain a plesiosaur-type animal, and in any case plesiosaurs were not fish but reptiles that breathed air, making it unlikely for them to surface as seldom as they apparently did. Loch Ness researcher Robert Rines died in November 2009, after expressing his belief that the monster he had sought and possibly documented for over thirty years may have itself expired, since the number of its appearances had fallen sharply. Global warming might have been a factor, he said.

In 2004 Greg Long's book *The Making of Bigfoot: The Inside Story* was published to considerable controversy in the cryptozoology community. Long had unearthed evidence that the 1967 Roger Patterson Bigfoot film, taken at Bluff Creek, California, was actually a hoax perpetrated by Patterson, with his friend Bob Hieronimus wearing a special costume to pose and walk like the unknown creature. Patterson's brother said the film clip was sold for $100,000. Patterson, who had died in 1972, was not around to dispute the allegations, but Patterson's partner, Bob Gimlin, was quoted as saying, "If it was a hoax, it was a hoax to me, too. And I'm pretty hard to fool."[31] It was also written that Patterson was known to be a shady character who had previously cultivated an interest in Bigfoot and had already gone looking for the beast and shot trial footage; he was not some ordinary woodsman who just happened to have brought a movie camera with him on a casual wilderness outing. Believers denounced the book, saying the 1967 film was not the only evidence for Bigfoot—what about the footprints? But around the same time a Ray Wallace, who died in 2002, was said to have faked with cutouts the original footprints in Humboldt County, California, that had inspired the name "Bigfoot" in 1958. The plot thickened with the claim that it had been Wallace's costumed wife, Elna, whom Roger Patterson had photographed at Bluff Creek. Of the 1967 Patterson footage no hard proof has been established one way or another.

Aside from this confusion, the fact remains that no bipedal primate has been conclusively identified in western North America. While there are large tracts of untouched forest and mountain range in the region, the incursions of loggers, tree planters, skiers, snowmobilers, prospectors, hunters, hikers, vacationers, and even marijuana growers have not resulted in any incontrovertible demonstration of Bigfoot's actuality. Naturalists have pointed out that for a viable Bigfoot or Sasquatch population there would have to be an adequate genetic pool in the form of at least a hundred animals—probably enough for the species to be seen more often than implied by the relatively scant number of witnesses. The plausible testimonies of Bigfoot glimpses that have been recorded over the decades—and there are not a few—have been far outnumbered by the obviously fabricated or imagined visions that have been posted on the Internet. In an age where nearly everyone carries some form of video camera and worldwide online publicity is available to all, no modern equivalent of the shaky, haunting images captured by Roger Patterson—honestly or not—has ever been made.

Yet even accepting that a few people cynically exploited the occult fascination with the unexplained that was so pervasive in the sixties and seventies, it must be said that most of those who stoked that fascination, and most of those who shared in it, were sincere. Erich von Däniken and the cryptozoologists might be distinguished from people who sought exorcisms or who consulted Ouija boards, but there was nonetheless an element of religious devotion in their work. They believed. They believed when up against personal ridicule, professional dismissal, and the stubborn elusiveness of substantiation. Peter Byrne, Charles Berlitz, Ivan T. Sanderson, John Keel, Raymond Bayless, Martin Ebon, and D. Scott Rogo were not hacks trying to get rich off a cult whose adherents they privately held in contempt; they were as intrigued as anyone by their subjects and did their idiosyncratic best to convince as many others as they could. Sanderson, Keel, Rogo, Ebon, and Bayless were actually associates who frequently quoted one another's books and bolstered one another's research. As much as the Committee for the Scientific Investigation of Claims of the Paranormal might have disavowed it, there is still something admirable about the way they stuck to their theories. In 2008, shortly before he passed away, the Loch Ness monster hunter Robert Rines told a Boston magazine he had no regrets about his quest and the derision he had faced for it. "They can just call me crazy, and that's okay by me. At least I won't go to jail for it, like Galileo."[32]

For the millions of readers and viewers excited by the possibilities of Bigfoot or the Bermuda Triangle, of clairvoyance or *Chariots of the Gods?*, the occult did not have to be something evil or ugly. It could also be hopeful, a promise of a reordered universe, or a remade natural world, or a reshaped body of knowledge. And there was yet more of the occult that configured the possibilities of the universe, nature, and human understanding into faiths even more elaborate than science or pseudoscience could come up with. Some of those faiths were eccentric, some of those faiths were outrageous, and some of them, unfortunately, were unspeakable.

6

Devil in the Flesh

Yes, the demons are real. I saw them, I felt their presence, and I heard them.
—David Berkowitz

In recent years there has been a rapidly spreading interest in this country in the occult, mysticism, 'black magic,' witchcraft and the worship of 'the Satanic majesty,'" related a *New York Times* article of July 6, 1971. "With California taking the lead, the interest, or obsession, has spread to colleges, hippie gathering places and even to suburban housewives."[1] Datelined from a small New Jersey community, the report was titled "'Satan Cult,' Death, Drugs Jolt Quiet Vineland, NJ." It was there that the body of twenty-year-old Michael Newell had been found bound and submerged in a local pond. According to his alleged killers, Newell had belonged to an underground satanic group and wanted to die a violent death, which they had provided for him. His goal, they claimed, was to enter the afterlife and assume command of forty leagues of demons. "Close to three centuries after the hanging of the witches of Salem," noted the newspaper, "witches seem to be turning up all over—in Brooklyn, in Nassau County, New York, and here in Vineland."[2]

The *Times* story had accurately judged the pervasiveness of the occult in the era. For millions of people, young and old, rural and urban, the occult was entertainment enjoyed through music, books, movies, television, games, and what-if conversations in classrooms, workplaces, and private homes. It was a vicarious thrill. But for millions of others the occult was something to be actively practiced, even if they did not always consider their practices occult at all. In the latter half of the sixties and throughout the seventies a wide swath of the Western populace took up the occult as a way of life, some of it in forms so mild it would eventually be incorporated into conventional medicine and psychology, and elsewhere in extreme manifestations that, together with the entire onslaught of occult pop culture and ephemera, would awake a sleeping giant of political and religious reaction that has not yet been stilled. Sometimes the occult was a means to live. For Michael Newell of New Jersey and many others, it turned out to be a means to die.

Other influential institutions besides the *New York Times* had taken notice of the occult. On November 15, 1972, an address by Pope Paul VI, "Confronting the Devil's Power," examined diabolism from the highest office of the Catholic Church. "What are the Church's greatest needs at the present time?" asked the Pontiff. "Don't be surprised at Our answer and don't write it off as simplistic or even superstitious: one of the Church's greatest needs is to be defended against the evil we call the Devil . . . . Sin in its turn becomes the occasion and the effect of interference in us and our work by a dark, hostile agent, the Devil . . . . This matter of the Devil and of the influence he can exert on individuals as well as on communities, entire societies or events, is a very important chapter of Catholic doctrine which should be studied again."[3] Thus millions of believers, and millions more wavering agnostics, heard a confirmation of Satan's reality from the most important living Christian in the modern world. Reckless youth from the American suburbs thought there really were demons; so did the bishop of Rome. The occult was reaching nearly everyone.

It had not come out of nowhere. The receptiveness of the public in advanced industrial societies to matters of the paranormal, the mystical, and the magical went back over one hundred years. The resurgence of interest that came after 1966 was an extension and a synthesis of several strands of belief that had arisen in the previous century; sometimes these roots were paid explicit tribute by latter-day exponents, and sometimes they had gone off on new tangents their originators could never have foreseen. Their furthest origins lay in European and English Romanticism, as well as in their American cousin, Transcendentalism. Those philosophies of personal and intellectual liberation, combined with the rise of an educated middle class, encouraged (or at least tolerated) new searches for understanding that were encapsulated in the founding documents and personalities of the modern occult movement.

Eliphas Lévi (1810–1875, born Alphonse Constant) is usually cited as the pivotal figure in the occult revival that began in his native France, with the publication of his *Dogme et ritual de la haute magie* in 1856. Lévi constructed a comprehensive theory of magic that drew on Kabbala texts of Judaic mysticism and medieval *grimoires* of magical instruction, among many other sources. As much as anything, Lévi and those he influenced— Aleister Crowley was an early admirer—were bibliophiles who thrived in a rich print culture and assiduously sought out old and rare manuscripts from the time of Gutenberg or before. Lévi's illustration of *The Goat of Mendès*, a winged, cross-legged, cloven-hoofed human hybrid with a pentagram on its forehead, remains one of the most reproduced occult pictures and was a familiar sight in occult emporia a hundred years after his death. Helena Blavatsky (1831–1891) was an eccentric Russian-born adventuress who, with her American disciples, established the Theosophical Society in 1875 based on the stew of Egyptian and Hindu religious teachings she claimed to have studied in her worldwide travels. Theosophy was purported to be an overarching metaphysical system that could bring enlightenment and supernatural powers to its adherents; branches of the society were still extant during the twentieth century's occult wave. And Spiritualism, the belief in viable communication with the dead, enjoyed a tremendous vogue that began in the United States around 1850 and spread across the Atlantic. Spiritualist meetings were especially popular after the U.S. Civil War and during World War I, when bereaved families attempted to contact loved ones who had been killed in battle. The family of the adolescent boy from Cottage City, Maryland, whose 1949 episode of apparent possession inspired *The Exorcist*, came from a Spiritualist background.

Following World War II, the Orientalism that had long informed occult doctrines was greatly boosted by millions of soldiers' overseas service in Asia. Now the Hindu, Buddhist, and Taoist traditions that had once been directly encountered by only a few were exposed to many ordinary Westerners, some of whom eventually returned to spread their knowledge, with Los Angeles and San Francisco prime terminals of entry. In addition, the small Asian enclaves in those and other cities were slowly opening themselves and their cultures to their surrounding populations, and in 1965 the U.S. government had rescinded its discriminatory system of immigration quotas, allowing more immigrants from the East. As Zen Buddhism had shaped the American bohemianism of the fifties and sixties, the flowery wisdom of the transplanted Lebanese poet Kahlil Gibran (1883–1931) also served for average Americans as a gateway to the mysteries of the East; dog-eared editions of Gibran's *The Prophet* were common accessories in campus coffeehouses of the era, succeeded by Robert Pirsig's *Zen and the Art of*

Motorcycle Maintenance (1974) and Alan Watts's *Tao: The Watercourse Way* (1975). Zen, Taoism, and Gibran could hardly be categorized as occult, yet they fostered a climate where foreign, quasi-religious instruction could increasingly find willing (and paying) audiences.

Much the same could be said of yoga and its relatives. These too caught on at the same time as the occult, and with much of the same demographic. Yoga had been developed in India centuries before Christ and had been gradually seeping into Western consciousness since 1893, when it had been demonstrated at the Chicago Columbian Exposition. In contrast to the reactive techniques of conventional medicine, yoga was about maintaining a balance between mind and body as a way to preventive or holistic health: a regimen of bends, stretches, and contemplative poses that reacquainted the yogic with his or her own inner serenity. By the sixties, yoga, the Chinese calisthenics of t'ai chi, and the hands-on procedures of acupuncture and shiatsu massage had gained a foothold in North America and were being touted as worthwhile alternatives to the pharmaceutical and surgical options typically offered to the unwell. Acupuncture was recognized as a legitimate medical expense by the U.S. Internal Revenue Service in 1973, and the celestial rites of intercourse prescribed in the Hindu Tantric scriptures gained acolytes during the sexual revolution. Again, such disciplines were far removed from parapsychology or Christian demonism, yet in those years they all seemed to belong to the same broad, nebulous field of unknown or unusual interests that disproportionately attracted the young and the experimental. Yoga studios, health food stores, and occult shops could often be found in the same neighborhoods being patronized by the same clientele.

Transcendental Meditation (TM) was a newer phenomenon that nevertheless had become part of the trend toward religious values outside Western monotheism. The TM movement was led by its Indian teacher Mahesh Prasad Varma (c. 1918–2008), better known as the Maharishi Mahesh Yogi, a spiritual lecturer and physics graduate who founded the Spiritual Regeneration Movement in 1958. The Maharishi's main lesson was of daily meditation practice, focused on the individual's private and undisclosed mantra (sound or word based on the names of Hindu deities), which promised to uplift its practitioners to their fullest human potential. Improved mental health, world peace, and even the ability to levitate were touted as possible benefits of TM. Considered a channel to the divine by some and pure quackery by others, TM's visibility was raised considerably in August

1967, when all four Beatles, fresh from making *Sgt. Pepper's Lonely Hearts Club Band*, attended a public engagement of the Maharishi's in Bangor, Wales. In January the following year, the quartet studied at the Maharishi's retreat in Rishikesh, India, accompanied by their wives, fellow rock celebrities Mike Love of the Beach Boys and English minstrel Donovan, and Mia Farrow, after she had concluded acting in *Rosemary's Baby*. The Beatles eventually withdrew from TM and the Maharishi—among other of their disillusionments, he was rumored to have made unwanted advances on Mia Farrow's sister, Prudence—but the relaxing and regenerating routine of meditation had already caught on with hundreds of thousands of people. Throughout the seventies, TM's popularity spread, with the founding of Maharishi International University in 1971 and its introduction into the state school curriculum of New Jersey (this was halted by court order a few years later, on grounds of bringing religion into the public sphere). Even today, the word "mantra" has become synonymous with any word repeatedly invoked for near-holy purposes.

An alternative route to heightened consciousness was promoted through the writings of trained anthropologist Carlos Castaneda (c. 1925–1998). Castaneda's *Don Juan* trilogy described firsthand his instruction by a mysterious shaman of the Yaqui Indian tribe who lived in the hills of northwest Mexico: *The Teachings of Don Juan* (1968), *A Separate Reality* (1971), and *Journey to Ixtlan: The Lessons of Don Juan* (1972) sold millions of copies and were translated into seventeen languages. Much of this success was due to Don Juan's apparent endorsement of ingesting hallucinogenic plants as a way to attain higher planes of experience, a prescription that millions of young people equated with their own recreational use of marijuana, LSD, and other drugs.

Certainly, the rise of both the occult and the drug culture had coincided to a significant degree; the U.S. National Commission on Marijuana and Drug Abuse, formed in 1970, concluded that 25 million Americans had tried cannabis at least once, and estimated that 40 percent of those between the ages eighteen and twenty-five were occasional or regular marijuana smokers. Such numbers likely included many of the same people who held Ouija board sessions, read the horrific conjurations of H. P. Lovecraft, and listened to the macabre lyrics of Alice Cooper. In *A Separate Reality*, Castaneda wrote that "for the American Indian, perhaps for thousands of years, the vague phenomenon we call sorcery has been a serious, bona fide practice, comparable to that of our science. Our difficulty in understanding it stems, no doubt, from the alien units of meaning with which it deals."[4] A review of the same title in *Natural History* magazine said that Castaneda "draws you into the weird world of witches. It reveals an inside view of how witchcraft works."[5] Castaneda himself avoided publicity of all kinds, lending a special mystique to his accounts. Some critics suggested they had been falsified or at least substantially embellished, but whatever their veracity, many people accepted his stories as offering insightful perspectives on both psychotropic drugs and spiritual revelation, and the relationship between the two.

Others put their faith in more tangible objects. Into the seventies some occult retailers began selling crystals, not as jewelry or ornamentation but for their supposed extra-aesthetic properties. Various gems had already been designated as birthstones (garnet for January, emerald for May, topaz for November, etc.), and crystal balls, of course, had long been connected with divinatory capacities, but in the collected prophecies of Edgar Cayce, which held a devoted fandom decades after his death, they had been mentioned frequently as having once been integral to the advanced civilization of Atlantis. Under the continued influences of Cayce and his Atlantean visions, items of quartz and other stones were acquired partly as attractive objects in themselves but also as instruments of spiritual enhancement. Gradually, the healing or psychic forces contained in crystals—and the related concept of "pyramid power," whereby pyramidal shapes were said to direct positive energy toward whatever living thing was situated under them—became other avenues for believers to travel in search of awareness and growth. Numerous books on pyramid power were published in the seventies, and crystals especially were to be very marketable occult-related products for many years thereafter.

Fortune-telling, too, came in several forms during the occult era. The interest in Asian traditions that popularized Zen Buddhism and yoga revived the stone-casting rites of the Chinese *I Ching*, or Book of Changes. Each roll of the stones (sticks or coins could also be used) indicated one of sixty-four symbolic hexagrams that, when distilled down to six final combinations, were held to represent the caster's future life course from which he or she could make relevant decisions. So Fire over Earth (*Li* over *K'un*) stood for *Chin*, or successful development; Heaven over Fire (*Chi'ren* over *Li*) stood for *T'ung Jen*, or friendliness; Mountain over Earth (*Ken* over *K'un*) warned of *Po*, or disintegration, and so on. An unknowable number of lives were transformed in ways large and small because of what the Book of Changes foretold. The *I Ching* was both timeless Confucian revelation and hip counterculture fad.

Similarly, Tarot cards harked back to the European Renaissance of alchemy and magic while occupying a firm place in the inventories of head shops and occult stores of jet-age North America. As a means of divination the Tarot system dated back to eighteenth-century France, using designs from Italian cards of four centuries before, which in turn could be traced to the Egyptian library of Alexandria; there were many Tarot decks, but most were based on twenty-two trump cards and four suits of wands, pentacles, swords, and cups. Like the *I Ching*, the mystique of the Tarot lay less in the reliability of its predictions than in the attractiveness of its ritual, and of the cards themselves. Upon its reissue in 1971 the most popular Tarot deck in America was the classic 1910 Rider-Waite version, designed by Arthur Edward Waite and rendered by Pamela Colman Smith, both members of the Order of the Golden Dawn. The ex-Golden Dawn affiliate Aleister Crowley had created his own Tarot, with illustrations by Frieda Harris, which was another steady seller when it was made available for retail in 1969. The Rider-Waite and Crowley editions were among many commercially produced by the U.S. Games Systems firm, formed in 1968, and these were followed by Native American, Erotic, Egyptian, and Mayan Tarot decks. A number of instructional Tarot books were available, including Eden Gray's *A Complete Guide to the Tarot* (1970), F. D. Graves's *The Windows of Tarot* (1973), and the inevitable *The Sexual Key to the Tarot* by Theodore Laurence (1973).

Tarot cards became some of the most familiar occult accessories in the seventies. "Currently in America there is a phenomenal interest in Tarot fortune-telling cards," asserted Stuart Kaplan in the pamphlet that accompanied the Rider-Waite deck. "Tarot cards are currently sought by college students and teenagers, housewives, businessmen, professional people—indeed, persons from all walks of life . . . . Teenagers revel in Tarot parties. Adults attend Tarot luncheons, charitable benefits and even Tarot picnics at which card readings are performed."[6] The complex patterns of arranging and displaying them, and the art of explaining what the myriad of arrangements and displays might say about the "Querent," or seeker, were often beyond the amateur Tarot reader. Instead it was the sheer visual beauty of the designs, and their evocation of another world—a separate reality, as Carlos Castaneda's Don Juan might put it—where Death, the Devil, the Lovers, the Hanged Man, the Hierophant, and the Last Judgment were elemental descriptors of human action, that held the imaginations of Tarot users. One's life seemed more profound if it could be explained in a language of Kings, Queens, Knights, Pages, and ravaged castles (the Tower), nude figures (the Star and the World), and robed angels (Temperance), rather than the mundane idioms of job, school, car, or home. Tarot cards were seen on the sleeves of hit records: Bob Dylan's *Desire* (1975) and Blue Öyster Cult's *Agents of Fortune* (1976), featuring "(Don't Fear) The Reaper," while *Led Zeppelin IV* (1971), featuring "Stairway to Heaven," had an adaptation of the Hermit illustrated across its inner foldout.

Yet there was an oracular method that became more ubiquitous during the occult era than the Tarot and the *I Ching* combined. It had the same basis in archaic tradition as yoga and Transcendental Meditation, yet it turned into an everyday habit for millions of modern people. It was decidedly as cryptic and as arcane as Zen Buddhism, yet it was mass-marketed to middle-class readers and consumers. It was about as subjective as the effects of psychedelic drugs, yet it was perfectly legal and even facetiously endorsed by the U.S. government. The occult was never more mainstream or less threatening than when, at innumerable singles bars, cocktail parties, and high school dances, a hopeful introduction began with the question "What's your sign?"

Astrology was the most common occult pastime of the sixties and seventies—so much so that people who would never have spared a thought for "Sympathy for the Devil," Bigfoot, or *The Omen* could still consider themselves mystically inclined. The protest rallies and consciousness-raisings that marked the youth movement—on top of its new music, hairstyles, and sex mores—were seen as heralds of the astrological Age of Aquarius, a term many commentators casually used to describe the counterculture as a whole. "Aquarius/Let the Sunshine In," the 1969 Fifth Dimension hit song from the 1967 musical *Hair*, conveyed the terminology of houses, planets, stars, and alignments across the airwaves of Top 40 radio. Serious astrologers, indeed, had stated that humankind was presently undergoing the end of the Piscean age and the beginning of a fresh 2,170-year cycle, although the calculations were vague enough to put the cosmic turning point anywhere from the year 1904 to February 4, 1962. By 1969 astrology columns were featured in 1,200 American newspapers (which then had about 40 million readers) and many more around the world. Astrology was everywhere, all the time.

And it was timeless. Studying the skies for their impact on human affairs was as old as humankind: the sun and the moon had clear effects on harvests and seas, so it was reasoned that the other objects in the heavens had equal significance. Various systems of star watching were developed by ancient Chinese, Indians, Mayans, and Babylonians. Astrology and astronomy arose together, and both were the domain of the learned and the exalted (the New Testament's Wise Men, who followed a star to the nativity of Jesus, were observing astrological indicators). The twelve signs of the zodiac, and the attributes of the constellations that dominated the nocturnal skies of each season, were codified by the Greek Ptolemy in the second century AD and remained a principal basis for magical and alchemical knowledge into the Renaissance. But as men of reason such as Galileo, Copernicus, and Tycho Brahe found more predictable, less intuitive patterns in the passages of planets and suns, astrology declined as a meaningful science and moved further into the occult.

Its resuscitation as a popular art began in the late nineteenth century, when the American aristocrat Evangeline Adams began dispensing horoscope readings to wealthy clientele—she successfully beat a charge of fortune-telling in New York by impressing the judge with her astrological divinations—and others in Europe and North America began designing more and more elaborate star charts to anticipate the future of nations, famous people, and world events. In the next decades astrology books and radio programs earned wide followings, and *American Astrology* magazine was founded in 1933, featuring the innovation of horoscopes that applied to anyone born under a particular birth sign. By the sixties, thousands of astrologers were selling their services in the United States alone, most prominent among them the very successful freelancers Sydney Omarr, Linda Goodman, Jeane Dixon, Carroll Righter, and Constella (née Shirley Spencer).

Horoscopes became matters of routine conversation, whether seriously considered or not; astronauts aboard Apollo 9 in March 1969 had theirs read to them from Mission Control in Houston for a chuckle. Apart from well-paid syndicated newspaper columnists, the production of zodiacal trinkets, mass-market astrological paperbacks, and arcane astrological guidebooks for the do-it-yourselfer became a sizable industry. "We sell 2000 a month of the 'A to Z Horoscope Maker' at $12 a copy," enthused occult publisher Carl Weschcke in 1971. "It was 400 copies eleven years ago."[7] In many ways the fashion for astrology mirrored that of the self-help trend, where the private concerns of the individual were paramount. Of course the counsels of astrologers were usually bland, ambiguous suggestions that defied falsification—who looked back on their old horoscopes to check whether they'd come true? But the advice to a Libra, a Scorpio, or a Leo published in the daily newspaper was explicitly about *you*, and some observers admitted that, whatever its predictive powers, astrology seemed to provide a richer psychological language for the contemporary person to use than he or she might find in more rational therapies. It wasn't that destiny was determined by the stars, but that the stars were a vehicle by which people could articulate their own sense of who they were. If the seventies were not the Age of Aquarius but the Me Decade, then the acceptance of astrology had surely propelled that fixation on the self. A 1976 Gallup poll found that 32 million Americans thought astrology to be a creditable form of knowledge.

For critics, however, astrology remained an aspect of the occult wave, and one most indicative of public gullibility. The position of stars and planets relative to an observer on Earth had zero influence on anyone's personal disposition or life course, they said; there was absolutely no evidence that astrology "worked" as a means of foretelling the future. In 1975 *The Humanist* magazine ran a formal statement, "Objections to Astrology," signed by 186 scientists, an early defense of rationalism that soon led to the formation of the Committee for the Scientific Investigation of Claims of the Paranormal. "Scientists in a variety of fields have become concerned about the increased acceptance of astrology in many parts of the world," began the declaration. "We, the undersigned—astronomers, astrophysicists, and scientists in other fields –wish to caution the public against the unquestioning acceptance of the predictions and advice given privately and publicly by astrologers. Those who wish to believe in astrology should realize that there is no scientific foundation for its tenets."[8] Yet the signs of the zodiac were still displayed on the clothes, personal belongings, and household décor of millions of people during the occult era, just as millions more glanced at their horoscopes every day and semi-seriously identified themselves as Libras, Virgos, and Cancers. Notwithstanding the accumulated facts of physics, astronomy, and biology, for many years astrology was the most open of all hidden practices.

Witchcraft, in contrast, was still weird. But as the occult had risen in prominence, so had "practicing witches": individuals or groups of people who openly claimed to observe the precepts of medieval magic and to use its accoutrements of ritual and worship in their personal faith. The numbers of active witches in the sixties and seventies probably numbered fewer than 10,000 in Europe and North America, but, unlike their inspirations of centuries past, they could freely admit to their beliefs and even welcome inquiries from the press (the British law that imposed a one-year jail sentence for telling fortunes had been repealed in 1951). Novels and films, including *Rosemary's Baby*, *The Brotherhood of Satan*, and *Race with the Devil*, exaggerated the nefarious activities of witches but nonetheless made them seem plausible in modern American society. For reporters and the curious, the sheer novelty of anyone living, dressing, or casting spells as a witch in the twentieth century was an entertaining distraction that, most of the time, brought on none of the zeal for exposure and punishment it had once inspired.

The persecutions, tortures, and executions of witches that had swept Europe during the early Renaissance had usually been considered a manifestation of superstition and hysteria, driven by the religious schism of the Reformation and social crises like the Black Death. But in 1921, the British anthropologist Margaret Murray's *The Witch-Cult in Western Europe* put forward the new thesis that many of those condemned as witches had in fact been members of a pre-Christian fertility religion, whose secret ceremonies and objects of veneration (forest gatherings and goats, for instance) had been attacked by vindictive Catholics and Protestants as devil worship. In other words, witches were real, but they were not the servants of Satan their prosecutors had contended they were. Though the historical validity of Murray's views was not universally recognized by scholars, a few people found them credible enough to "resurrect" witchcraft as a living sect. Englishman Gerald Gardner came forward as a witch in 1949, announcing that he was part of an underground organization whose covens met in the present-day United Kingdom; his *Witchcraft Today* (1954) was an influential manual of what he called "Wicca," a sort of neo-paganism that celebrated nature and life instead of the devil and death. Sybil Leek was another well-known practitioner of Wicca, who in *Diary of a Witch* (1968) described her lineage in witchcraft that went back to the year 1134. Leek became famous through the seventies as an author on astrology and ghosts as well.

Outsiders noted that the customs of Gardner, Leek, and their latter-day followers were more invented than revived, and that these customs varied widely from circle to circle. Some forms of paganism probably had existed in medieval Europe before being uncovered by the church—indeed, the Christian festivals of Christmas, Easter, and Halloween were adapted from seasonal "sabbats" that took place around December 21 (Yule), April 21 (Eostre), and October 31 (Samhain)—but most of the rituals undertaken in the occult era were based on a very conjectural understanding of historical evidence. For those who participated in it, witchcraft was a refreshingly upbeat alternative to the dour denials of mainstream Christianity or Judaism, promising an engagement with the natural world and a mastery of natural conditions (weather, health, human desires) on which other religions rarely delivered. As environmental awareness came to the fore from the sixties onward, Wicca's devotion to the divinity of nature took on a greater urgency. Liberated people of the era got a bonus thrill from the way that the most exotic Wiccan rituals were conducted "skyclad," or nude, and that some even involved ceremonial sex. Wiccan or neo-pagan groups that began in the sixties and seventies included the Asatru Free Assembly, the Church of All Worlds, the Church of Circle Wicca, the Aquarian Tabernacle Church, the Church and School of Wicca, and something called the New Reformed Orthodox Order of the Golden Dawn.

But it was the centrality of the Great Mother Goddess to Wicca that made it most relevant in the seventies. Just as astrology could be tied to self-help, so witchcraft was an offshoot of women's liberation. While Margaret Murray's positing of a clandestine fertility cult had its doubters (she went on to assert that Joan of Arc and Thomas Becket, archbishop of Canterbury, had been among the cultists), there was little doubt that many thousands of people had been executed as witches in Europe, the majority of them female. This could be called a gender-specific genocide. Most of the women put to death were subject to excruciating torture and humiliating bodily inspection in an effort to extract confessions of carnal relations with demons or Satan himself—all of which, of course, was conducted by men, who claimed to be acting with only the highest intentions of advancing theological knowledge and enforcing God's law. With the feminist movement of the sixties and seventies, this authentic sexual abuse and the less verifiable folklore of Wicca combined for a female-centered witchcraft that revered both the Great Mother Goddess and the ideals of women's strength and independence.

Some "Dianic" (all-female) covens were formed, but even co-ed Wiccan bodies were led by priestesses and revered a female deity. One important Wiccan body was the Covenant of the Goddess, formed in San Francisco in 1975, an early leader of which was the woman born Miriam Simos but by then known as Starhawk. Starhawk's 1979 book, *The Spiral Dance: A Rebirth of the Ancient Religion of the Great Goddess*, became a key text of feminist Wicca. "For women, the Goddess is the symbol of the inmost self, and the beneficent, nurturing, liberating power within woman," Starhawk wrote. "The cosmos is modeled on the female body, which is sacred . . . . To invoke the Goddess is to awaken the Goddess within, to become, for a time, that aspect we invoke . . . . A woman's body, its odors, secretions, and menstrual blood, are sacred, worthy of reverence and celebration."[9] *The Spiral Dance* defined witchcraft (or just "the Craft") in political terms, a spiritual resistance lobby that promoted gender equality, herbal medicine, sustainable environmentalism, and similar progressive causes. In her 1979 study of the Wiccan and neo-pagan movements, *Drawing Down the Moon*, Margot Adler added, "The Witch . . . is an extraordinary symbol—independent, anti-establishment, strong, and proud. She is political, yet spiritual and magical. The Witch is woman as martyr; she is persecuted by the ignorant; she is the woman who lives outside society and outside society's definition of woman."[10] Disparate groups of Wiccans and neo-pagans, Dianic and otherwise, met and continued to practice across North America and Europe into subsequent decades.

Witchcraft, astrology, the Tarot, the *I Ching*, crystals, Transcendental Meditation, yoga, and Zen Buddhism were somewhat controversial in their heydays of the sixties and seventies. So were other assorted occult interests, or psychotherapeutic methods derived from drug-inspired mysticism and Asian religion: numerology, graphology, karma, Rolfing, rebirthing, Erhard Seminars Training (EST), and the practices of California's Esalen Institute. But they were all fundamentally harmless. Some may have been based on weak science, others on watered-down principles borrowed from very old and very distant cultures, and still more on middle-class susceptibility to the exotic and the faddish. None of them, though, led directly to lawbreaking or violence. They were on the social fringes, not over the legal limits. But other tangents of the occult were definitely dangerous, definitely criminal, and some turned sickeningly fatal.

As early as May 1966 headlines around the world reported the sad case of Bernadette Hasler, a seventeen-year-old Swiss girl who had been taken up into a bizarre sect called the Seekers of Mercy. Entrusted by her parents to the group for several years, Bernadette was deemed by them to have held a sexual relationship with the devil and was put through weeks of degradation and beatings as part of her "exorcism." She died as a result of the sustained deprivations and physical punishments she had suffered, which had involved being whipped and forced to eat her own feces. The two leaders of the Seekers of Mercy, defrocked priest Josef Stocker and his common-law wife, Magdalena Kohler, were, along with four disciples, convicted of inflicting injuries causing death. In her diary the isolated and traumatized Bernadette had confessed to consorting with Satan but entered a poignant wish as well: "I would like to have a friend my age, and if I cannot have a friend, I would like at least to have a cat or a parakeet to whom I could talk."[11]

Ten years later, in Klingenberg, West Germany, two Catholic priests were sentenced for negligent manslaughter after they had conducted a ten-month exorcism of twenty-three-year-old Anneliese Michel, who, they claimed, had shown signs of demonic possession. Anneliese had starved to death under their treatment, based on a ritual prescribed in 1614, and weighed sixty-eight pounds when she died of malnutrition and dehydration. Recordings of her hellish cursing and shrieks were played as evidence of her condition; she had raged in the voices of Emperor Nero, Judas Iscariot, and Cain, from the Book of Genesis. Anneliese's devoutly Catholic parents Josef and Anna were also found to be complicit in her death. In the wake of the story, Munich's Cardinal Joseph Ratzinger conceded that the seventeenth-century rite of exorcism warranted revision. Ratzinger later became Pope Benedict XVI.

In the late sixties and throughout the seventies, farmers across the United States and Canada reported mysterious cases of animal mutilation, which attracted the attention of the press and raised concerns about an occult connection to the episodes. On September 9, 1967, the body of a three-year-old Appaloosa horse named Snippy (also called Lady) belonging to rancher Harry King of southern Colorado was found missing its heart and other organs, with no nearby signs of blood, footprints, or other animal activity. The King family voiced suggestions that the horse's death and the strange condition of its remains were linked with a recent UFO outbreak in the area. The same year, in West Virginia, John Keel heard stories of inexplicably killed and dismembered local livestock, which he repeated in *The Mothman Prophecies*. But over the next twelve years a wave of cattle mutilations—tallied anywhere from a few hundred to a few thousand—struck across the Great Plains of Montana, Kansas, and Oklahoma and into the Canadian province of Alberta. In the autumn of 1974, farmers in South

Dakota and Nebraska found numerous of their cows dead and weirdly dissected: missing eyes, tongues, lips, reproductive organs, and seemingly drained of blood. Now the suspicion shifted to satanic cults, which, it was alleged, may have been killing the beasts and using their blood and body parts in blasphemous rituals. Who else, it was said, could destroy the cattle so stealthily and then remove their flesh with near-surgical precision?

Police and veterinarians who investigated the mutilations arrived at a different conclusion. No satanic covens were uncovered near the farmlands in question, and the cattle and horses' deaths were likely attributable to disease, the consumption of poisonous plants, or lightning strikes. Scavengers, among them wolves, coyotes, skunks, foxes, magpies, and ravens, were the probable cause of the missing organs—the soft tissue being easier to rend and chew than the exterior hide—and, as the animals' carcasses bloated from internal gases, the bites and wounds caused by predators would look neater than immediately after being made. Blood and internal fluids would pool in the underside of the bodies, giving the appearance of exsanguination. In 1979 the U.S. Department of Justice began to conduct Operation Animal Mutilation for the state of New Mexico, led by former FBI man Kenneth Rommel, which eventually concluded that the horses and cows had died from natural causes and that the odd absence of eyes or genitalia was the work of other, smaller animals. Yet the willingness of ranchers and others to believe in a conspiracy of cow-killing Satanists was indicative of how far the occult idea had spread, and the constructed satanic motives of blood ceremonies and violation of bovine sex organs showed how deeply Middle America had absorbed, and even elaborated on, occult mythology.

So-called cattle mutilations resulted in no criminal charges, but the criminal intent assumed to be behind them reflected the reality that there was assuredly a new upsurge of occult crime. In fact, occult crime itself was new: analysts had hitherto explained individual arsonists, rapists, and murderers in terms of sociology (poverty, prejudice, addiction, exclusion) or psychology (Freudian sexual neuroses). The most infamous serial killers, like Jack the Ripper, Peter Kürten ("the Vampire of Düsseldorf"), Albert DeSalvo ("the Boston Strangler"), and Ed Gein (a model for Norman Bates in *Psycho*), were obviously sick and sadistic men whose actions were sourced in the darkest recesses of their very damaged minds. By the sixties, though, some murders could not be counted as simply the work of psychopaths, degenerates, or alienated loners. Police and civilians were faced with dangerous people whose demons may not have been internal.

Between December 1968 and October 1969 five people were stabbed or shot by an unknown assailant around San Francisco, California. A survivor of one of his assaults reported that the attacker was a man whose hood was inscribed with a zodiac sign. During this time the killer contacted local newspapers with details of the crimes and also included a message written in a strange symbolic code. When finally deciphered, the error-filled message read in part: "I like killing people because it is so much fun it is more fun than killing wild game in the forrest . . . the best part of it is thae when I die I will be reborn in paradice and the I have killed will become my slaves."[12] The letters were signed "Zodiac," and there were also phone calls to police from someone identifying himself as "the Zodiac killer." After the murders stopped and no suspects had been apprehended there were still contacts from a man claiming to be Zodiac, and claiming responsibility for up to thirty-seven deaths, between 1971 and 1974; in the last letter to the *San Francisco Chronicle*, he wrote, "I saw and think 'The Exorcist' was the best saterical comidy that I have ever seen [*sic*]."[13] Whether the last correspondence came from the actual killer or only a disturbed prankster has never been conclusively proven (the Zodiac killings remain unsolved), but here was an investigation forced to look beyond motives of mere criminal insanity or sexual perversion. More such cases would follow.

In New York City between July 1976 and July 1977, six people were killed and seven wounded by David Berkowitz. Before his capture, newspaper headlines named him "the .44 Caliber Killer," but he too wrote taunting letters to police and reporters, which he signed with an occult symbol, calling himself "the Son of Sam." "Sam loves to drink blood," he told Captain Joseph Borrelli of the New York Police Department by mail. "'Go out and kill,' commands father Sam . . . I feel like an outsider. I am on a different wave-length than everybody else—programmed too kill [*sic*]."[14] To columnist Jimmy Breslin, he declared he was "thirsty, hungry, seldom stopping to rest; anxious to please Sam. I love my work. Now, the void has been filled."[15] David Berkowitz's victims were fewer in number than those of other serial killers, but his terrorizing of an entire metropolis in its most crisis-wracked decade, and his bizarre statements preceding and following his arrest, placed him firmly into the annals of occult crime.

After his apprehension, Berkowitz, a chubby, innocuous-looking twenty-four-year-old postal worker, was examined by psychiatrists and gave voluble accounts of his misdeeds and his own background. Pronounced sane and sentenced to 365 years in prison in 1978, he kept a diary that gave further autobiographical details. Initially, Berkowitz spun a twisted tale of the six-thousand-year-old "Sam Carr" (based on his real neighbor of the same name), whose dog commanded him to kill. Police who searched his squalid apartment found writings Berkowitz had scrawled on its battered walls:

> *In this hole lives the Wicked King*
> *Kill for my Master*
> *I turn children into Killers*[16]

In his prison journal Berkowitz appeared to be battling with another entity within him, who interjected its voice into the convict's more reflective writings: "I am Abaddon the Destroyer . . . I am the demon from the bottomless pit here on earth to create havoc and terror. I am War, I am death. I am destruction! . . . I am he the Son of Sam who fears nothing I destroy! I am kind I am hell I am death."[17] In February 1979, however, Berkowitz confessed that his tales of Sam Carr and the demons were hoaxes, and a more plausible but scarcely reassuring version of his personal problems began to come forward.

Berkowitz was an illegitimate child adopted by another couple, his adoptive mother died when he was fourteen, and an eventual reunion with his birth mother proved disappointing. Some of his murderous impulses seemed to have grown out of influences from popular culture. "I was obsessed with 'Rosemary's Baby,'" he said years after his killing spree. "I felt like it was speaking directly to me."[18] In his jail diary he had remembered, "After reading that book Hostage to the Devil by Malachi Martin I have no doubt that I am a person who has been visited by an alien force or being." (*Hostage to the Devil: The Possession and Exorcism of Five Living Americans* was published in 1976 as a nonfiction effort to capitalize on the huge success of *The Exorcist*.) In the early seventies a directionless Berkowitz had joined the U.S. Army and was stationed in South Korea, but he gradually became enamored of the hippie ethos. "The world is all fucked up (thanks Nixon)," he wrote to a friend in January 1972. "We've got to have some peace. The only thing on my mind is Drugs, Music, Pollution, Poverty, Peace and Love."[19] Refusing to carry a gun the next month, he quoted the title of a Black Sabbath song in another letter: "I'll have to prove that I'm a conscientious objector, which I am . . . . Because now I'm an individual again. Free from the war pigs and there [*sic*] evil ways."[20] He signed another message "Master of Reality," the name of Sabbath's 1971 album. "You remember that guy from New York, Son of Sam, who was killing all the chicks?" asked Black Sabbath vocalist Ozzy Osbourne in 2004. "When they got into his apartment, he supposedly had the lyrics to [Sabbath song] 'After Forever' written on his wall. I thought, 'Fuck me, are we going too far?'"[21]

Berkowitz's demons and talking dogs were either made-up alibis or sincere delusions, but some researchers suggested he had been caught up in genuine satanic rituals. The sons of the real Sam Carr, Michael and John, were said to have recruited Berkowitz into a local cult and participated with him in the murders of 1976 and 1977. "Son of Sam," in this theory, referred to the pagan deity Samhain. "We made a pact, maybe with the Devil, but also with each other," Berkowitz told it in 1993. "We're soldiers of Satan now. I was just too far in, too loyal, too much playing the role of the soldier and trying to please people."[22] While Berkowitz was the only person ever prosecuted for the Son of Sam killings (and he had originally admitted to all six), both John and Michael Carr died mysteriously after Berkowitz's arrest, and some Son of Sam eyewitnesses reported assailants who looked markedly different from Berkowitz himself. Imprisoned for life, Berkowitz today has attracted a small following of disciples who revere him for his penitence and born-again Christianity.

Scattered across America in the sixties and seventies were less remembered murders linked in some way to the occult: insanity pleas that claimed the defendants had demonic hallucinations, or media scares reporting individual killers who belonged to and acted on behalf of a larger satanic network. There was the New Jersey youth bound and drowned by two friends in his bid to take control of an army of demons after death. There were the two hitchhiking youths from Wyoming who killed and cannibalized a social worker who had given them a ride. There was a twenty-two-year-old Floridian, a self-described Satanist, who stabbed her friend to death. There were the devil-worshipping Californian kids who killed and mutilated a motorist whose car they hijacked in Orange County. Ironically, the most infamous occult murders of all are the ones with the most inflated occult substance.

Between July 27 and August 26, 1969, members of the Charles Manson "Family" killed nine people, including seven on the two successive nights of August 9 and 10. The apparently random nature of the murders, and their extreme violence, marked a watershed moment in the counterculture and in the American national psychology. "Everything was unmentionable but nothing was unimaginable," journalist and author Joan Didion recalled of the Tate-LaBianca aftermath in her memoir, *The White Album*. "There were twenty dead, no, twelve, ten, eighteen. Black masses were imagined, and bad trips blamed. I remember all of the day's misinformation very clearly, and I also remember this, and wish I did not: *I remember that no one was surprised.*"[23] As the background of Manson and his codefendants emerged following their arrests and trial, the swirl of coincidence, conflation, and sheer creepiness surrounding the case made it the most lingering and chilling single event of the entire occult period.

Some of the reasons for this were obvious at the time, while others were discovered later on. The savagery of the killings, committed with guns, knives, and ropes. The bloody writing of "POLITICAL PIGGY," "RISE," "PIG," "DEATH TO PIGS," and "HEALTER SKELTER" found at the crime scenes. The word "WAR" carved into Leno LaBianca's body. Sharon Tate's advanced pregnancy at the time of her death from multiple stab wounds. The "hood" draped over the body of Jay Sebring (accidentally, it came out). Tate's husband, Roman Polanski, director of the hit occult movie *Rosemary's Baby*. Sebring's revealed taste for kinky sex and occult role-play. Psychic Peter Hurkos's early (and thoroughly inaccurate) "reading" of the Tate carnage.

Then the web of intersection grew outward. Charles Manson had conceived his deadly plans through his interpretation of lyrics from Beatles songs; the Beatles had met *Rosemary's Baby* star Mia Farrow through their shared study of Transcendental Meditation; ex-Beatle John Lennon was murdered outside his New York home of the Dakota Apartments, where some of *Rosemary's Baby* had been filmed. The association of Family member Bobby Beausoleil (who killed music teacher Gary Hinman) with the San Franciscan filmmaker and occult figure Kenneth Anger; Anger's later collaborations with members of the Rolling Stones and Jimmy Page of Led Zeppelin; Family member Lynette "Squeaky" Fromme's attempted communication with Led Zeppelin in 1975 (noted by Zeppelin publicist Danny Goldberg) before she tried to shoot U.S. president Gerald Ford. The Family's base at California's remote Devil's Canyon. Killer Charles "Tex" Watson's announcement to victim Wojciech Frykowski: "I am the Devil and I'm here to do the Devil's business."[24] Manson's explanation for shaving off his hair after his conviction: "I'm the Devil, and the Devil always has a bald head."[25] Serving a life sentence, Manson revealed he had instructed the killers to write "something witchy" at the Sharon Tate residence.[26] Shortly after the deaths of his wife and the four others at his home, Roman Polanski told investigators, "It could be some type of witchcraft, you know."[27]

Yet neither Charles Manson nor any of his followers were serious students of the occult. Like hundreds of thousands of disaffected young people in the late sixties, they had absorbed a mixture of antiestablishment rhetoric and unorthodox spirituality, as well as a miasma of psychotropic drugs, before conducting their massacres, but none of it added up to a coherent occult sensibility. Manson was poorly educated and barely literate, had been in and out of institutions most of his life, and had experienced the brutal racial divisions and sexual violence of the American penal system over many years. Ultimately, it turned out that Manson's rationale for the murders was to incite an all-consuming race war—Helter Skelter—from which his whites-only group would rise out of the Californian desert to take over the ruined civilization blacks would prove unable to administer. Given his personal history as a criminal and convict, this turned out to be the least unlikely motive.

Into our own time, a tiny clique of followers continues to insist that the innocent Manson was scapegoated for his countercultural views by a vindictive establishment. Though Charles Manson was certainly capable of murder, it remains an uncomfortable fact that none of the seven Tate-LaBianca victims were physically dispatched by him. During his trial some members of the Family had sought to deflect blame from Manson by claiming the Tate killings were an independent effort to exonerate Bobby Beausoleil, already in custody, in order to "prove" Gary Hinman's killer was still at large and leaving bloody messages. Later it was argued that the Tate slaughter (in which Manson was not present) was directed by Tex Watson in an attempt to wrest control of the Family from Manson, while the LaBianca murders represented Manson's reclaiming of his authority (the husband and wife were tied up by Manson before being stabbed to death). It was, indeed, Tex Watson who shot Steven Parent. It was Tex Watson who shot and knifed Jay Sebring and knifed Sharon Tate. It was Tex Watson who bludgeoned and stabbed Wojciech Frykowski. Tex Watson, Susan Atkins, Patricia Krenwinkel, and Leslie Van Houten committed all the murders of August 9 and 10, 1969. The world's most dreaded "mass murderer" did not kill the people for whose deaths he is usually held responsible. Instead of the apocalypse he envisioned, and which he enjoined his young disciples to initiate, was pretty much the same one he had inhabited since his adolescence.

The occult legend of the Charles Manson murders loomed over the seventies and down to the present day, furthered by a 1973 television movie, *Terror on the Beach*, about a family's harassment by a Manson-like youth gang, and then the publication of prosecutor Vincent Bugliosi's 1974 true-crime bestseller *Helter Skelter*, followed by its 1976 TV adaptation, in which actor Steve Railsback's wild-eyed portrayal was so compelling as to become the general public's standard image of Manson himself. The occult rumors regarding cattle mutilations trailed in Manson's bloody wake, as did the new archetypes of the satanic hippie and the cult of drug-crazed, long-haired killers. Some stories of the occult era were entertaining and even fun. The Manson madness was no such story: it was the occult at its most destructive and most frightening.

Cults such as Charles Manson's were society's underlying bogey of the occult era. Very few of them were ever tied to murder or crime—and the Manson Family itself could barely qualify as a cult—but most made the broader public uneasy nevertheless. In a time when the appeal of traditional faiths was diminishing, the growing numbers of believers in new and eccentric creeds stood for the shifting cultural mood that had affected all areas of human activity: the authority of parents, the military, the schools, capitalism, the government, the family, and now even the church were being challenged. Alongside this was the problematic freedom of worship mandated by secular social systems. How did a "cult" differ from a "religion"? Didn't Christianity itself begin with a mere handful of followers, who were often persecuted for their strange tenets and ways of life? For many cults in the occult years, their greatest point of contention was with the tax-exempt status that was guaranteed to all religions by the state. If Roman Catholics, Baptists, Episcopalians, Muslims, and Orthodox Jews were free to observe their own doctrines, why not converts to the Church of God, the Church of Armageddon, the Unification Church, and the Movement of Spiritual Inner Awareness?

Many cults came and went during the late sixties and seventies. Some took off from a Christian tradition, others from Hinduism or Buddhism, still more from some obscure synthesis of philosophy, science, intuition, and the charisma of a single preacher or guru. Their proselytizing succeeded most among young people: dropouts, drug users, the aimless, the restless, and those with time on their hands. Cults offered answers, a sense of community, and a home to those with none of these; many were actual communes living off the land in an attractive escape from the crowds, pollution, and moral chaos of city life. It also mattered that the interest in the supernatural represented by the occult, in magic, unexplainable phenomena, and suppressed versions of history, provided fertile ground for cult recruitment. Predisposed to accept alternative realities, newcomers found the truths espoused by cultists to be as credible as many of the ideas they had already been exposed to on the streets of Greenwich Village and Haight-Ashbury and in their chemically expanded consciousnesses.

Familiar from their solicitation drives at airports in the seventies, the robed, shaven-headed Hare Krishnas, officially known as the International Society for Krishna Consciousness (ISKON), taught a strict form of Hinduism and lived together in separate, ascetic communes, having first appeared in the United States in the mid-sixties. Ex-Beatle George Harrison's hit song "My Sweet Lord" featured a joyous chorus of "Hare Krishna" in 1970. Around the same time, Jesus People USA proclaimed a Christian message of love and personal fulfillment among youth. Such organizations were regarded by most laypeople with bemusement, annoyance, or grudging tolerance. The most shocking cult-related episode of the seventies was the mass suicide of over 900 people (one-third of them under age eighteen) at the Reverend Jim Jones's People's Temple in Jonestown, Guyana, on November 18, 1978. Significantly, though, the People's Temple had begun as a liberal branch of mainstream Protestantism, had gradually become more radical under Jones's ministry, and was only classed as a cult after the Jonestown catastrophe. So where, again, did "religion" leave off and "cult" begin?

This was the question most applied to Scientology. Sometimes called the "science fiction religion," from the pulp stories authored by its founder, Lafayette Ronald Hubbard (1911–1986), the Church of Scientology had been founded in Los Angeles in 1954 and slowly gained adherents in the United States and Europe over the next twenty years. An early associate of Hubbard's, bizarrely, was the rocket engineer Jack Parsons, who himself subscribed to the Thelema code conceived by Aleister Crowley. Scientology was based on Hubbard's voluminous writings and lectures, which combined metaphysics, psychotherapy, and a grand narrative of interplanetary history; Scientology was not so much a style of worship as a method of achieving individual clarity through the realization of one's incorporeal essence, or Thetan. Through the sixties and seventies, as Scientology grew around the world, it had come under the scrutiny of various governments for financial malfeasance and the rigorous control—some called it brain-washing—the organization exercised over its members. It may not have been part of the occult, but it decidedly acquired a reputation as a cult.

Scientology's growth was such that it had even inspired breakaway factions, the most disquieting of which was the Process Church of the Final Judgment. In 1963 husband-and-wife Scientologists Robert Moor and Mary Anne Maclean left Hubbard's assembly to form a therapeutic system called Compulsions Analysis in London, England; they established themselves in the Bahamas, then at a commune in Xtul, Mexico, then back to London, and in 1970 moved to North America and set up chapters in Toronto, Chicago, Boston, and New Orleans. Renamed the Process (Moor now went by the name Robert de Grimston), the church performed social work among the poor and homeless but drew attention for its trinity of gods: Jehovah, Lucifer, and Satan. Overruling all three was Christ, who would finally complete the unification of the competing deities. "The three Gods represent three basic patterns of reality," de Grimston stated in a Process pamphlet. "Within the framework of each pattern there are count-less variations and permutations, widely varying grades of suppression and intensity. Yet each one represents a fundamental problem, a deep-rooted driving force, a pressure of instincts and desires, terrors and revulsions."[28] The Process's incorporation of Christianity's arch-villains into its own theology, its emphasis on sex, de Grimston's own Mephistophelean appear-ance, and the church members' black robes, goat's-head jewelry, and other occult artifacts led many to think they were full-fledged Satanists.

Strange or sinister though they may have seemed, de Grimston, Maclean, and their acolytes really believed in a sort of futuristic Christianity rather than archaic diabolism. In time the Process would be tied to both the Manson Family (two Process members visited Charles Manson in jail after his 1969 incarceration) and the Son of Sam (it was said to be the devil-worshipping cult into which David Berkowitz supposedly fell). The first connection did result in the Process running quotations from Manson in its 1969 publication, *Death*, alongside an essay by English author Malcolm Muggeridge. "Death is peace from the world's madness and paradise is my own self," Manson rambled to his interlocutors. "Death as I lay in my grave of constant vibration, endless now. Prison has always been my tomb."[29] The second accusation is entirely bogus. By 1974 the marriage of de Grimston and Maclean had ended and de Grimston was ousted from the group, which never had more than a thousand members worldwide; the Process evolved into the Foundation Faith of God and later into the Best Friends Animal Society, an animal welfare organization based in Utah. In 1990 de Grimston, by then long apart from the Process, reflected in a letter to a former associate, "The inclusion of Satan as one of our archetype characters made us fair game, besides which it made good copy! But we were harmless, and may even have done some good along the way. A few unhappy misfits found friends in the Process; and some just plain lonely souls found congenial company."[30]

While the Process could thus not be classed as bona fide Satanism, Satanism did exist, both historically and in the occult era. Even the medieval and Renaissance witch hysteria may likely have caught some authentic devil worshippers, in an age when the devil was the most obvious symbol of rebellion available to ordinary folk. In his 1975 study *The Powers of Evil*, scholar Richard Cavendish admitted, "It is likely that among the thousands of innocent victims falsely accused of witchcraft in the past there were a few who worshipped Satan in all reality. Anyone who did not already know how to go about it was amply supplied with information by the witch-trials."[31] Satanism was not Wicca or a fertility religion but reverence paid to Christianity's monstrous antagonist, usually involving obscene parodies of the Catholic liturgy. Among its scant confirmed instances is an orgiastic group that met and committed ritual murder within the court of Louis XIV in seventeenth-century France, and later in the same country there were clandestine ceremonies of defrocked priests and female supplicants whose rites featured inverted crosses, prayers recited backward, communion wafers, and drinks of foul materials, and which climaxed with various forms of heterosexual, homosexual, and bestial copulation. This Satanism (referenced in passing in Blatty's *The Exorcist*) was plainly derived from a very conflicted erotomania that had no sanctioned release in the culture of the time—the practitioners' sexual gratification had somehow become inextricable from highly orchestrated acts of sacrilege. Such were the psychosocial urges most often concluded to have underlain this obscure and illicit faith, until 1966, when the Church of Satan was inaugurated by Anton Szandor LaVey.

LaVey became one of the most famous, if not *the* most famous, personalities of the occult wave of the sixties and seventies, and his visibility to the generations that came of age in those years is comparable to that of the legendary Aleister Crowley. The Church of Satan and its literature were familiar to anyone who looked into the occult. Its trademarked Sigil of Baphomet (an inverted pentagram with a goat's head inside it), though not an original design, became a widely recognized emblem of black magic and Satanism that showed up on clothes, record albums, and personal accessories; even the upper windows of the house at 112 Ocean Avenue in Amityville, New York, looked a little goatish when studied closely. For many people of that period, the mere existence of Anton LaVey and his church was proof that the world really was going to hell.

Like Crowley, LaVey sought publicity through whatever media was available to him. Like Crowley, LaVey cultivated a glaring, intimidating persona and made no apologies for himself or his philosophy. Like Crowley, LaVey boasted of his irreverent values and scandalous lifestyle. Like Crowley, LaVey openly disdained the teachings of mainstream religion. Unlike Crowley, however—and unlike the traditional Satanists—LaVey did not believe in supernatural forces and was not much interested in simply inverting Christian ritual. LaVey's doctrine borrowed from Crowley's "Do what thou wilt" but stripped it of the cosmic poetry and hocus-pocus: the Church of Satan resembled the Objectivism of Ayn Rand more than the Magick of Aleister Crowley and was far removed from the Helter Skelter of Charles Manson. These distinctions were not always apparent to casual observers. For most of his very public but very contrived career, Anton LaVey was as close as America wanted to come to having its own Antichrist.

LaVey's first major press coverage came on January 31, 1967, when local reporters in his home of San Francisco ran the story that he had officiated at the satanic wedding of Judith Case and John Raymond, at LaVey's base, a Victorian house at 6114 California Street. Case, twenty-six, was described as a "New York socialite" (her father was a prominent Republican in the state), while Raymond, thirty-five, was a "radical journalist." "By the power of Satan, I now confer the possession of each other upon you," LaVey pronounced. "Take the woman."[32] The ceremony's altar was formed by the nude body of one Lois Murgenstrumm. In May of the same year LaVey was seen providing a satanic baptism for his three-year-old daughter, Zeena, and in December a satanic funeral was held for U.S. naval officer Edward Olsen. Anton LaVey appeared on *The Tonight Show* on October 3, 1967, with the San Franciscan rock group Jefferson Airplane as musical guests.

The Year One of Anno Satanas, LaVey declared as his notoriety grew, had been ushered in with the witch festival Walpurgisnacht (April 30) of 1966—just after the publication of *Time* magazine's "Is God Dead?" issue.

Soon he was attracting titillated reporters and figures from show business. Buxom Hollywood star Jayne Mansfield was photographed with LaVey as a publicity stunt and was killed in a car accident shortly thereafter. LaVey said he had torn a photograph of Mansfield, separating her imaged head from her body, some time before she was decapitated in the crash. Las Vegas showman and Frank Sinatra pal Sammy Davis Jr. was more deeply involved. Davis had already dabbled in the occult, through sex parties in which Jay Sebring sometimes participated: "I'd read enough about it to know that [the partiers] weren't Satanists, they were bullshit artists and they'd found an exotic way they could ball each other and have an orgy," he remembered in his autobiography, *Why Me?* "It was all fun and games and dungeons and dragons and debauchery and as long as the chick was happy and wasn't really going to get anything sharper than a dildo stuck into her, I wasn't going to walk away from it."[33]

Anton LaVey, though, was no dabbler, as Davis found when they met in 1968. LaVey told him, "Don't get involved with this unless you really want to commit yourself to something."[34] So Sammy Davis painted one of his fingernails red as a satanic symbol and displayed it in public appearances. "Evil fascinated me," he looked back. "I was ready to accept the wildness, the rolling in the gutter, and having to get up in the morning and wash myself clean." His infatuation was brief, however. "One morning after a 'coven' that wasn't quite fun and games, without anyone telling me to, I got some nail polish remover and I took off the red fingernail."[35]

LaVey courted yet more attention with the release in 1968 of a long-playing record of his performances on organ, *The Satanic Mass.* A nudie exploitation film of one of his satanic ceremonies, *Satanis: The Devil's Mass,* was produced the next year. LaVey was frequently photographed wearing a black cape and horns; his shaved scalp and goatee already made him look devilish enough. In 1969 Avon Books contracted him to write *The Satanic Bible,* its title alone perhaps the ultimate affront to middle-American moral codes. By then the leader of the Church of Satan was being dubbed "the Black Pope." *The Satanic Bible,* with its black cover and Baphomet logo, sold hundreds of thousands of paperback copies (not counting the many that were nervously flipped through in the stores or shoplifted out of them) and was followed by *The Compleat Witch* in 1971 and *The Satanic Rituals* in 1972. On August 24, 1971, he posed with a human skull for the cover of the popular pictorial magazine *Look.* LaVey published the church's newsletter,

The Cloven Hoof, and asserted that the Church of Satan had some 10,000 active followers in grottoes around the world.

What message, exactly, was LaVey preaching? Essentially, his Satanism advocated what he called "the worship of life" rather than the worship of the devil. He rejected the millennia of guilt and duty impressed by Judeo-Christian dogma in favor of "the fullest gratification of the ego on this plane of existence." Like its better-known competitor, *The Satanic Bible* began with several basic commandments, for example: "Satan represents indulgence instead of abstinence!" "Satan represents responsibility to the responsible, instead of concern for psychic vampires!" "Satan represents man as just another animal, sometimes better, more often worse than those that walk on all fours, who because of his 'divine spiritual and intellectual development' has become the most vicious animal of all!"[36] Within its pages—divided into "the Book of Satan," "the Book of Lucifer," "the Book of Belial," and "the Book of Leviathan"—LaVey further upended Christian exhortations. "Blessed are the strong, for they shall possess the earth," he decreed. "Hate your enemies with a whole heart, and if a man smite you on one cheek, SMASH him on the other!"[37] God may have been already dead, but LaVey wanted to kick at His corpse.

Much of this was adapted from the writings of Aleister Crowley, Ayn Rand's novel *Atlas Shrugged*, and a seldom-read 1896 treatise of social Darwinism by the pseudonymous Ragnar Redbeard, *Might Is Right* (likely candidates for the latter's authorship were New Zealander Arthur Desmond or Chicago businessman Jacob Loeb). In *The Satanic Rituals*, LaVey even invoked H. P. Lovecraft's amoral Cthulhu gods: "His tales constantly remind the reader that humanity is but a short step from the most depraved and vicious forms of bestiality . . . . This theme of a constant interrelationship between the constructive and destructive facets of the human personality is the keystone of the doctrines of Satanism."[38] LaVey explained that he had formed his satanic principles as a photographer for the San Francisco police in the fifties, where his daily and nightly work at the scenes of suicides, senseless crimes, and tragic accidents revealed to him the absence of a just deity or divine intervention. By the early sixties he had acquired an expanding audience among San Francisco's many circles of eccentrics and people interested in the occult (including filmmaker Kenneth Anger), who attended his lectures on werewolves, vampires, and the paranormal. Eventually, someone told him that by legally incorporating his teachings and listeners into a formal church, it would be chartered under the state of California and therefore free from tax laws.

It was this kind of opportunism that characterized LaVey in his role as magus of the Church of Satan. The autobiography he recited for eager journalists, it emerged over many years, was riddled with deceptions, and his administration of the church was driven by naked greed at least as much as inventive philosophy. Into the seventies LaVey sold priesthoods in the church, which in 1975 prompted the less cynical among his flock to renounce him and form their own Temple of Set, led by Michael Aquino; other "reformers" left the Church of Satan for the ephemeral religions of the Church of the Satanic Brotherhood and the Ordo Templi Satanis. According to purists, LaVey was not properly faithful to the real Satan but was only using satanic gimmickry to promote his own secular agenda.

Anton Szandor LaVey had, in fact, been born Howard Stanton Levey in Chicago in 1930. He was descended from Ukrainians, not the Transylvanians he claimed. He said he had run away to join the circus as a young person and worked as an animal tamer and as an organist at burlesque shows, where he'd had an affair with a young Marilyn Monroe; LaVey kept exotic animals and was certainly a capable keyboardist, but there the truth ended. He had never been a police photographer; he did not play oboe in the (nonexistent) San Francisco Ballet Orchestra; the Church of Satan did not begin on April 30, 1966, but later that year; he had never appeared as Satan in *Rosemary's Baby*; Jayne Mansfield had not been decapitated in her auto fatality; the Church of Satan's international membership was probably never more than a few hundred, most of whom signed up for the occult excitement and then quickly lost interest.

In his defense, LaVey was strict in his opposition to violence and any form of ritual killing, notably animal sacrifice, and warned members that any criminal conviction warranted expulsion from church ranks. The Church of Satan was, at a fundamental level, about hedonism and self-realization, and in that sense his fabrications were justifiable efforts to mythologize himself and his worldview—efforts that did pay off during the prime phase of his celebrity. LaVey took pains to dissociate himself with allegedly "satanic" murderers like the Charles Manson Family: "Kooks and creeps out of their minds on drugs," he called them.[39] Oddly, while building his church and highlighting its fixture of nude female altars, he had even enlisted future Manson killer Susan Atkins, then employed as a San Francisco stripper, in some of his public observances. "His gaze was as intense as any I'd ever seen, even though his mouth was smiling," Atkins reminisced of LaVey in her prison memoir, *Child of Satan, Child of God*, although she complained to her boss, "I don't go for this Satan stuff."[40] After its early sensationalism faded away and dissident Satanists had left the fold, the Church of Satan receded further into the where-are-they-now files, even as satanic movies, books, and music became some of the most popular releases of the era. When LaVey died on October 29, 1997, in San Francisco's St. Mary's Hospital, the Church of Satan had been mostly forgotten, and the Black Pope himself had still resided in his now-dilapidated house on California Street, eking out a meager living from continued sales of *The Satanic Bible* and playing hoary pop tunes like "Telstar" and "Yes, We Have No Bananas" on his instruments. Ultimately, Anton LaVey was more a showman than a shaman, whose true allegiance to Mammon was overshadowed by his professed hostility to God.

Yet this was the paradox of the substitute faiths that arose in the occult age of the sixties and seventies. Zen Buddhism, Transcendental Meditation, astrology, Wicca, Scientology, the Process, the Church of Satan—all of them had promised a better life for believers, if only they went along with the program and remained mindful of its core values. But what religion didn't offer the same bargain? Just as it is possible to be a perfectly good and kind human being without belief in a scriptural God, surely it was just as possible to be selfish and satisfied without Anton LaVey's Satan, or to be serene and wise without Buddha, or to experience an altered consciousness without Carlos Castaneda's Don Juan, or to anticipate the future without the zodiac or the Tarot, or to love nature without the Mother Goddess. What made the occult so contentious were its radical portrayals of a mystical beyond or an intangible human essence; the notions that there *was* a mystical beyond or an intangible human essence had already long enjoyed a broad acceptance among billions of people. And in a grand irony of historic dimensions, it was from some of those who had confidently accepted the beyond and the intangible that the greatest and most forceful response to the occult would come.

7

World of Wonders

A general attraction to the supernatural, extending beyond narrowly defined funda-
mentalism, lies at the heart of the profound divide not only between religious America
and secular Europe but also between devout religious believers and secularists within
the United States.
—Susan Jacoby, *The Age of American Unreason*

The crop of new churches, cults, and crackpots that had sprung up
during the occult era also generated a corollary appreciation among
the young for that original sandal-wearing, long-haired flower child who
went around making everyone uptight with his constant raps on peace
and love—Nazareth's favorite son, Jesus Christ. Just when millions of high
school and college kids were looking into black magic and the devil, a
smaller subset was off on an opposite trip. Some of what the "Jesus Freaks"
explored was little different from the various vehicles on which thousands
of hippies and dropouts had already embarked to take their personal
cosmic journeys, whether through LSD, Transcendental Meditation, the
Process Church of the Final Judgment, or Krishna Consciousness. But
others came out of the traditional stream of Protestant evangelicalism and
hewed more closely to old-fashioned biblical orthodoxies. In the late sixties
one such ministry appeared in a very hotbed of the counterculture, on the
Los Angeles campus of the University of California. It was called the Jesus
Christ Light and Power Company, and it was led by Hal Lindsey.

Lindsey, then forty-one, was a Houston-born missionary who had experienced his own religious conversion as a young adult, around 1955, and
entered the Dallas Theological Seminary. He had already served with the
U.S. Coast Guard and had lived, by his subsequent admission, the wanton
exploits of a sailor and riverboat captain, but after obtaining his master's

degree in theology in 1962, he began to work for the Campus Crusade for Christ, spreading the Gospels to audiences of college and university students around the United States. He was on his second marriage and had started a family. When he left the Campus Crusade to form his own Jesus Christ Light and Power Company, he had been witness to the occult tide that was sweeping over popular imagination, and wanted to address prospective converts in an urgent idiom that would suit their proven receptiveness to heavy concepts and the imminence of ecstasy. It had to be, he knew, "a direct account of the most thrilling, optimistic view of what the future could hold for any individual."[1] With a colleague, Carole C. Carlson, Lindsey began to write a book. "As I wrote," he explained later, "I'd imagine that I was sitting across the table from a young person—a cynical, irreligious person—and I'd try to convince him that the Bible prophecies were true. If you can make a young person understand, then the others will understand too."[2] The resultant work was published in 1970 by the specialist Christian publisher Zondervan Press; it was titled *The Late Great Planet Earth.*

"All around the world today the increase in the mystic, occult, and even devil-worship is so pronounced that people are beginning to question what it's about," Lindsey and Carlson asserted, no doubt alarmed by the spate of press received by Anton LaVey and his Church of Satan. "There are churches in some of the major cities of America which actually incorporate into their 'religious ceremonies' the worship of the devil . . . . We believe that we are seeing, with all the other signs, the revival of Mystery, Babylon—not just in astrology, but also in spiritism, a return to the supernatural, and in drugs."[3] *The Late Great Planet Earth* was based on Lindsey's interpretations of scriptural forecasts from the Old and New Testaments, a branch of evangelical theology known as Dispensationalism; the book connected the social and geopolitical turmoil of 1970 with biblical descriptions of the events or trends that would signify the coming end of the world. The occult craze was one indicator, but the growth of a European Common Market, the besieged state of Israel, and the superpower standoff between the United States and the Soviet Union were others. *Planet Earth* became the best-selling American nonfiction book of the decade. Over ten million copies were retailed, and Lindsey's visions of the impending Apocalypse were his subject in many subsequent efforts, all of them hugely successful: *Satan Is Alive and Well on Planet Earth* (1972), *There's a New World Coming* (1973), *When Is Jesus Coming Again?* (1974), *The Terminal Generation*

(1976), and *The 1980s: Countdown to Armageddon* (1980). This was a level of popularity rarely seen in the mainstream publishing industry and virtually unknown among religious houses. "If I had been writing fifteen years earlier, I wouldn't have had an audience," Lindsey said to *Publishers Weekly* magazine in 1977. "But a tremendous number of people were beginning to worry about the future, and they were looking everywhere for answers. The turn to the occult, astrology, eastern religion, and other movements reflected the fear of what was going to happen in the future. And I'm just part of that phenomenon."[4]

Lindsey had found an angle for communicating his beliefs that neatly corresponded with the public's interest in the sensational and the fantastic. Instead of just repeating the well-worn Christian lessons of charity and forgiveness, he imparted a here-and-now suspense to biblical texts, citing the occult fancies of the contemporary era as spiritually reckless contraventions of ancient warnings. In *Satan Is Alive and Well on Planet Earth*, Lindsey and Carlson cautioned, "God condemns the practice of astrology, which began in ancient Babylon," adding with unintentional irony, "It was a pseudo-science as well, which has been proven absurd in the light of modern science."[5] In the same book the authors stated, "Any complicity with demon activity, whether it be ouija boards, tarot cards, horoscopes, crystal balls, palm readings, or fortune telling, makes one vulnerable to demon influences. I have encountered cases where heavy demon influence began this way."[6] In a 1977 profile of Lindsey in the periodical *People*, his teenage daughter Jenny reported that she and her twin sister nearly left a friend's slumber party when some girls wanted to hold a séance. "We finally convinced the others that the Devil is real and not to be meddled with," she was quoted.[7] In the years after *Rosemary's Baby*, *The Exorcist*, and *The Omen*, the alarms of Hal Lindsey and his offspring carried weight.

And they reached beyond the Christian faithful. *The Late Great Planet Earth* was turned into a documentary film in 1977, with narration by Orson Welles and featuring commentary by Lindsey himself. With dramatized portrayals of scenes from the Book of Revelation juxtaposed with authentic news footage of modern world leaders and current events, *The Late Great Planet Earth* was a slick production that drew a profitable mainstream audience. Around the same time other biblical topics received the same treatment, with *In Search of Noah's Ark* (1976) and *In Search of Historic Jesus* (1979), both produced by Sunn Classic Pictures, which had also put out ostensibly factual films on the paranormal, such as *The Mysterious*

Monsters, *The Outer Space Connection*, and *The Bermuda Triangle*. Clearly, even old-time religion could have box-office potential when it was framed as another avenue of the occult—unusual, ominous, and even a bit scary.

By the late seventies, of course, old-time religion was on the verge of a major comeback. In 1979 the American Moral Majority lobby group was formed, and the following year the conservative Republican Ronald Reagan was elected president of the United States. Led by Jerry Falwell, a telegenic pastor from Lynchburg, Virginia, the Moral Majority was a response to the perceived permissiveness and moral decay of American society over the previous years, the most provocative demonstrations of which had been the decriminalization of abortion, the availability of explicit pornography, the teaching of evolution in public schools, and the new openness of homosexuality. These were the obvious targets of the conservative mobilization, but the mass marketing of the occult was among the many other bogeys that had spurred the activism of Hal Lindsey, Jerry Falwell, and their followers, which in turn had played a significant role in propelling Reagan to the White House. Ouija boards, Black Sabbath, and the Church of Satan had drawn many converts since the mid-sixties, but they had built up enemies as well. Now the enemies were speaking out. "God is going to judge America," assured Assemblies of God evangelist David Wilkerson in 1985, "for its violence, its crimes, its backslidings, its murdering of millions of babies . . . its cheatings, its robbings, its dirty movies, and its occult practices."[8] In 1980 Falwell's Moral Majority could claim a mailing list of 2.5 million people, and over one million Americans watched his weekly *Old Time Gospel Hour* TV program.

The paradox here was that the march of the Christian soldiers across the political landscape of the United States, to the extent that it represented a reaction to the excesses of the liberal counterculture, had the net effect of replacing one quirky religiosity with another. That replacement has held into our own century. Up until 1980 the occult and its aficionados had been generally identified with progressives and the left: conservative writer David Frum has called the seventies "the golden age of cranks,"[9] with the decade's manias for astrology, the Bermuda Triangle, and *Chariots of the Gods?*, while in their 2004 book *The Rebel Sell*, Canadian commentators Joseph Heath and Andrew Potter noted, "*Morning of the Magicians*, ufology, ancient space god theory, Druidic rituals, the search for Atlantis, theosophy, Scientology, Rosicrucianism—there seemed to be no limit to the credulity of the countercultural rebels."[10] Yet as the pendulum began to swing the other way, the strangely irrational beliefs of the occult buffs were confronted not with a sober materialism but with beliefs that were, in their own manner, just as irrational and often just as strange. Both the occult and the surging Christian fundamentalism were based on a millennial outlook—the idea that the world was on the brink of some great transformation that would finally come about when everyone saw the light, or the darkness, as the case might have been—and both the occult and Christian fundamentalism energetically pursued that millennial breakthrough. The difference was that Christian fundamentalists were also gaining access to public office and the corridors of power.

As early as 1968 Richard Nixon had courted the well-known Reverend Billy Graham while campaigning for election, but after Ronald Reagan's ascendancy, the ties binding the Moral Majority and its ilk to the U.S. conservative movement were particularly apparent. In 1980 Reagan spoke to Pentecostal minister Jim Bakker on the latter's PTL (Praise the Lord) television network, saying, "We may be the generation that sees Armageddon."[11] In a 1984 debate with the Democratic candidate for presidency, Walter Mondale, Reagan qualified, "No one knows whether those prophecies [from the Book of Revelation] mean that Armageddon is a thousand years away or the day after tomorrow."[12] It was later revealed that Reagan, as commander-in-chief, was wont to digress on the subject of interplanetary invasion when discussing national security with General Colin Powell of the Joint Chiefs of Staff. "Here come the little green men again," Powell would nudge his aides.[13] In 1983 Reagan described America's Cold War adversary, the Soviet Union, as "the evil empire." Reagan's wife, Nancy, had frequently consulted astrologer Joan Quigley for advice, and her husband's travel schedules were sometimes altered according to the favorability of the stars.

After Ronald Reagan left office in 1989, American religion and politics continued to mix, with undertones that continued to evoke the occult. In 1992 the Reverend Pat Robertson, another TV preacher whose expansive audience neared Jerry Falwell's, ran in the Republican presidential primary and denounced feminism as "a socialist, anti-family political movement that encourages women to leave their husbands, kill their children, practice witchcraft, destroy capitalism and become lesbians."[14] After the mass shooting at Columbine High School in Littleton, Colorado, in 1999, another would-be Republican president, Alan Keyes, declared, "Our problem is that a spirit of death is stalking the land . . . . It doesn't come from the barrel of a gun; it comes from the deep pit of hell that we are allowing to replace what ought to be the reverence for God and truth in the hearts of this society."[15] A third GOP presidential primary candidate, Rick Santorum, was revealed in 2012 to have addressed the students of Florida's Ave Maria University in 2008: "This is a spiritual war. And the Father of Lies has his sights on what you would think the Father of Lies, Satan, would have his sights on: a good, decent, powerful, influential country—the United States of America."[16]

While Christian conservatives gained ground by using a vocabulary of Satan and Armageddon, the occult itself evolved. After 1980 the genre spread even further and more broadly throughout pop culture, in ways that could sometimes hardly be traced back to antecedents of the sixties and seventies. In some mediums the occult's shock-value quotient was jacked up to catch the attention of a market already jaded by Kiss or *The Amityville Horror*, whereas in other areas the occult was rendered almost benign, with its most devilish themes downplayed or dispensed with altogether. Depending on where it was found, the occult could be viewed as anything from a positive force for spiritual change to a sweeping criminal conspiracy that presented an immediate menace to public safety.

Rock music became more satanic than ever, both by design and by accident. After a drug-sodden dismissal from the original Black Sabbath in 1979, Ozzy Osbourne started a solo career that heavily promoted the singer's persona as a rock 'n' roll Prince of Darkness, beginning with the 1980 release of his *Blizzard of Ozz* album, boasting the gothic threnodies of "Crazy Train," "Suicide Solution," and the cathedral doom of his classic ode to the Great Beast, "Mr. Crowley." For many years Osbourne added to his evil reputation with a variety of publicity coups, few of them deliberate, including the 1981 death by plane crash of his young guitarist Randy Rhoads, Osbourne's biting the heads off a live dove and bat, his drunken urination on the revered Alamo shrine in San Antonio, Texas, in 1982, and his equally stupefied attempted murder of his wife in 1989. In recent years Ozzy has been seen as a lovably addled husband and father of reality television.

AC/DC's vocalist Bon Scott died from alcoholic misadventure in 1980, but the band paid him tribute with its most successful work (and one of the best-selling records of the rock era), 1980's *Back in Black*, a kind of funereal party album that included the monolithic title song, plus the no-apologies "Have a Drink on Me" and the demonic tolling of "Hells Bells." Led Zeppelin stayed disbanded after the death of drummer John

Bonham (also alcohol related) in 1980, but the band's "Stairway to Heaven" was subject to scrutiny for its alleged encryption with backward messages in praise of Satan. In 1982 Californian legislators regarded the assertions in a Committee on Consumer Protection and Toxic Materials; the same year a Louisiana pastor named Jacob Aranza published a pamphlet titled *Backward Masking Unmasked: Backward Satanic Messages of Rock and Roll Exposed*. "The potential for manipulation of people completely unaware of what is going on here is truly staggering," Assemblyman Phillip Wyman, a California Republican, was quoted.[17] Led Zeppelin's record company denied the backward masking claims, as did the group's surviving members, more angrily: "I mean, who on earth would have ever thought of doing that in the first place?" singer and lyricist Robert Plant said in *Rolling Stone* magazine in 1990. "Especially with 'Stairway.' I mean, we were so proud of that thing, and its intentions are so positive, that the last thing one would do would be . . . I find it foul, the whole idea, you know? But . . . it's very American. Nowhere else in the world has anybody ever considered it or been concerned or bothered at all about that."[18] In the United States, lawsuits related to rock lyrics and backward masking were launched in 1985 against Ozzy Osbourne for his song "Suicide Solution" and in 1990 against Judas Priest, for its album *Stained Class*; both cases were dismissed.

A second and third generation of performers influenced by Led Zeppelin, Blue Öyster Cult, Alice Cooper, and Black Sabbath did big business for decades after 1980 and found increasingly elaborate means to outrage parents and other authorities—or parents and authorities found the means for them. Occult imagery and catchphrases were prominent on the album covers and in the music of major acts Mötley Crüe (*Shout at the Devil*, 1983), Metallica ("The Call of Ktulu," 1984), Judas Priest ("Devil's Child," 1982), and Iron Maiden (*The Number of the Beast*, 1982), while the groups Slayer, Candlemass, Celtic Frost, Megadeth, Mercyful Fate, W.A.S.P., Exodus, and Venom were categorized in the niches of "death metal" or "black metal." Stylistically, such bands were pretty derivative, with their central gimmick of taking the dissonance, volume, tempi, or mysticism of earlier artists a few unholy steps further: Mercyful Fate and Celtic Frost made Black Sabbath sound like the Beatles, and whereas you had to dig a little to uncover the occult implications of Led Zeppelin or Blue Öyster Cult, W.A.S.P., Venom, and Slayer were hitting you over the head with pentagrams.

In 1985 a group of Washington political spouses created the Parents'
Music Resource Center (PMRC), which advocated the placement of
warning labels on albums said to carry pornographic, violent, or satanic
songs. The PMRC's Tipper Gore, wife of Senator Albert Gore, authored
the book *Raising PG Kids in an X-Rated Society* in 1987 and referenced
the music professor Joe Stuessy's *Heavy Metal User's Manual*, which had
argued, "Most of the successful heavy metal projects one or more of the
following basic themes: extreme rebellion, extreme violence, substance
abuse, sexual promiscuity/perversion . . . Satanism."[19]

Such scares did little to hurt the commercial appeal of the occult in rock
music; if anything they probably helped. The next field of heavy metal artists
came with names like Pantera (*Vulgar Display of Power*, 1992), Cradle of
Filth (*The Principle of Evil Made Flesh*, 1994), Godsmack (*Faceless*, 2003),
and Slipknot (*All Hope Is Gone*, 2008). Trent Reznor, formerly of the industrial rock band Nine Inch Nails, made headlines with his 1994 conversion of the Sharon Tate home at 10050 Cielo Drive in Los Angeles into a
private recording studio. A handful of extreme Norwegian metal groups
were charged with the arson of churches. The most notorious rocker of
this era was Marilyn Manson, whose corrosive, obscenity-laced albums
Smells Like Children (1995) and *Antichrist Superstar* (1998) stoked parental
anxieties and whose touring spectacles set new standards for theatrical
offensiveness: ripping up Bibles onstage were some of Manson's milder
stunts, and fans bought official Marilyn Manson T-shirts imprinted with
slogans like "Bigger Than Satan" and "Everyone Will Suffer Now." Manson,
true name Brian Warner, was serving up shock rock for kids to whom the
androgyny of David Bowie and the grotesqueries of Alice Cooper were
positively quaint. Yet soon enough even his provocations lost their impact.
As garish or as degenerate as figures like Marilyn Manson, Trent Reznor,
and Slipknot strained to appear, the occult had become such a staple motif
of rock 'n' roll that there were few real fears left for them to raise among the
wider public. As the music industry slowly dissolved with the advent of the
Internet, death metal and satanic anthems turned into just another couple
of micro-tastes to rip and burn.

Publishing had completely absorbed the occult—or was it the other way
around? The stratospheric careers of Stephen King and Anne Rice made
horror fiction one of the most reliably lucrative fields in the industry from
the late seventies onward. King added to his tally of hit volumes with *Pet
Sematary* (1983), *It* (1986), and *The Tommyknockers* (1987), while Rice's

undead oeuvre expanded to *The Vampire Lestat* (1985) and *The Queen of the Damned* (1988). Authors V. C. Andrews (*Flowers in the Attic*, 1979; *Petals on the Wind*, 1980; *If There Be Thorns*, 1981), John Saul (*The God Project*, 1982; *Hellfire*, 1986; *Creature*, 1989), Clive Barker (*The Damnation Game*, 1985; *The Hellbound Heart*, 1986; *Weaveworld*, 1987), and James Herbert (*The Lair*, 1979; *The Dark*, 1980; *Shrine*, 1983) won their own loyal readerships by churning out novels of paranormal mystery, supernatural evil, and neo-gothic chills.

Nonfiction titles of the unknown and the unknowable scaled the best-seller lists too, except these were classified under a new label. After 1980, bookstores' occult stocks began to be filed on shelves headed "New Age," and specialty occult shops became, in turn, New Age centers. New Age became the overarching term for subjects formerly considered occult, but the darkest materials of the earlier category had been jettisoned for more positive writings that were, in essence, a sort of spiritual self-help. There was New Age music to complement New Age books, comprising peacefully abstract instrumentals not much different from elevator Muzak. Astrology, Wicca, crystals, yoga, and meditation were highlighted in the New Age industry, along with reincarnation, channeling, astral projection, and angels; Aleister Crowley and the Bermuda Triangle were now tucked away in the corners.

The most famous New Ager was the actress and dancer Shirley MacLaine, whose autobiographical books *Out on a Limb* (1983), *Dancing in the Light* (1985), and *Going Within: A Guide for Inner Transformation* (1989) recounted her worldwide adventures in psychic self-discovery. MacLaine was, if nothing else, candid in acknowledging how flaky many of her stories seemed to be (standing on a beach and exulting "I am God!" for instance), but millions of readers admired her fearless voyages across the cosmos in search of her truest being and sought to emulate her with voyages of their own. In *Out on a Limb*, MacLaine began, "This book is about a quest for my self—a quest which took me on a long journey that was gradually revealing and at all times simply amazing. I tried to keep an open mind as I went because I found myself gently but firmly exposed to dimensions of time and space that heretofore, for me, belonged in science fiction or what I would describe as the occult. But it happened to me."[20]

Ironically, MacLaine had been William Peter Blatty's model for the independent-minded actress and mother Chris MacNeil in *The Exorcist*. When the inspiration came to light, MacLaine's daughter, Sachi, was teased by schoolmates for having been a victim of demonic possession, and MacLaine even claimed (over Blatty's strong denial) that a blurred photo of Sachi was used for *The Exorcist*'s cover. To film critic Mark Kermode, in 1997 Shirley MacLaine clarified that Chris MacNeil "was Bill's idea of what he thought I was . . . I am *not* that. I agree with Gandhi, strangely enough, that the only devils we really have are the ones rattling around in our own hearts. I don't believe the Devil is out there. I think the potential for doing mean and evil things is what's in here."[21] Sachi Parker herself later wrote, "Maybe Blatty did use me as a reference when he was sketching the basic outlines of the character. But that was as far as it went. I don't recall ever walking like a crab or spitting vomit from my revolving head, or doing anything untoward with a crucifix."[22]

A subsequent New Age blockbuster was James Redfield's 1993 book *The Celestine Prophecy*, which combined the shamanistic anthropology of Carlos Castaneda with Shirley MacLaine's guides to inner transforma-tion. In a G-rated incarnation, the occult was once again a huge player in publishing with the 1997 release of J. K. Rowling's *Harry Potter and the Philosopher's Stone*, the first of a series that eventually became the most successful fiction franchise of all time. Clearly reflecting the fantastic land-scapes and magical hierarchies of J. R. R. Tolkien's Middle Earth, Rowling's rich narratives were written for boys and girls but struck a chord with adults as well, not always supportively. An evangelical Christian named Billy James Hargis spoke for many in his cohort when he complained in 2001, "The biblical god simply doesn't fit into [Harry Potter's] world of wizards, witches, and other gods."[23] By this time the occult, the New Age, and the Apocalypse were all challenging one another for commercial preeminence within the book business, between Stephanie Meyer's *Twilight* series, begun in 2005 (teenage vampires and werewolves), and Tim LaHaye's *Left Behind* titles, which first came out in 1995 (biblical rapture and end times). Even Ira Levin, whose *Rosemary's Baby* had initiated the modern boom in occult books, was reduced to penning a forgettable sequel, *Son of Rosemary*, in 1997. In 2002, just five years before his death, Levin seemed to regret what his imaginary mother and child had wrought upon the culture. "I feel guilty that 'Rosemary's Baby' led to 'The Exorcist,' [and] 'The Omen,'" he said in a newspaper interview. "A whole generation has been exposed, has more belief in Satan. I don't believe in Satan. And I feel that the strong funda-mentalism we have would not be as strong if there hadn't been so many of these books . . . . Of course, I didn't send back any of the royalty checks."[24]

Cinema and television have continued to thrive on horror and the occult. The successes of the so-called slasher films *Halloween* (1978), *Friday the 13th* (1980), and *Nightmare on Elm Street* (1984) led to a long train of sequels and rip-offs of each. These depicted homicidal maniacs rather than devil-worshipping cultists and were marked by an increasing emphasis on explicit violence and bloody special effects more than any theological insights or artistic merit, but they no doubt inherited the interests of theatergoers by then well prepared for their graphic shocks. A severely expurgated cut of *The Exorcist* was finally aired on CBS TV in 1980—before the revolution in home video that made the original movie accessible to every household—and came prefaced with the network affiliate's solemn warnings from clergymen and other experts warning of its undimmed power to offend.

In 1993 Fox Television premiered *The X-Files*, a weekly drama in which two FBI personnel investigated a different occult or paranormal case every episode: vampires, monsters, aliens, cults, werewolves, and a compendium of other mysteries. *The X-Files* was like an updated version of *The Night Stalker*, with the attractive young agents Mulder and Scully in place of grizzled reporter Carl Holchak, only with an ongoing subplot of government conspiracy: the show's taglines were "The Truth Is Out There" and "Trust No One." The program was enormously popular for almost ten years and spawned several movie versions. A later favorite was the occult film *The Blair Witch Project* (1999), about young hikers exploring a backwoods legend of witchcraft and ritual murder, shot and marketed as a pseudo-documentary in the manner of the old *In Search Of . . .* reenactments. This technique, more and more plausible in an age when personal video devices are ubiquitous, has been appropriated for the box-office bonanzas of *Paranormal Activity* (2007) and its numerous sequels. Aside from its own direct descendants, *The Exorcist* has stood as the inspiration for an entire class of possession flicks, among them *Lost Souls* (2000), *The Exorcism of Emily Rose* (2005), based on the Anneliese Michel case of 1976, *The Last Exorcism* (2010), and *The Devil Inside* (2012).

Today the occult has its own television networks, with various cable channels including Syfy and Space airing original and classic horror and science fiction movies and TV shows around the clock. Other cable series offer extended story lines of haunted houses (*American Horror Story*), civilizations overrun by zombies (*The Walking Dead*), or vampires (*True Blood*). What stands out in all this programming are the staggering production values invested into realistically presenting inherently unrealistic, not to say absurd, premises. The housebound believability so carefully constructed by Roman Polanski and William Friedkin in *Rosemary's Baby* and *The Exorcist* has been hijacked in service of preposterous scenarios that rely on digital imagery, advanced makeup and prosthetic effects, and soap-operatic narrative complexity to keep viewers tuning in, which they do in impressive numbers. Monsters and devils are now so acceptable to mainstream audiences that their existence alone can no longer sustain a plot; there must be extra elements of postmodern irony or gruesome violence to hold down the channel surfers. The occult was something that was once best appreciated at midnight on Walpurgisnacht or Halloween. Thanks to the five-hundred-channel universe, it is today with us 24/7, 365.

And it has started earlier. Children's exposure to the occult has been the subject of concern since adolescent suicides had been traced to the Dungeons & Dragons game in the late seventies, which led to the formation of the parents' group BADD (Bothered About Dungeons and Dragons) in 1983. Around the same time, arcade and home video games increasingly diverted young people's spending money away from comic books but continued to employ macabre graphics and premises, as in the quarter-gobbling Wizard of Wor and the landmark 1996 PlayStation franchise *Resident Evil*, which led to several follow-up games, as well as action figures and feature films. Kids who still enjoyed reading were caught up in R. L. Stine's best-selling *Goosebumps*, a line of spooky-funny paperbacks produced from 1992 to 1997, with titles like *Phantom of the Auditorium*, *The Horror at Camp Jellyjam*, and *It Came from Beneath the Sink*. The *Goosebumps* collection has sold over three hundred million copies and has also been adapted for movies, TV, and video games. Nowadays children can play with Magic: The Gathering decks of cards (the games parallel the D&D universe of wizards, spells, and castles) and with dolls from the Monster High set (glamorous teen girls styled as Draculaura, Frankie Stein, and Clawdeen Wolf); or they can plow through the scarifying adventures of the Poison Apple and Beast Quest book series. Of course it is hard to say whether any of these are promulgating dangerously occult notions, yet there *is* something significant in their current popularity, and in the familiar grade school sight of little kids wearing black hats, T-shirts, and backpacks decorated with cute monsters and skulls—small people who are at the beginning of their lives, yet who are already immersed in stories and symbols that celebrate its end.

The unexplained and the paranormal have also kept up to date. As the widespread fascination with demonic possession dwindled down after 1980, it was replaced with the comparably eerie subject of alien abduction. Whitley Strieber's book *Communion* (1987) was pitched as a true-life account of his actual encounter with extraterrestrials that came into his bedroom on the night of December 26, 1985, and took him away to their spacecraft, where they performed bizarre medical experiments on him. Strieber could only recall this much later, under hypnosis, but his tale posited that these therapeutic revelations were the best confirmation that his abduction had been genuine—surely an experience so traumatic would be buried by the conscious mind, only to be extracted through intensive psychoanalysis. Many readers agreed: *Communion* sold 10 million copies, and numerous other descriptions of intimate alien contact, supposedly authentic, appeared in bookstores. Many others, though, felt Strieber, who was already an established writer of horror and science fiction, was merely capitalizing on the fashion for dream therapy by putting a veneer of New Age psychobabble on a yarn for which he had absolutely no physical corroboration. "This book is part of a deplorable trend in publishing," novelist and physicist Gregory Benford was quoted in a *Publishers Weekly* article on the appeal of *Communion*. "It is catering to the flagrant irrationalities of the public with tarted-up Potemkin-Village science. The reemergence of the Shirley MacLaine . . . subgenre is a chastening reminder that we are not, in fact, a deeply rational society in spite of our technology. I regard these people as unwittingly in the same camp as the Fundamentalists."[25]

Erich von Däniken's ancient astronaut theory has been periodically resuscitated or revised by other writers, who take different historical facts and spin them into wildly conjectural alternatives to the standard chronologies of humankind. New takes on the Bible and the life of Jesus were advanced by Michael Baigent and Richard Leigh in *Holy Blood, Holy Grail* (1982) and *The Dead Sea Scrolls Deception* (1991), and hitherto unknown lost civilizations were explored in Graham Hancock's *Fingerprints of the Gods* (1995) and *The Message of the Sphinx* (1996). All were huge bestsellers. Dan Brown's novel *The Da Vinci Code* (2003) was another publishing phenomenon, exposing to millions the presumed darkest secrets of the Catholic Church and those of various occult societies who were in on the conspiracy. Erich von Däniken himself has continued to stump for his claims from *Chariots of the Gods?* and other works, which are still repeated and expanded on by himself and others in books, on television, and through the Internet.

The Internet is where most cryptozoology now resides. In the heyday of Bigfoot, the Mothman, and the Loch Ness monster, the topic of strange, undiscovered species struggled for acceptance, against much doubt expressed by journalists, lawmen, and scientists. Now those rejections can be completely bypassed for an online audience. Amateur videos of hairy humanoids or living dinosaurs are well represented on YouTube and other websites, in addition to cable TV shows that present found footage of ghosts, poltergeists, and mysterious animals in action. As with every other sensational fact posted on the World Wide Web, and every video clip edited to blow the lid off some previously covered-up occurrence, such material is untroubled by the normal processes of peer review and independent scrutiny. Indeed, the paranormal of the seventies has become the normal of today, insofar as it is now almost impossible for critics and skeptics to track down and disprove every last fraud, conspiracy theory, monster photo, or alien abduction case streamed onto the Internet. Were he alive today, Charles Fort would have no need to write a *Book of the Damned*; he would be posting daily updates to his blog and Photoshopping any images he needed to back up his entries. The hard evidence is as rare as it ever was, but the rumors, suppositions, embellishments, and pure hoaxes have multiplied and roam free in cyberspace.

Perhaps the one area where the occult has most flourished is in that of criminology. Since 1980 a large number of investigations into murder and other misdeeds have focused on the perpetrators' satanic motivations, while among nonprofessional citizens the general fear of "satanic killers" has become commonplace and at times has risen to the level of mass hysteria. In fact, only a very few cases of occult-related murders or other serious assaults have ever been verified—and even then the occult elements have been superficial—but after Charles Manson, the Zodiac Killer, and the Son of Sam, the specter of cruel violence enacted in the name of the devil has been all too readily believable.

In 1984, in the town of Northport, New York, on Long Island, a teenaged boy named Gary Lauwers was killed by two young acquaintances, Jimmy Troiano and Ricky Kasso, while drinking beer and taking drugs in a local wood during a late-night party. Troiano and Kasso were arrested, and Kasso hung himself in jail shortly afterward. Police and reporters who looked into the case found a broad circle of youths dabbling in the pop occult conventions of the era: they listened to Black Sabbath, Led Zeppelin, and AC/DC (a handcuffed Kasso was photographed wearing an AC/DC jersey), made a pilgrimage to the infamous DeFeo/Lutz house in nearby Amityville, and scribbled pentagrams and 666 graffiti. Witness Albert Quinones stated that before stabbing Lauwers, Kasso commanded his victim:

Say you love Satan!

What was most disturbing in the Northport murder was not so much the young age of the murderers, and less their high-school-dropout appropriations of occult language and ceremony, as the open knowledge of Lauwers's death that was shared among many area teens for some two weeks before police were contacted. The tabloid press and its TV equivalents made much of the case's satanic overtones, but the Long Island kids' worse problems were their boredom, their alienation from authority, and their jaded indifference to the stupid, seedy crime that had been committed in their midst.

A considerably more destructive reign of terror was served in Los Angeles over 1984 and 1985 by Richard "The Night Stalker" Ramirez, who was eventually apprehended and charged with thirteen murders as well as several more violent sexual assaults and attempted murders. Pentagrams and satanic writing had been spray-painted at some of the murder scenes, and he had forced some of his victims to plead for mercy from Satan rather than God. While his case was tried, Ramirez openly boasted of his satanic inspiration. To photographers he displayed the pentagrams he had inked on his palms, and he cited AC/DC's "Night Prowler" from *Highway to Hell* as his personal anthem. Anton LaVey later claimed Ramirez had paid him homage on a 1978 journey to the Church of Satan's headquarters in San Francisco. "I thought Richard was very nice, very shy," LaVey recalled.[26]

Found guilty and sentenced on November 9, 1989, a defiant Ramirez harangued the court: "You maggots make me sick! Hypocrites one and all. We are all expendable for a cause. No one knows that better than those who kill for a policy, clandestinely or openly, as do the governments of the world which kill in the name of God and country . . . . I am beyond good and evil . . . . Legions of the night, night breed, repeat not the errors of the Night Prowler and show no mercy. I will be avenged. Lucifer dwells in all of us."[27] Once again, the media emphasized the killer's self-confessed Satanism over his other pathologies: he was an epileptic and a heavy drug user, and as a youngster he had been shown photos of battlefield rapes and decapitations by his cousin, a Vietnam veteran. The clinical truth was that at bottom Richard Ramirez was a demented sadist for whose impulses the occult provided a convenient rationalization. He and similar killers were not more interesting because they were obsessed with Satan; they showed how obsession with Satanism had spread even to the marginal and the delinquent.

By the time of Ramirez's trial, America, or at least the more credulous portion of it, was gripped by a full-scale "Satanic panic." The occult murders, occult music, occult movies, and occult mayhem that had captivated the country for over twenty years now collided with the fundamentalist Christianity that had arisen since 1979; something had to give. Back in 1972 author Mike Warnke's book *The Satan Seller* had purported to be a firsthand document of a criminal underworld of Satanists, who kidnapped, tortured, and killed as part of their practices, but it was the publication in 1980 of the memoir *Michelle Remembers* that really kicked off the Satanism scare. Credited to the pseudonymous Michelle Smith in conjunction with her psychiatrist (and husband) Dr. Lawrence Padzer, *Michelle Remembers* told the amazing story of Michelle's childhood victimization by satanic cultists while growing up in the provincial capital of Victoria, British Columbia, in 1954 and 1955. Like Whitley Strieber's recollection of alien abduction, Michelle's testimony had been brought out in a trance state, in her case administered by Padzer. From her subconscious came accounts of being trapped in a cage with snakes, of being placed in a coffin with a corpse, of watching unholy rites held by robed Satanists (including her mother), of being left among the bodies of murdered and mutilated infants, and of a range of other terrifying brutalities. The ugly and obscene descriptions in *Michelle Remembers* became the templates for a new class of crime: satanic ritual abuse (SRA).

In August 1983 the McMartin Preschool in Manhattan Beach, California, was at the epicenter of an explosive criminal investigation into satanic ritual abuse visited upon the children entrusted to its care. Several members of the facility's staff (four of them members of the McMartin family) were arrested. Tots who attended the McMartin Preschool said they had been forced to participate in sexual acts, had witnessed human and animal sacrifices, were compelled to consume blood, urine, and excrement, were forced into cannibalism, and had seen horrific satanic ceremonies conducted in hidden tunnels within the building's underground. For a culture accustomed to the bloody rampages of Charles Manson, the shameless perversities of Anton LaVey, and the no-holds-barred gross-outs of *The Exorcist*, such combinations of cruelty, vulgarity, and the occult were no longer surprising. The devil had long since ceased being personified as a goateed, debonair gentleman who spoke charmingly and presented would-be servants with scrolled contracts to sign—the Satan of Hal Lindsey, Michelle Smith, and the McMartin Preschool was wholly vile and wholly evil.

Over three hundred children from the McMartin Preschool were diagnosed as victims of satanic ritual abuse. Seven McMartin employees (including founder Virginia McMartin, her daughter Peggy Buckey, and grandchildren Ray and Peggy Ann Buckey) were subject to criminal charges, and the lengthy case against them dragged on until 1989, at a cost to the state of California of some $15 million. In the end all charges were dropped. What had happened? The initial complaint of sexual abuse had been launched by mother Judy Johnson, who was later institutionalized with paranoid schizophrenia and who died in 1986 from chronic alcoholism. Psychiatrist Lawrence Padzer and his wife, Michelle, authors of *Michelle Remembers*, had been consulted by parents as the case unfolded, and children from the school had been interrogated by therapists who acted out abusive scenes with anatomically correct dolls and prompted them with leading questions about what their caregivers had supposedly done to them: Did he ever make you . . . ? Did she say she would hurt you if . . . ? Did he take off his clothes . . . ?

Yet while the McMartin trial went forward with all its outrageous testimony and repulsive allegations, America's satanic panic spread. Over thirty other day-care centers in the United States were investigated for satanic ritual abuse, over one hundred communities were rocked by SRA stories, and dozens of teachers, preschool workers, and babysitters across the country were charged. The scandals were featured on the TV news program *20/20* and a special show hosted by crusading journalist Geraldo Rivera, and they received exclamatory coverage in *People*, *Time*, and other magazines. Quickie books and pamphlets were issued to exploit the cultural anxiety: *Satan's Underground* (1988), *The Edge of Evil* and *Suffer the Child* (both 1989), and *Painted Black: The Alarming True Story of How Satanic Crime Is Terrorizing Our Communities* (1990) and *Satan's Children* (1991). More rumors about secret satanic societies infiltrating every strata of American life circulated. There was the backward masking in the heavy metal music of Ozzy Osbourne and Judas Priest; there were the manifest occult themes in the Dungeons & Dragons board game; there were new reports of cattle mutilations; there were tales of motorists who were stopped and nearly accosted by circles of robed figures on lonely roads at night; there were countless walls spray-painted with pentagrams, inverted crosses, and the number 666; in 1982 the Procter & Gamble toiletry company had been forced to launch a lawsuit against Guy Sharpe, an Atlanta lay preacher, who had detected 666 and other satanic insignia hidden in the firm's corporate logo.

In hindsight it was obvious that much of the satanic panic was an unintentional consequence of the occult boom of the sixties and seventies. Most commentators of the period attributed the scare to a loose and vaguely current category of heavy metal and horror movies, without specific mention of how the widely the occult had been represented in the books, music, films, television, recreation, and news stories of the previous twenty years. The satanic panic was not a sudden irruption of irrationality but a natural and probably inevitable result of a media saturation that was by then so deep that few were still noticing it. For a long time the public had been bombarded with messages of what Satan and Satanists were like, of the words, images, and symbols associated with devil worship, and especially of how children were Satan's favorite victims. It had all finally proved too much for some people.

The supposed sexual sadism and underground networks of the abusers took off from the fiction of Ira Levin and William Peter Blatty, while the abusers' apparent penchants for convoluted rites sounded like extreme versions of the Church of Satan's publicity showcases. Similarly, the willingness to believe children's wildest stories of satanic ritual abuse—or the willingness to plant them in the minds of the kids themselves—must have derived in part from Flora Rheta Schreiber's *Sybil*, which had helped inspire the admissibility of "recovered memory" in psychiatric patients. As with the contemporaneous alien abduction claims of the decade, many episodes of sexual abuse (satanic or otherwise) were recalled from the subconscious minds of troubled individuals, helped along by therapists eager to uncover their subjects' inner demons. It had happened with *Sybil*; it had happened with Michelle Smith; it happened with the children of the McMartin Preschool. Satanic ritual abuse was the product of an unholy mix of cultural influences that could be traced to quite particular sources, but the influences had spread so far that believers no longer recognized them for what they were.

The dismissal of charges against the McMartin staff, even as criminal trials in other SRA cases continued and satanic urban legends mushroomed, pointed to a gradual backlash against the entire obsession. The scattering of recognized satanic churches in America were quick to say that they had never brought children into their rituals and they had never condoned violence or blood sacrifice; Michael Aquino's Temple of Set threatened legal action against the authors of *Michelle Remembers* for implying that it did. Within the psychiatric profession and among the general population, serious concerns arose about the efforts of social workers and other specialists to coach people in "recollecting" horrible abuses they had never really undergone, and about the consequences for luckless friends or relatives who became suspected of having inflicted them. At their most extravagant the satanically panicked had cited figures of as many as 50,000 American children kidnapped and killed by diabolic cults *every year*, which finally proved too much for even the most sympathetic police departments. Anything even approaching this number, it was pointed out, would be a national emergency, and there was no physical evidence (bodies, clothes, cultists' bloodstained altars) that would remotely indicate a widespread network of satanic pedophiles and murderers. In 1992 FBI man Kenneth V. Lanning wrote in an advisory to investigators: "After all the hype and hysteria is put aside . . . most satanic/occult activity involves the commission of NO crimes [or] relatively minor crimes such as trespassing, vandalism, cruelty to animals, or petty thievery."[28] Others saw in the satanic panic a resemblance to earlier witch hunts like the anticommunist Red Scare and even the anti-Semitic pogroms that had marred European history: in each instance, an imagined or minority other had served as a useful scapegoat for inherent tensions that were already plaguing society.

By the epoch of the satanic panic, American society was plagued by some real tensions indeed. The presidency of Ronald Reagan had been marked by his stepped-up War on Drugs, which reversed the previous decade's increasing liberalization of marijuana laws; now an entire class of young, indulgent, or unconventional people was implicated as potential criminals to whom their peers were warned to Just Say No. The Cold War renewed its intensity with saber-rattling between Reagan's United States and the Soviet gerontocracy, and the prospect of nuclear conflict and its aftermath once again terrified Europeans and North Americans. Technological and economic change meant industry towns across Canada and America lost their traditional blue-collar employment bases, and Satan was a handy villain for Rust Belters who could otherwise find no one to confront for layoffs and downsizing—where better to spray-paint a pentagram than on the front gate of an abandoned factory?

Ethical scandals in Washington (the Iran-Contra affair), on Wall Street (junk bonds and insider trading), in the U.S. banking system (the savings and loan debacle), and even within the Christian conservative movement (tawdry personal revelations about TV evangelists Jim Bakker and Jimmy Swaggart) also laid the groundwork for the satanic panic. "What is perceived by Americans in their worries about moral decline is the growing moral corruption in society," theorized sociologist Jeffrey Victor in *Satanic Panic: The Creation of a Contemporary Legend* (1993). "In the experience of the average American today, the moral corruption of society is encountered throughout the institutions of American society. In recent decades, Americans have encountered lying on a grand scale in national politics."[29] From these verified instances of corruption, it was not such a leap to believe that other organizations, such as schools and churches, might themselves have been harboring dark secrets behind their lawful, wholesome exteriors.

As the most paranoid fantasies of Satanism diminished and diffused outward into the broader currents of North American life after the McMartin trial, the occult boom of 1966 to 1980 could be placed into a longer perspective. It had not sprung out of nothing after 1965, nor did it stop cold in 1981, but it eventually stood as a singular episode of modern culture. Anyone who had lived through it, particularly as a young adult, would recall that the occult had been a vogue of the sixties and seventies; even those who had never succumbed to its allure can remember it being part of their mental environment. The fourteen-year centrality of the occult in the popular media and mass sensibility was a legitimate phenomenon whose underlying origins and enduring legacies have become a chapter of social history that reveals much about where society has been and where it might yet travel.

As early as 1919, Sigmund Freud in his essay "The 'Uncanny'" anticipated how the dormant psychological instincts of contemporary men and women could be awoken by unexpected stimuli: "Let us take the uncanny associated with the omnipotence of thoughts, with the prompt fulfillment of wishes, with secret injurious powers and with the return of the dead," he argued. "We—or our primitive forebears—once regarded such things as real possibilities; we were convinced that they really happened. Today we no longer believe in them, having *surmounted* such modes of thought. Yet we do not feel entirely secure in these new convictions; the old ones live on in us, on the look-out for confirmation."[30] In the same work Freud seemed to predict the juxtaposition of the everyday with the paranormal that would be achieved with such devastating effect by the authors of *Rosemary's Baby* and *The Exorcist*: "The imaginative writer may have invented a world that, while less fantastic than that of the fairy tale, differs from the real world in that it involves supernatural entities such as demons or spirits of the dead . . . . However, if the writer has to all appearances taken up his stance on the ground of common reality . . . he betrays us to a superstition we thought we had 'surmounted'; he tricks us by promising everyday reality and then going beyond it."[31]

The other great psychologist of the twentieth century, Carl Jung, also gave thought to the occult. Throughout his writings he expressed an interest in psychic aberrations and the clinical plausibility of clairvoyance or telepathy, but he too foresaw how easily the notion of supernatural evil could erupt through the rational surface of modern existence. Devils and demons were elements of humanity's collective unconscious, he opined, serving as symbols of our deepest phobias and most hateful potentials, which seemed to have been realized with World War II and the Final Solution. "The Church has the doctrine of the devil," he wrote in *Psychology of the Transference* in the watershed year of 1945, "of an evil principle, whom we like to imagine complete with cloven hoofs, horns, and tail, half man, half beast, a chthonic deity apparently escaped from the rout of Dionysus, the sole surviving champion of the sinful joys of paganism. An excellent picture, and one which exactly describes the grotesque and sinister side of the unconscious; for we have never really come to grips with it and consequently it has remained in its original savage state . . . . The frightful records of our age are plain for all to see, and they surpass in hideousness everything that any previous age, with its feeble instruments, could have hoped to accomplish."[32]

During the occult heyday serious commentators viewed the trend in different lights. Some saw it as a welcome break from the orthodoxies of conventional religion; others took the occult as evidence of a regrettable generational dumbing-down. "The current interest of youth in astrology, clairvoyance and the occult is no coincidence," Canadian philosopher of media and technology Marshall McLuhan was quoted in 1969. "Psychic communal integration, made possible at last by the electronic media, could create the universality of consciousness foreseen by Dante when he predicted that men would continue as no more than broken fragments until they were unified into an inclusive consciousness. Mysticism is just tomorrow's science dreamed today."[33] Buddhist teacher Alan Watts was also positive. "What is constructive and meaningful about the return of occultism is that for the first time, masses of young Americans are learning that life can have a goal of something else besides producing and consuming junk, that life should be directed at spiritual ends . . . . What's pleasurable to thinking persons today are active mind-body disciplines like yoga or meditation."[34] Theodore Roszak's sympathetic 1969 study, *The Making of a Counter Culture*, took note of how youth were turning away from the causes and campaigns of their elders: "Is the youthful political activism of the sixties any different from that of the thirties? If the difference shows up anywhere, it reveals itself in the unprecedented penchant for the occult, for magic, and for exotic ritual which has become an integral part of the counter culture . . . . Perhaps, after all, the age of ideology is passing, giving way to the age of mystagogy."[35]

But author Owen Rachleff (*The Occult Conceit*, 1971) complained that "most occultniks are either frauds of the intellectual and/or financial variety, or disturbed individuals who frequently mistake psychosis for psychic phenomena."[36] In 1972 sociologist Marcello Truzzi likewise questioned the depth of the new occult fad. "If we fully believed in demons," he wrote in *Sociological Quarterly*, "we certainly would not want to call them up . . . . [The popularity of the occult suggests] a kind of victory over the supernatural, a demystification of what were once fearful and threatening cultural elements. What were once dark secrets known only through initiation into arcane orders are now exposed to everyman."[37]

Later on, some thinkers stated that the occult fixation represented a quest by present-day people to reconnect with the old reassurances of ceremony and ritual. A culture devoid of grand cosmic stories or larger-than-life heroes and villains was an empty one, maintained anthropologist Joseph Campbell; despite its malevolent characters and frightening tales, the occult offered a comforting mythology. And the dominance of science and technology, epitomized by space travel, threatened that mythology into a volatile reaction. In 1979 Campbell commented on the acceptance of Hal Lindsey's *The Late Great Planet Earth* and the dogmas it upheld: "The sense of the apocalypse is very widespread," he acknowledged. "We hate ourselves so much that we take delight in the destruction of people . . . . The mystical theme of the space age is this: the world, as we know it, is coming to an end. The world as the center of the universe, the world divided from the heavens, the world bound by horizons in which love is reserved for members of the in-group—that is the world that is passing away . . . . Our divided, schizophrenic worldview, with no mythology adequate to coordinate our consciousness and unconscious— that world is coming to an end."[38] To ward off atheism, Campbell thought, Christians had been forced to summon the last resort of the Antichrist.

Later still it was said that the occult fascination inflicted lasting damage on America's national intelligence. However fun or frivolous the subjects may have once seemed, the enthusiasm of millions for poltergeists, possession, and parapsychology resulted in a dramatic lowering of the country's erstwhile intellectual standards. In *The Age of American Unreason* (2008), Susan Jacoby objected this way: "Even when the entertainment media are not promoting a particular version of religion, they do promote and capitalize on widespread American credulity regarding the supernatural. In recent years, television has commissioned an unceasing stream of programs designed to appeal to a vast market of viewers who believe in ghosts, angels, and demons . . . . The American marketing of the Apocalypse is a multimedia production, capitalizing on fundamentalism and paranoid superstition."[39] And astronomer Carl Sagan, an original member of the Committee for the Scientific Investigation of Claims of the Paranormal, summed up in *The Demon-Haunted World* (1995):

> Yes, the world *would* be a more interesting place if there were UFOs lurking in the deep waters off Bermuda and eating ships and planes, or if dead people could take control of our hands and write us messages. It would be fascinating if adolescents were able to make telephone handsets rocket off their cradles just by thinking at them, or if our dreams could, more often than can be explained by chance and our knowledge of the world, accurately foretell the future.
>
> These are all instances of pseudoscience. . . . With the uninformed cooperation (and often the cynical connivance) of newspapers, magazines, book publishers, radio, television, movie producers, and the like, such ideas are easily and widely available.[40]

What, then, was the occult wave all about? From different angles it could be viewed as a by-product of the protest generation and the drug culture; or it was a backlash against the supremacy of science; or it was a desperate rearguard response to the decline of mainstream faiths; or it was a show business ploy that caught on with a surprisingly big audience across a surprisingly wide spectrum of formats. In retrospect it is clear how many disparate facets of the occult served to reinforce its visibility as a whole: occult symbols displayed on rock album covers, serial killers who quoted occult rock groups, popular books about supposedly occult serial killers, board games which were based on popular occult books, hit movies that featured occult board games, and so on. The occult constantly referenced, echoed, and overlapped itself. Nothing succeeds like success, and for several years, nothing succeeded like satanic success.

Complementing the occult in the media was the occult in popular myth. Some of the most widespread stories of the paranormal and the diabolical came not from professional artists or reporters but a truly spooked public. The soul selling of Led Zeppelin; Alice Cooper grossing out his audience; the true story behind *The Exorcist*; Anton LaVey on the set of *Rosemary's Baby*; the purported consequences of dabbling with Ouija boards or Dungeons & Dragons; the satanic basis for cattle mutilation; satanic ritual abuse—such tales had not been started by hoaxers or publicity agents but by ordinary citizens projecting their own fears onto legitimate news and commercial culture. The occult years witnessed the flourishing of the urban legend.

The legacy of all this should be obvious. Certainly, the entertainment we consume today, crowded with zombies, vampires, wizards, shadowy sects, and earth-shaking revelations, is descended from the best-selling and blockbusting occult legends of the sixties and seventies. Certainly, our readiness to accept the wildest conspiracy theories about the international order and the darkest rumors about the prominent and the powerful comes from how the occult sowed seeds of doubt in what we had previously assumed to be a measurable, definable thing known as reality. The occult changed how we think and what we believe.

Yet the ultimate implications of the occult are finite. Even supposing its inherent premises to be true—and time and again, they have been shown to be false—the occult would not obviate the ordinary, material issues that have always concerned us. One or two authenticated cases of demonic possession would still be less impactful than the millions of cases of disease and accidents that occur every year. A few exposed criminal satanic cults could never be guilty of as much wrongdoing as financial crooks, drug cartels, national armed forces, or global terrorists have demonstrably committed over the last few decades. A captured Bigfoot or Loch Ness monster would not much sway the continued debates over natural resources and environmental degradation. Proven telepathic or psychokinetic ability in some individuals could hardly keep pace with the rapid advances in digital communication and electronic tools, which have affected how billions of people around the globe interact. A documented vista of Hell could be no more nightmarish than the epilogues of wars, famines, and disasters we have seen recorded in countless places from the beginning of history. And which sort of ritual abuse is more prevalent: children coerced into satanic orgies, or children abused by Catholic priests? Women voluntarily serving as naked altars in San Francisco, or women involuntarily receiving circumcisions in Africa? Which religious manias have done more harm: isolated groups of eccentrics practicing what they think is witchcraft, or whole populations of the faithful imposing what they are convinced is God's will? How, practically, would mass transcendence end poverty or hunger or despair? How would some final revelation of a supreme being, or an Antichrist, change how we really go about our daily lives? How much of our homes, families, or innermost thoughts would we really abandon just because the devil appeared in the White House, or handcuffed in court, or singing backward on a rock album?

It isn't that *The Exorcist* is no longer a terrifying movie, that "(Don't Fear) The Reaper" isn't a memorable song, that thoughts of the Sasquatch aren't unnerving on an outdoor hike, or that Aleister Crowley and Anton LaVey weren't remarkable people. It isn't that pagan or Asian religions aren't rich in story and symbolism, or that intuitive pathways to knowledge and health aren't more attractive than the dreary dictates of school and hospital. It isn't that Tarot cards and astrological charts aren't beautiful to look at, that Dungeons & Dragons isn't an absorbing pastime, that Stephen King is any less original a writer, or that David Berkowitz is any less psychopathic a murderer. The point, though, is that the occult of 1966 to 1980 offered a compelling but limited vision of humankind's location in the universe—one steeped in the past, in naïveté and fear and reaction, rather than a future of enlightenment and hope and inspiration. It was a very imaginative, very colorful, and very dead end. That it held our attention as intensely and for as long as it did is a testament to both the enchantments of the occult tradition and the traditional will to enchantment of the human race.

Timeline of the Occult Era

1966

- J. R. R. Tolkien's *Lord of the Rings* grows in popularity among US college students.

- Previous year's elimination of race-based immigration quotas in the US allows more Asian newcomers, fostering greater public awareness of Buddhist, Hindu, and other non-Eurocentric religious traditions.

- April 8: *Time* magazine cover asks, "Is God Dead?"

- Jane Roberts's *How to Develop Your ESP Power* is published.

- May: Josef Stocker and associates are charged with murdering Bernadette Hasler during "exorcism" ritual, Switzerland.

- June–July: Anton LaVey forms the Church of Satan, San Francisco.

- *Eerie* (Warren comic) debuts.

- Parker Brothers firm purchases the rights to market Ouija boards; sales are high.

- September: Wave of Mothman sightings begins in West Virginia.

- *Dark Shadows* (TV series) premieres.

1967

- January 31: Anton LaVey conducts the first wedding ceremony of The Church of Satan, San Francisco.

- New Reformed Orthodox Order of the Golden Dawn is formed in San Francisco.

- May: Ira Levin's novel *Rosemary's Baby* is released.
- June 1: *Sgt. Pepper's Lonely Hearts Club Band* is released, featuring cover photo of Aleister Crowley.
- September 9: Discovery of oddly dismembered horse initiates cattle mutilation rumors.
- International Society for Krishna Consciousness opens San Francisco office.
- October 3: Anton LaVey appears on *The Tonight Show*.
- October 20: Roger Patterson films alleged Bigfoot, Bluff Creek, California.
- November: Rolling Stones' *Their Satanic Majesties Request* is released.

1968

- January: Beatles and friends visit India to study under the Maharishi Mahesh Yogi.
- February: Stills from Patterson's Bigfoot film appear in *Argosy* magazine.
- June: *Rosemary's Baby* (film) is released.
- Neo-pagan group Church of All Worlds is formed.
- Sea serpent "Ogopogo" is filmed in British Columbia's Lake Okanagan.
- August: "The Spreading Mystery of the Bermuda Triangle" is published in *Argosy*.
- Sybil Leek's *Diary of a Witch* is published.
- September: Carlos Castaneda's *The Teachings of Don Juan* is published.
- December: First attack by "Zodiac" is recorded in California.
- December 5: Rolling Stones' *Beggars Banquet*, featuring "Sympathy for the Devil," is released.

1969

- Anton LaVey's *The Satanic Bible* is published by Avon Books.
- July: Rolling Stone Brian Jones is found dead, age twenty-six.
- August 9 and 10: Charles Manson Family members commit Tate-LaBianca murders.

- September: *Scooby-Doo, Where Are You!* (cartoon series) debuts on CBS.
- *Vampirella* (Warren comic) debuts.
- Rod Serling's *Night Gallery* (TV series) debuts.
- December: The American Association for the Advancement of Science accepts the Parapsychological Association into its membership.
- December 6: Fan is stabbed to death by Hells Angels at a Rolling Stones concert, Altamont, California.

1970

- February: Black Sabbath's *Black Sabbath* album is released.
- February: Erich von Däniken's *Chariots of the Gods?* is released (English translation).
- Jane Roberts's *The Seth Material* is published.
- September 18: Black Sabbath's *Paranoid* album is released.
- Process Church of Final the Judgment establishes North American chapters.
- Ken Russell's film *The Devils* is released.
- Hal Lindsey's *The Late Great Planet Earth* is published by Zondervan.
- September: Kathryn Paulsen's *The Complete Book of Magic and Witchcraft* is published.
- October 5: *Led Zeppelin III* is released, featuring quotations from Aleister Crowley on the vinyl grooves.
- Anton LaVey's *The Compleat Witch* is published.

1971

- January: Comics Code is relaxed to permit depiction of vampires, werewolves, monsters, and other macabre elements.
- Ballantine Books publishes new paperback editions of H. P. Lovecraft anthologies.
- February 21: Alice Cooper's *Love It to Death* album is released.
- May: William Peter Blatty's *The Exorcist* is published by Harper & Row.

- *The Mephisto Waltz* (film) is released.
- Thomas Tryon's novel *The Other* is published.
- Zilpha Keatley Snyder's *The Headless Cupid* (juvenile novel) is published.
- Rider-Waite Tarot deck is made available by U.S. Games Systems.
- Carlos Castaneda's *A Separate Reality* is published.
- Erich von Däniken's *Gods from Outer Space* is published.
- August: Black Sabbath's *Master of Reality* album is released.
- August 24: Anton LaVey appears on the cover of *Look* magazine.
- October: Franken Berry and Count Chocula cereals are retailed.
- November: Alice Cooper's *Killer* album is released.
- November 5: Led Zeppelin's fourth album is released, featuring "Stairway to Heaven."

1972

- Zilpha Keatley Snyder's *The Witches of Worm* (juvenile novel) is published.
- Hal Lindsey's *Satan Is Alive and Well on Planet Earth* is published.
- June: Stanford Research Institute begins conducting experiments in remote viewing.
- June: *Time* magazine cover story, "The Occult Revival," appears.
- June: Alice Cooper's album *School's Out* is released.
- June: Carlos Castaneda's *Journey to Ixtlan: The Lessons of Don Juan* is published.
- July: *The Exorcist* is published in paperback.
- Mike Warnke's book *The Satan Seller*, alleging widespread crimes of satanic cults, is published.
- *The Legend of Boggy Creek* (film) is released.
- August 8: Underwater photo of alleged Loch Ness monster is taken.
- September: *Black Sabbath Vol. 4* is released.

- November 15: Pope Paul VI delivers his address "Confronting the Devil's Power."
- December: LaVey's *The Satanic Rituals* is published.
- *The Possession of Joel Delaney* (film) is released.

1973

- February 25: Alice Cooper's album *Billion Dollar Babies* is released.
- Thomas Tryon's *Harvest Home* is published.
- May: Flora Rheta Schreiber's *Sybil* is published.
- June: *The Legend of Hell House* (film) is released.
- Psychic Uri Geller appears on *The Tonight Show*.
- TV movie *Satan's School for Girls* is aired.
- TV movie *Don't Be Afraid of the Dark* is aired.
- November: Black Sabbath's album *Sabbath Bloody Sabbath* is released.
- December: Rolling Stones' "Dancing with Mr. D."
- December 26: William Friedkin's film *The Exorcist* is released.

1974

- January–June: *The Exorcist* breaks box-office records.
- April: Stephen King's debut novel, *Carrie*, is published.
- April: Blue Öyster Cult's album *Secret Treaties* is released.
- Jane Roberts's *The Nature of Personal Reality: A Seth Book* is published.
- Dungeons & Dragons is first retailed by Tactical Studies Rules.
- September–November: More cattle mutilation scares occur in the US Midwest.
- October: *It's Alive* (film) is released.
- October: *The Devil's Triangle* (documentary film) is released.
- November 25: Documentary *Monsters! Mysteries or Myths?* is aired.
- November: Vincent Bugliosi's account of the Manson murders, *Helter Skelter*, is published.

- November: Charles Berlitz's *The Bermuda Triangle* is published.
- *The Night Stalker* (TV series) is aired.

1975

- January: *Satan's Triangle* (TV movie) is aired.
- February: *The Outer Space Connection* (documentary film) is released.
- Temple of Set breaks away from the Church of Satan.
- March: *Escape to Witch Mountain* (film) is released.
- Wiccan group Covenant of the Goddess is formed, San Francisco.
- *Environmental Atlas of Washington State*, published by the US Army Corps of Engineers, acknowledges possible existence of Bigfoot.
- June: *Race with the Devil* (film) is released.
- John Keel's *The Mothman Prophecies* is published.
- October: Stephen King's *Salem's Lot* is published.

1976

- January: Black Sabbath's *We Sold Our Soul for Rock 'n' Roll* is released.
- April 12: Anne Rice's *Interview with the Vampire* published.
- April 30: Committee for the Scientific Investigation of Claims of the Paranormal is formed, Buffalo, New York.
- May: Blue Öyster Cult's album *Agents of Fortune*, featuring "(Don't Fear) The Reaper," is released.
- June: *The Omen* (film) is released.
- June: *The Amazine World of Psychic Phenomena* (documentary film) is released.
- July: "Son of Sam" claims his first victim, New York City.
- Anneliese Michel dies after exorcism ritual, West Germany.
- *In Search Of . . .* (TV series) debuts.
- *Helter Skelter* (TV miniseries) is broadcast.
- October: *Look What's Happened to Rosemary's Baby* (TV sequel to 1967 film) is aired.

- September: Stephen King's *Firestarter* is published.

- September: Ozzy Osbourne's *Blizzard of Ozz* album, featuring "Mr. Crowley," is released.

- November: *Michelle Remembers*, purported memoir of co-author Michelle Smith's childhood experiences of satanic ritual abuse, is published.

- December: Led Zeppelin disbands following death of drummer John Bonham, amid tabloid rumors of a "Zeppelin curse."

Notes

Introduction: The Return of the Repressed

1. "Toward a Hidden God." *Time*, April 8, 1966, 98.

Chapter 1: Diabolus in Musica

1. Derek Taylor, *It Was Twenty Years Ago Today* (New York: Simon & Schuster, 1987), 33.

2. Somerset Maugham, *The Magician* (London: Penguin Classics, 1992), 7.

3. Lawrence Sutin, *Do What Thou Wilt* (New York: St. Martin's Press, 2000), 425.

4. Aleister Crowley, *The Book of the Law* (York Beach, ME: Samuel Weiser, 1976), 14.

5. Keith Richards, *Life* (New York: Little, Brown, 2010), 205.

6. Ibid., 222.

7. Marianne Faithfull, with David Dalton, *Faithfull: An Autobiography* (Boston: Little, Brown, 1994), 186.

8. Ibid., 187.

9. Ibid., 159.

10. Richards, *Life*, 253.

11. David Dalton, ed., *The Rolling Stones: The First Twenty Years* (New York: Alfred A. Knopf, 1981), 111.

12. Faithfull, *Faithfull*, 186.

13. George Case, *Led Zeppelin FAQ* (New York: Backbeat, 2011), 193.

14. George Case, *Jimmy Page: Magus, Musician, Man* (New York: Hal Leonard, 2007), 148.

15. Case, *Led Zeppelin FAQ*, 192.

16. Case, *Jimmy Page*, 154–155.

17. Case, *Led Zeppelin FAQ*, 191–192.

18. Case, *Jimmy Page*, 179.

19. Albert Goldman, "Rock in the Androgynous Zone," *Life*, July 30, 1971, 16.

20. George Case, *Out of Our Heads: Rock 'n' Roll Before the Drugs Wore Off* (New York: Backbeat, 2010), 86.

21. Bob Greene, *Billion Dollar Baby* (New York: Atheneum, 1974), 47.

22. Ace Frehley with Joe Layden, *No Regrets: A Rock 'n' Roll Memoir* (New York: Gallery Books, 2011), 77.

23. "The Year in Review," *Guitar World*, January 1994, 16.

24. Dan Epstein, "Black Magic," *Guitar World*, July 2001, 66–67.

25. Black Sabbath, *Reunion* (CD liner notes by Phil Alexander), 1998.

26. www.blacksabbath.com/history.html

27. Jim Miller, original ed., *The Rolling Stone Illustrated History of Rock & Roll* (New York: Random House, 1992), 460.

28. Epstein, "Black Magic," 64.

29. Nicholas Schaffner, *The British Invasion: From the First Wave to the New Wave* (New York: McGraw-Hill, 1982), 199.

30. Brad Tolinski, "Iron Men," *Guitar World*, August 1992, 79.

31. Epstein, "Black Magic," 69.

32. Steven Rosen, *Black Sabbath* (London: Sanctuary, 2002), 61.

Chapter 2: Bad Words

1. "Going to the Opera With . . . Ira Levin," *Opera News*, October 1997, 36.

2. Ibid.

3. Margalit Fox, "Ira Levin, 78, of 'Rosemary's Baby,' Dies," *New York Times*, November 14, 2007, B11.

4. Stephen King, *Danse Macabre* (New York: Berkley Books, 1981), 319.

5. Thomas J. Fleming, "Rosemary's Baby" (book review), *New York Times*, April 30, 1967, 39.

6. "Going to the Opera With . . . Ira Levin," *Opera News*, October, 1997, 36.

7. Bradley J. Birzer, *J. R. R. Tolkien's Sanctifying Myth: Understanding Middle-Earth* (Wilmington, DE: ISI Books, 2002), 16.

8. Lovecraft, H. P., "The Dreams in the Witch House," *The Best of H. P. Lovecraft: Bloodcurdling Tales of Horror and the Macabre* (New York: Ballantine, 1982), 318.

9. William Peter Blatty, *The Exorcist: From Novel to Film* (New York: Bantam Books, 1974), 6.

10. Ibid., 22.

11. Ibid., 21.

12. "After 40 Years, Grisly 'Exorcist' Book Gets a Rewrite," *Weekend Edition Saturday* (National Public Radio broadcast), October 29, 2011.

13. Ibid.

14. Webster Schott, "The Devil and Little Regan," *Life*, May 7, 1971, 20.

15. Peter S. Prescott, "Fear Can Be Fun," *Newsweek*, May 10, 1971, 112–113.

16. R. Z. Sheppard, "Brimstone by the Numbers," *Time*, June 7, 1971, 96.

17. "After 40 Years, Grisly 'Exorcist,' ... " *Weekend Edition Saturday*.

18. Martin Pedersen, "New York's Magickal Childe," *Publishers Weekly*, September 13, 1991, 54.

19. Blatty, *The Exorcist: From Novel to Film*, 16.

20. Jay Anson, *The Amityville Horror* (New York: Prentice-Hall, 1977), 310.

21. Diana Jean Schemo, "'Amityville' Prisoner Says Movie Money Tainted Defense," *New York Times*, June 25, 1992.

22. Ibid.

23. "Amityville Braced for Another 'Horror,'" ABC News, April 15, 2005.

24. Jason Lynch, "Amityville Ghosts," *People*, April 18, 2005.

25. Jane Roberts, *The Unknown Reality: A Seth Book* (New York: Prentice-Hall, 1978).

26. Anne Rice, *Interview with the Vampire* (New York: Knopf, 1976), 280.

27. Tim Underwood and Chuck Miller, eds., *Fear Itself: The Horror Fiction of Stephen King* (New York: New American Library, 1984), 20.

28. "After 40 Years, Grisly 'Exorcist,' ... " *Weekend Edition Saturday*.

29. Michael Mewshaw, "Novels and Stories," *New York Times*, March 26, 1978, BR4.

Chapter 3: Sin Cinema

1. Roman Polanski, *Roman* (New York: Morrow, 1984), 263.

2. Ibid.

3. Ibid., 265.

4. Ibid., 272.

5. Ibid.

6. "Going to the Opera With . . . Ira Levin," *Opera News*, 36.

7. Mia Farrow, *What Falls Away* (New York: Nan A. Talese, 1997), 108.

8. Polanski, *Roman*, 274.

9. Farrow, *What Falls Away*, 111.

10. Stanley Kauffmann, *Before My Eyes: Film Criticism and Comment* (New York: Harper & Row, 1971), 85.

11. Farrow, *What Falls Away*, 123.

12. Polanski, *Roman*, 265.

13. Lawrence Wright, "Sympathy for the Devil," *Rolling Stone*, September 5, 1991, 62.

14. Blatty, *The Exorcist From Novel to Film*, 4.

15. Ibid., 41.

16. Mark Kermode, *The Exorcist* (BFI Modern Classics) (London: British Film Institute, 1997), 41.

17. Blatty, *The Exorcist From Novel to Film*, 37.

18. Ron Lackmann, *Mercedes McCambridge: A Biography and Career Record* (Jefferson, NC: McFarland, 2004), 116.

19. Kermode, *The Exorcist*, 66.

20. Ibid., 78.

21. Blatty, *The Exorcist From Novel to Film*, 278.

22. Stanley Kauffmann, *Living Images: Film Comment and Criticism* (New York: Harper & Row, 1975), 255–256.

23. Roger Ebert, *Roger Ebert's Movie Home Companion* (New York: Andrews, McMeel & Parker, 1986), 174.

24. Vincent Canby, "Blatty's 'Exorcist' Comes to the Screen," *New York Times*, December 27, 1973, 46.

25. Vincent Canby, "Why the Devil Do They Dig 'The Exorcist'?" *New York Times*, January 13, 1974.

26. Eugene C. Kennedy, "A Priest Takes a Look at the Devil and William Blatty," *New York Times*, August 4, 1974, 95.

27. Ebert, *Roger Ebert's Movie Home Companion*, 173.

28. John Kenneth Muir, *Terror Television: American Series, 1970–1999* (Jefferson, NC: McFarland, 2001).

29. King, *Danse Macabre*, 152.

30. Lynn Haney, *Gregory Peck: A Charmed Life* (New York: Carroll & Graf, 2004), 366.

31. Harry Medved with Randy Dreyfuss, *The Fifty Worst Films of All Time (And How They Got That Way)* (New York: Popular Library, 1978), 172.

Chapter 4: Little Devils

1. Laura Levine, email to author, July 2012.

2. Ibid.

3. Bill Hanna, with Tom Ito, *A Cast of Friends* (Dallas: Taylor Publishing, 1996), 143.

4. Hal Erickson, *Television Cartoon Shows: An Illustrated Encyclopedia, 1949 through 2003* (Jefferson, NC: McFarland, 2005), 25.

5. Randy Duncan and Matthew J. Smith, *The Power of Comics: History, Form, and Culture* (New York: Continuum, 2009), 62.

6. Jon B. Cooke, *Comic Book Artist Collection, Volume 1* (Raleigh, NC: TwoMorrows Publishing, 2000), 27.

7. Bernie Wrightson, Bruce Jones, et al., *Creepy Presents Bernie Wrightson: The Definitive Collection of Bernie Wrightson's Stories and Illustrations from the Pages of* Creepy *and* Eerie (Milwaukie, OR: Dark Horse Comics, 2011), 8.

8. "He Chose His Own Adventure," *Newsweek*, March 17, 2008.

Chapter 5: Stranger Than Science

1. Peter Byrne, *The Search For Bigfoot: Monster, Myth or Man?* (New York: Pocket Books, 1976), 48–49.

2. Ibid, 230.

3. Mel Allen, "The Gift," *Yankee*, March–April 2011.

4. Donnie Sergent and Jeff Wamsley, *Mothman: The Facts Behind the Legend* (Proctorville, OH: Mark S. Phillips, 2002), 51.

5. John Keel, *The Mothman Prophecies* (New York: Tor, 2002), 16.

6. Byrne, *The Search for Bigfoot*, 180.

7. Charles Fort, *The Book of the Damned: The Collected Works of Charles Fort* (New York: Jeremy P. Tarcher/Penguin, 2008), 1019.

8. Tom Wolfe, *Mauve Gloves & Madmen, Clutter & Vine, and Other Stories, Sketches,and Essays* (New York: Farrar, Straus & Giroux, 1976).

9. Nat Freedland, *The Occult Explosion* (New York: G. P. Putnam's Sons, 1972), 237.

10. Paul H. Smith, *Reading the Enemy's Mind: Inside Star Gate; America's Psychic Espionage Program* (New York: Tom Doherty Associates, 2005), 59.

11. King, *Danse Macabre*, 209.

12. D. Scott Rogo, *The Haunted Universe* (New York: Signet, 1977), 5.

13. Keel, *The Mothman Prophecies*, 266.

14. John Moorhead, "Dissolving the Bermuda Triangle Case," *Christian Science Monitor*, May 7, 1975, 23.

15. "A Deadly Triangle," *Time*, January 6, 1975, 70.

16. Charles Berlitz, *Without a Trace* (Garden City, NY: Doubleday, 1977), 105.

17. Ibid., 17.

18. "A Deadly Triangle," *Time*, 70.

19. "The Extra-Terrestrial Profit Picture," *New York*, May 7, 1973, 80.

20. Erich von Däniken, *The Gold of the Gods* (New York: G.P. Putnam's Sons, 1973).

21. "Chariots of the Gods?" (book review), *Choice*, May 1970.

22. Daniel Loxton, "Ancient Aliens," *Skeptic*, 13, 2007, 84.

23. "Attacking the New Nonsense," *Time*, December 12, 1977.

24. Kendrick Frazier, "Science and the Parascience Cults," *Science News* 109, 1976, 346–350.

25. Ibid.

26. Ibid.

27. Ibid.

28. E. Lynne Wright, *Disasters and Heroic Rescues of Florida: True Stories of Tragedy and Survival* (Guilford, CT: Insider's Guide, 2006), 78–79.

29. Daniel Loxton, "Ancient Aliens," *Skeptic*.

30. Frazier, "Science and the Parascience Cults," 346–350.

31. Lynn Rosellini, "Not So Big After All," *U.S. News & World Report*, January 25, 1999, 61.

32. Douglas Martin, "Inventor Pursued Loch Ness Monster," *Edmonton Journal*, November 15, 2009, E7.

Chapter 6: Devil in the Flesh

1. Edward C. Burks, "'Satan Cult,' Death, Drugs Jolt Peaceful Vineland, NJ," *New York Times*, July 6, 1971, 35.

2. Ibid.

3. www.catholic-pages.com/morality/devil-p6.asp

4. Carlos Castaneda, *A Separate Reality: Further Conversations with Don Juan* (New York: Simon & Schuster, 1971), 10.

5. William Madsen and Claudia Madsen, "A Separate Reality" (book review), *Natural History*, June 1971.

6. Stuart R. Kaplan, introduction to the Rider Tarot deck instructions, U.S. Games Systems, September 1971.

7. Jerry M. Flint, "Rise in Occultism Viewed as Revolt Against Science," *New York Times*, September 10, 1971, 37.

8. *The Humanist*, September–October 1975, 4–6.

9. Starhawk, *The Spiral Dance: A Rebirth of the Ancient Religion of the Great Goddess* (20th Anniversary Edition) (San Francisco: Harper San Francisco, 1999), 127.

10. Margot Adler, *Drawing Down the Moon: Witches, Druids, Goddess-Worshippers, and Other Pagans in America Today* (New York: Viking Press, 1979), 183.

11. "Switzerland: Beating the Devil," *Time*, February 7, 1969.

12. Robert Graysmith, *Zodiac Unmasked* (New York: Berkley Books, 2002), 40.

13. Ibid., 161.

14. Dirk Cameron Gibson, *Clues from Killers: Serial Murder and Crime Scene Messages* (Westport, CT.: Praeger, 2004), 11–12.

15. Ibid, 15.

16. Elliott Leyton, *Hunting Humans: The Rise of the Modern Multiple Murderer* (Toronto: McClelland and Stewart, 1987).

17. Ibid.

18. Steve Fishman, "The Devil in David Berkowitz," *New York*, September 18, 2006, 32.

19. Leyton, *Hunting Humans*.

20. Ibid.

21. Matt Diehl, "The Holy Sabbath," *Rolling Stone*, April 21, 2004.

22. Fishman, "The Devil in David Berkowitz."

23. Joan Didion, *The White Album* (New York: Simon & Schuster, 1979), 41.

24. Vincent Bugliosi, with Curt Gentry, *Helter Skelter* (New York: W.W. Norton, 1974), 237.

25. Ibid., 594.

26. Jeff Guinn, *Manson: The Life and Times of Charles Manson* (New York: Simon & Schuster, 2013), 245.

27. Bugliosi, *Helter Skelter*, 84.

28. Adam Parfrey, ed., *Apocalypse Culture* (Los Angeles: Feral House, 1990), 166.

29. Timothy Wylie, *Love, Sex, Fear, Death: The Inside Story of the Process Church of the Final Judgment* (Los Angeles: Feral House, 2009) 253.

30. Ibid., 171.

31. Richard Cavendish, *The Powers of Evil* (London: Routledge & Kegan Paul, 1975), 214.

32. Bill Ellis, *Raising the Devil: Satanism, New Religions, and the Media* (Lexington: University Press of Kentucky, 2000), 169.

33. Sammy Davis, with Jane and Burt Boyar, *Why Me? The Sammy Davis Jr. Story* (New York: Farrar, Straus & Giroux, 1989), 208.

34. Ibid., 209.

35. Ibid.

36. Anton LaVey, *The Satanic Bible* (New York: Avon Books, 1969, 2005), 25.

37. Ibid., 33.

38. Anton LaVey, *The Satanic Rituals* (New York: Avon Books, 1972), 176.

39. Freedland, *The Occult Explosion*, 152.

40. Susan Atkins, with Bob Slosser, *Child of Satan, Child of God* (Plainfield, NJ: Logos International, 1977), 65–67.

Chapter 7: World of Wonders

1. Mark S. Sweetnam, "Hal Lindsey and the Great Dispensational Mutation," *Journal of Religion and Popular Culture*, July 2011, 217.

2. Jonathan Kirsch, "Hal Lindsey" (interview), *Publishers Weekly*, March 14, 1977.

3. Hal Lindsey, with Carole C. Carlson, *The Late Great Planet Earth* (Grand Rapids, MI: Zondervan, 1970), 124.

4. Lucretia Marmon, "Hal Lindsey Says the Wave of the Future Is Armageddon, and 14 Million Buy It," *People*, July 4, 1977.

5. Hal Lindsey, with Carole C. Carlson, *Satan Is Alive and Well on Planet Earth* (Grand Rapids, MI: Zondervan, 1972), 126.

6. Ibid., 152.

7. Marmon, "Hal Lindsey Says the Wave of the Future Is Armageddon..."

8. David Wilkerson, *Set the Trumpet to Thy Mouth* (New Kensington, PA: Whitaker House, 2001, orig. 1985), 12.

9. David Frum, *How We Got Here: The 70s: The Decade that Brought You Modern Life (For Better or Worse)* (New York: Basic Books, 2000), 131.

10. Joseph Heath and Andrew Potter, *The Rebel Sell: Why the Culture Can't Be Jammed* (Toronto: Harper, 2004), 137.

11. Lou Cannon, *President Reagan: The Role of a Lifetime* (New York: Simon & Schuster 1991), 248.

12. Ibid., 248.

13. Ibid., 42.

14. Robert Hughes, *Culture of Complaint: The Fraying of America* (New York: Oxford University Press, 1993), 31.

15. Charles W. Moore, "Evil Needs to Be Taken Seriously," *Calgary Herald*, May 7, 1999, A19.

16. Maureen Dowd, "Rick's Religious Fanaticism," *New York Times*, February 22, 2012, A23.

17. Case, *Led Zeppelin FAQ*, 200.

18. J .D. Considine, "Led Zeppelin," *Rolling Stone*, September 20, 1990, 56.

19. Robert Walser, *Running with the Devil: Power, Gender, and Madness in Heavy Metal Music* (Hanover, NH: Wesleyan University Press, 1993), 139.

20. Shirley MacLaine, *Out on a Limb* (New York: Bantam Books, 1983), 5.

21. Kermode, *The Exorcist*, 20.

22. Sachi Parker, *Lucky Me: My Life With—and Without—My Mom, Shirley MacLaine* (New York: Gotham Books, 2013), 52.

23. Glenn H. Utter and John Woodrow Storey, *The Religious Right: A Reference Handbook* (Santa Barbara, CA: ABC-CLIO, 2001), 143.

24. Fox, "Ira Levin, 78, of 'Rosemary's Baby,' Dies," B11.

25. Edward Beecher Claflin, "When Is a True Story True?" *Publishers Weekly*, August 14, 1987, 23–26.

26. Philip Carlo, *The Night Stalker: The True Story of America's Most Feared Serial Killer* (New York: Kensington Books, 1996), 238.

27. Ibid., 518.

28. Jan Harold Brunvand, *Encyclopedia of Urban Legends* (Santa Barbara, CA: ABC-CLIO, 2012), 550.

29. Jeffrey Victor, *Satanic Panic: The Creation of a Contemporary Legend* (Chicago: Open Court, 1993), 188–189.

30. Sigmund Freud, *The Uncanny*, translated by David McLintock (London: Penguin Classics, 2003), 154.

31. Ibid., 156–157.

32. Carl Jung, *The Psychology of the Transference*, Translated by R. F. C. Hull (Princeton, NJ: Princeton University Press, 1969), 28.

33. Freedland, *The Occult Explosion*, 16.

34. Ibid., 16–17.

35. Theodore Roszak, *The Making of a Counter Culture: Reflections on the Technocratic Society and Its Youthful Opposition* (New York: Anchor Books, 1969), 125.

36. "The Occult: A Substitute Faith," *Time*, 1972.

37. Ibid. (quoting *Sociological Quarterly*).

38. Joseph Campbell, *Thou Art That: Transforming Religious Metaphor* (Novato, CA: New World Library, 2001), 106–107.

39. Susan Jacoby, *The Age of American Unreason* (New York: Pantheon Books, 2008), 18–19.

40. Carl Sagan, *The Demon-Haunted World: Science as a Candle in the Dark* (New York: Random House, 1995), 13–14.

Bibliography

Books

Adler, Margot. *Drawing Down the Moon: Witches, Druids, Goddess-Worshippers, and Other Pagans in America Today*. New York: Viking Press, 1979.

Allen, Thomas B. *Possessed: The True Story of an Exorcism*. New York: Doubleday, 1993.

Anson, Jay. *The Amityville Horror*. New York: Prentice-Hall, 1977.

Atkins, Susan, with Bob Slosser. *Child of Satan, Child of God*. Plainfield, New Jersey: Logos International, 1977.

Basil, Robert, ed. *Not Necessarily the New Age: Critical Essays*. Buffalo: Prometheus Books, 1988.

Baugess, James S. *Encyclopedia of the Sixties: A Decade of Culture and Counterculture*. Santa Barbara, California: Greenwood Press, 2012.

Berlitz, Charles. *The Bermuda Triangle*. Garden City: Doubleday, 1974.

Berlitz, Charles, with J. Manson Valentine. *Without a Trace*. Garden City: Doubleday, 1977.

Blatty, William Peter. *The Exorcist*. New York: Harper & Row, 1971.

———. *The Exorcist From Novel to Film*. New York: New York: Bantam, 1974.

Booth, Martin. *A Magic Life: The Biography of Aleister Crowley*. London: Hodder & Stoughton, 2000.

Bugliosi, Vincent, with Curt Gentry. *Helter Skelter*. New York: W.W. Norton, 1974.

Byrne, Peter. *The Search For Bigfoot: Monster, Myth or Man?* New York: Pocket Books, 1976.

Carlo, Philip. *The Night Stalker: The True Story of America's Most Feared Serial Killer*. New York: Kensington Books, 1996.

Carpenter, Humphrey. *Tolkien: A Biography*. Boston: Houghton Mifflin, 1977.

Case, George. *Jimmy Page: Magus, Musician, Man: An Unauthorized Biography.* New York: Backbeat, 2009.

Castaneda, Carlos. *A Separate Reality: Further Conversations With Don Juan.* New York: Simon and Schuster, 1971.

———. *The Teachings of Don Juan: A Yacqui Way of Knowledge.* Berkeley: University of California Press, 1968.

Cavendish, Richard. *The Powers of Evil.* London: Routledge & Kegan Paul, 1975.

Chambers Dictionary of the Unexplained. Edinburgh: Chambers, 2007.

Cohen, Daniel. *The Encyclopedia of the Strange.* New York: Avon, 1985.

Coleman, David. *The Bigfoot Filmography: Fictional and Documentary Appearances in Film and Television.* Jefferson, North Carolina: McFarland, 2012.

Crowley, Aleister. *The Book of the Law.* York Beach, Maine: Samuel Weiser, Inc., 1976.

———. *Magic In Theory and Practice.* Book Sales, 1992.

Dalton, David, ed. *The Rolling Stones: The First Twenty Years.* New York: Alfred A. Knopf, 1981.

Däniken, Erich von. *Chariots of the Gods? Unsolved Mysteries of the Past.* New York: Putnam, 1970.

———. *In Search of Ancient Gods: My Pictorial Evidence For the Impossible.* London: Souvenir Press, 1974.

Davis, Sammy, with Jane and Burt Boyar. *Why Me? The Sammy Davis Jr. Story.* New York: Farrar, Straus, and Giroux, 1989.

De Camp, L. Sprague. *Lovecraft: A Biography.* New York: Ballantine, 1976.

Didion, Joan. *The White Album.* New York: Simon & Schuster, 1979.

Duncan, Randy, and Matthew J. Smith. *The Power of Comics: History, Form, and Culture.* New York: Continuum, 2009

Ebert, Roger. *Roger Ebert's Movie Home Companion.* New York: Andrews, McMeel & Parker, 1986

Erickson, Hal. *Television Cartoon Shows: An Illustrated Encyclopedia, 1949 through 2003.* Jefferson, North Carolina: McFarland, 2005.

Faithfull, Marianne, with David Dalton. *Faithfull: An Autobiography.* Boston: Little, Brown, 1994.

Farrow, Mia. *What Falls Away: A Memoir.* New York: Nan A. Talese, 1997.

Fort, Charles. *The Book of the Damned: The Collected Works of Charles Fort.* New York: Jeremy P. Tarcher / Penguin, 2008.

Freedland, Nat. *The Occult Explosion.* New York: G.P. Putnam's Sons, 1972.

Frehley, Ace, with Joe Layden. *No Regrets: A Rock 'n' Roll Memoir*. New York: Gallery Books, 2011.

Frum, David. *How We Got Here: The 70s: The Decade That Brought You Modern Life (For Better or Worse)*. New York: Basic Books, 2000.

Graysmith, Robert. *Zodiac Unmasked*. New York: Berkley, 2002.

Greene, Bob. *Billion Dollar Baby*. New York: Atheneum, 1974.

Guiley, Rosemary. *The Encyclopedia of Witches and Witchcraft*. New York: Facts on File, 1999.

Haney, Lynn. *Gregory Peck: A Charmed Life*. New York: Carroll & Graff, 2004.

Hanna, William, with Tom Ito. *A Cast of Friends*. Dallas: Taylor Publishing, 1996.

Heath, Joseph, and Andrew Potter. *The Rebel Sell: Why the Culture Can't Be Jammed*. Toronto: Harper, 2004.

Iommi, Tony, with T.J. Lammers. *Iron Man: My Journey Through Heaven and Hell With Black Sabbath*. Philadelphia: DaCapo, 2011.

Jacoby, Susan. *The Age of American Unreason*. New York: Pantheon Books, 2008.

James, Bill. *Popular Crime: Reflections on the Celebration of Violence*. New York: Scribner, 2011.

Kauffmann, Stanley. *Before My Eyes: Film Criticism and Comment*. New York: Harper & Row, 1980.

———. *Figures of Light: Film Criticism and Comment*. New York: Harper & Row, 1971.

Keel, John A. *The Mothman Prophecies*. New York: Tor, 2002.

Kermode, Mark. *The Exorcist (BFI Modern Classics)*. London: British Film Institute, 1997.

King, Francis X. *Witchcraft and Demonology*. London: Hamlyn, 1987.

King, Stephen. *Carrie*. Garden City: Doubleday, 1974.

———. *Danse Macabre*. New York: Berkley Books, 1981.

———. *Firestarter*. New York: Viking, 1980.

———. *The Dead Zone*. New York: Viking, 1979.

———. *Night Shift*. Garden City: Doubleday, 1978.

———. *Salem's Lot*. Garden City: Doubleday, 1975.

———. *The Shining*. Garden City: Doubleday, 1977.

———. *The Stand*. Garden City: Doubleday, 1978.

Lackmann, Ron. *Mercedes McCambridge: A Biography and Career Record*. Jefferson, North Carolina: McFarland, 2004.

LaVey, Anton. *The Satanic Bible*. New York: Avon, 1969.

———. *The Satanic Rituals*. New York: Avon, 1972.

Levin, Ira. *Rosemary's Baby*. New York: Random House, 1967.

Leyton, Elliott. *Hunting Humans: The Rise of the Modern Multiple Murderer*. Toronto: McClelland and Stewart, 1987.

Lindsey, Hal, with Carole C. Carlson. *The Late Great Planet Earth*. Grand Rapids, Michigan: Zondervan, 1970.

———. *Satan Is Alive and Well on Planet Earth*. Grand Rapids, Michigan: Zondervan, 1972.

Long, Greg. *The Making of Bigfoot: The Inside Story*. Amherst, New York: Prometheus Books, 2004.

Lovecraft, H.P. *The Best of H.P. Lovecraft: Bloodcurdling Tales of Horror and the Macabre*. New York: Ballantine, 1982.

MacLaine, Shirley. *Out on a Limb*. New York: Bantam Books, 1983.

Medved, Harry, with Randy Dreyfuss. *The Fifty Worst Films of All Time (And How They Got That Way)*. New York: Popular Library, 1978.

Medway, Gareth. *The Lure of the Sinister: The Unnatural History of Satanism*. New York: New York University Press, 2001.

Melton, J. Gordon. *The Encyclopedic Handbook of Cults in America (Revised Edition)*. New York: Garland Publishing, 1992.

Melton, J. Gordon, with Jerome Clark and Aidan A. Kelly. *New Age Almanac*. New York: Visible Ink, 1991.

Nathan, Debbie. *Sybil Exposed: The Extraordinary True Story Behind the Famous Multiple Personality Case*. New York: Free Press, 2011.

Nickell, Joe. *Tracking the Man-Beasts: Sasquatch, Vampires, Zombies and More*. Amherst, New York: Prometheus Books, 2011.

Orbanes, Philip. *The Game Makers: The Story of Parker Brothers From Tiddledy Winks to Trivial Pursuit*. Boston: Harvard Business School Press, 2004.

Parker, Sachi, with Frederick Stroppel. *Lucky Me: My Life With—and Without—My Mom, Shirley MacLaine*. New York: Gotham Books, 2013.

Paulsen, Kathryn. *The Complete Book of Magic and Witchcraft*. New York: Pentacle Press, 1980.

Polanski, Roman. *Roman*. New York: Morrow, 1984.

Quasar, Gian J. *Into the Bermuda Triangle: Pursuing the Truth Behind the World's Greatest Mystery*. Toronto: McGraw-Hill / International Marine, 2005.

Randi, James. *Flim-Flam! The Truth About Unicorns, Parapsychology, and Other Delusions*. New York: Lippincott & Crowell, 1980.

Rice, Anne. *Interview Wwth the Vampire*. New York: Knopf, 1976.

Richards, Keith, with James Fox. *Life*. New York: Little, Brown & Co., 2010.

Roberts, Jane. *The Education of Oversoul Seven*. Englewood Cliffs, New Jersey: Prentice-Hall, 1973.

———. *The Seth Material*. Englewood Cliffs, New Jersey: Prentice-Hall, 1970.

Robson, Peter. *The Devil's Own*. New York: Ace, 1969.

Rogo, D. Scott. *The Haunted Universe*. New York: Signet, 1977.

Rosen, Steven. *Black Sabbath*. London: Sanctuary, 2002.

Roszak, Theodore. *The Making of a Counter Culture: Reflections on the Technocratic Society and Its Youthful Opposition*. New York: Anchor Books, 1969.

Sagan, Carl. *The Demon-Haunted World: Science as a Candle in the Dark*. New York: Random House, 1995.

Savage, Candace. *Witch: The Wild Ride From Wicked to Wicca*. Vancouver: Greystone Books, 2000.

Schreiber, Flora Rheta. *Sybil*. Chicago: Regnery, 1973.

Serial Killers, by the Editors of Time-Life Books. Alexandria, Virginia: Time-Life Books, 1992.

Smith, Michelle, with Lawrence Padzer. *Michelle Remembers*. New York: Congdon & Lattes, 1980.

Smith, Paul H. *Reading the Enemy's Mind: Inside Star Gate—America's Psychic Espionage Program*. New York: Tom Doherty Associates, 2005.

Stanley, John. *Creature Features: The Science Fiction, Fantasy, and Horror Movie Guide*. New York: Berkley Boulevard Books, 2000.

Starhawk. *The Spiral Dance: A Rebirth of the Ancient Religion of the Great Goddess* (20th Anniversary Edition). San Francisco: Harper San Francisco, 1999.

Sutin, Lawrence. *Do What Thou Wilt: A Life of Aleister Crowley*. New York: St. Martin's Press, 2000.

Taylor, Derek. *It Was Twenty Years Ago Today: An Anniversary Celebration of 1967*. New York: Simon & Schuster, 1987.

Tryon, Tom. *Harvest Home*. New York: Knopf, 1973.

———. *The Other*. New York: Knopf, 1971.

Underwood, Tim, and Chuck Miller, eds. *Fear Itself: The Horror Fiction of Stephen King*. New York: New American Library, 1984.

Victor, Jeffrey S. *Satanic Panic: The Creation of a Contemporary Legend*. Chicago: Open Court, 1993.

Walser, Robert. *Running With the Devil: Power, Gender, and Madness in Heavy Metal Music*. Hanover: Wesleyan University Press, 1993.

Wolfe, Tom. *Mauve Gloves & Madmen, Clutter & Vine, and Other Stories, Sketches, and Essays*. New York: Farrar, Straus, & Giroux, 1976.

Wrightson, Bernie. *Creepy Presents Bernie Wrightson: The Definitive Collection of Bernie Wrightson's Stories and Illustrations From the Pages of* Creepy and Eerie. Milwaukie, Oregon: Dark Horse Comics, 2011.

Wylie, Timothy. *Love, Sex, Fear, Death: The Inside Story of the Process Church of the Final Judgment*. Los Angeles: Feral House, 2009.

Zinoman, Jason. *Shock Value: How a Few Eccentric Outsiders Gave Us Nightmares, Conquered Hollywood, and Invented Modern Horror*. New York: Penguin Press, 2011.

ARTICLES

"After 40 Years, Grisly 'Exorcist' Book Gets a Rewrite." *Weekend Edition Saturday* (NPR Radio Broadcast): October 29, 2011.

Allen, Mel. "The Gift." *Yankee*, March-April 2011.

"Astrology: Fad and Phenomenon." *Time*, March 21, 1969: 51.

"Attacking the New Nonsense." *Time*, December 12, 1977.

Boulware, Jack. "A Devil of a Time." *The Washington Post*, August 30, 1998: F1.

Burks, Edward C. "'Satan Cult', Death, Drugs Jolt Peaceful Vineland, NJ." *New York Times*, July 6, 1971: 35.

Canby, Vincent. "Blatty's 'Exorcist' Comes to the Screen." *New York Times*, December 27, 1973: 46.

Ibid. "Why the Devil Do They Dig 'The Exorcist'?" *New York Times*, January 13, 1974.

"A Deadly Triangle." *Time*, January 6, 1975: 70.

DeYoung, Mary. "The Devil Goes to Day Care: McMartin and the Making of a Moral Panic." *Journal of American Culture*, Volume 20, 1997: 19.

Ibid. "One Face of the Devil: The Satanic Ritual Abuse Moral Crusade and the Law." *Behavioral Sciences and the Law*, Volume 12, 1994: 389-407.

Fishman, Steve. "The Devil in David Berkowitz." *New York*, September 18, 2006: 32.

Fleming, Thomas J. "Rosemary's Baby" (Book review). *New York Times*, April 30, 1967: 39.

Flint, Jerry. "Rise in Occultism Viewed as Revolt Against Science." *New York Times*, September 10, 1971: 37.

Fox, Margalit. "Ira Levin, 78, of 'Rosemary's Baby,' Dies." *New York Times*, November 14, 2007: B11.

Frazier, Kendrick. "Science and the Parascience Cults." *Science News* 109, 1976: 346–350.

Goldman, Albert. "Rock In the Androgynous Zone." *Life*, July 30, 1971.

"Going to the Opera With . . . Ira Levin." *Opera News*, October 1997: 36.

Hayles, David. "From Exorcism to Redemption." *The Times* (London), January 29, 2011: 9.

"He Chose His Own Adventure" (Gary Gygax obituary). *Newsweek*, March 17, 2008.

Huston, Peter. "Satanic Panic: Creation of a Contemporary Legend" (Book review). *Skeptical Inquirer*, Spring 1994: 280.

Kennedy, Eugene C. "A Priest Takes a Look at the Devil and William Blatty." *New York Times*, August 4, 1974: 95.

Loxton, Daniel. "Ancient Aliens." *Skeptic*, Volume 13, 2007: 80–87.

———. "The Bermuda Triangle." *Skeptic*, Volume 10, 2003: 96–104.

———. "Bigfoot." *Skeptic*, Volume 11, 2004: 96–104.

Lynch, Jason. "Amityville Ghosts." *People*, April 18, 2005, Volume 63, Issue 15.

Marmon, Lucretia. "Hal Lindsey Says the Wave of the Future is Armageddon, and 14 Million Buy It." *People*, July 4, 1977.

Martin, Douglas. "Inventor Pursued Loch Ness Monster." *Edmonton Journal*, November 15, 2009: E7.

"The Occult: A Substitute Faith." *Time*, June 19, 1972: 68.

Schemo, Diana Jean. "'Amityville' Prisoner Says Movie Money Tainted Defense." *New York Times*, June 25, 1992.

Selby, Mike. "Misguided Myth Masks Tragedy." *Kimberley Daily Bulletin*, October 13, 2011: 7.

Sweetnam, Mark S. "Hal Lindsey and the Great Dispensational Mutation." *Journal of Religion and Popular Culture*, July 2011: 217.

"Towards a Hidden God." *Time*, April 8, 1966: 98.

Wright, Lawrence. "Sympathy For the Devil." *Rolling Stone*, September 5, 1991: 62.

Index

ABOUT THE AUTHOR

George Case is a writer on ideas and popular culture, and an acknowledged authority on the band Led Zeppelin. He has seven previous books on popular culture and contemporary history, including *Calling Dr. Strangelove: The Anatomy and Influence of the Kubrick Masterpiece* (2014), and the award-winning biography of Led Zeppelin legend Jimmy Page, *Magus, Musician, Man* (2007). He has also contributed several articles to the social science journal *Skeptic* and maintains a regular blog, *Essays and Ideas*. Case lives in Ottawa, Canada, with his family.

/